MEASURING UP

A MEMOIR OF FATHERS AND SONS

DAN ROBSON

VIKING

VIKING

an imprint of Penguin Canada, a division of Penguin Random House Canada Limited

Canada • USA • UK • Ireland • Australia • New Zealand • India • South Africa • China

First published 2021

www.penguinrandomhouse.ca

The author would like to acknowledge funding support from the
Ontario Arts Council, an agency of the Government of Ontario.

LIBRARY AND ARCHIVES CANADA CATALOGUING IN PUBLICATION
Title: Measuring up : a memoir of fathers and sons / Dan Robson.
Names: Robson, Dan, 1983- author.
Identifiers: Canadiana (print) 20200238671 | Canadiana (ebook) 20200238604 |
ISBN 9780735234697 (softcover) | ISBN 9780735234703 (EPUB)
Subjects: LCSH: Robson, Dan, 1983- | LCSH: Fathers and sons—Canada—
Biography. | LCSH: Fathers—Death. | LCSH: Bereavement—Psychological aspects. |
LCSH: Construction industry. | LCSH: Family-owned business enterprises. |
LCGFT: Autobiographies.
Classification: LCC BF575.G7 R65 2021 | DDC 155.9w37092—dc23

Book design by Matthew Flute
Cover design by Terri Nimmo

Manufactured in Canada

10 9 8 7 6 5 4 3 2 1

Penguin
Random House
VIKING CANADA

For Oliver Richard Robson

"For our house is our corner of the world. As has often been said, it is our first universe, a real cosmos in every sense of the word. If we look at it intimately, the humblest dwelling has beauty."

Gaston Bachelard, *The Poetics of Space*

Contents

Part I
Things Fall Apart

I

It begins with a phone call, as these things often do.

I've been asleep for only a few hours when the ring shakes me awake. I'm behind on a looming book deadline and have been working through most nights. I'm dazed, and my eyes feel too heavy to open—until the sharp cold-water splash of panic.

I'm supposed to meet my publisher at nine. *I've slept in.*

I grab the phone expecting to see that it's him, calling me from a table at Starbucks, wondering where I am. But the display says "Jai."

Jai?

Jai is my older sister. We're a year and a half apart. Two of three siblings. Our little sister, Jenna, is five years younger. We're close. Close enough to know that neither would ever call me at seven a.m.

It's that rare feeling that reaches beyond worry. You feel it in your chest. *Something is wrong.*

I answer.

"Jai?"

"Dan. Are you awake?"

Jai rarely betrays emotion when she speaks. She's either happy or annoyed. That's it, two modes. But this is different. She's rushed. She's scared.

"Mom just called. Something happened to Dad."

"What?"

"She thinks he had a stroke. He's okay. But they've taken him to the hospital. She wants us to meet her there."

It's the kind of news you know exists. You know it will come, one day—but you never expect it. Then it crushes you from the blind side.

Jai lives in the east end of Toronto. We agree to meet at Jenna's condo in the west end, since it's on the way to the hospital in Mississauga. Our mother's a nurse. She's requested that the ambulance take our dad straight to a facility that specializes in strokes.

To me that means she doesn't *think* it's a stroke. Mom knows.

I dress quickly while Jayme, my partner, turns towards me in bed, trying to catch up and trying to slow me down.

"It's probably just something small," she says.

Her father had a scare with his heart a couple of months ago. But it was just a warning shot. It's likely something like that, she says.

"Yeah," I say. "Probably."

But I'm running down the stairs. I have to go and I'm not sure when I'll be back.

"You need to take care of Henry," I say. He's our seven-month-old Goldendoodle.

I stuff my laptop into my bag, hoping to get some work in—hoping Jayme's right. Probably. But it's self-preservation. The sound of my heart beating deep in my ears tells me it's not true. *Bump, bump— bump, bump—bump, bump.*

"Okay, love you," I shout from the door. "Call you soon."

Mom is in the waiting room when my sisters and I arrive. She is alone and looks scared. She's pale. I've never seen her like this before.

Dad fell on the floor beside the bed, she tells us. She'd been down-stairs, and when she came into their room she found him there. He tried to get up, but couldn't. He tried to speak, but couldn't. She called the ambulance. She stayed beside him, holding him until they arrived.

He must have been terrified.

Time is a blur now. A nurse tells us that a doctor wants to see us in a private room.

Mom used to work in an ER. She shakes her head, squeezes her lips tight, and then her voice breaks.

"It's never good when they want to take you to a room," she says.

She's never flinched. She's witnessed it all, no problem. But now she's falling apart. I try to calm her as we wait in a lamplit room with two brown couches and flowers on side tables. I've never been more afraid.

I hold my breath when the doctor opens the door. He is a serious-looking man, probably in his sixties. The hospital's lead neurosurgeon. The title sounds important. Reassuring.

He tells us that Dad is out of surgery and that it has gone well.

I breathe, quietly—but it feels like a gasp after being held under water.

He's suffered a large stroke, the doctor says. They managed to find the problem, and he's stable. But there's no telling what the outcome will be until he wakes up.

He seems positive. This is the *lead guy*. This man *knows*.

There is some swelling around his brain and that needs to go down, the doctor tells us. Best-case scenario, he'll recover well—although he'll probably need some rehabilitation. But the damage could be much worse and there's a chance the damage could be severe.

"We won't know until he wakes up," the doctor says again.

A nurse takes us out of the bad-news room and down a white hallway, through double doors and into a very serious-looking area filled with beeping machines, blue curtains, and busy people walking around in gowns and masks. I try not to look between the curtains as we pass, but I hear a muffled sob and see hunched figures over a bed. I look at the ceiling. We pass another bed. Then the nurse turns and leads us in.

My father lies on his back, eyes closed.

There is an oxygen mask on his face, and tiny wires and tubes running from his body into the grey beeping machines beside him. But it looks oddly familiar.

For several years when I was young and scared of everything, I'd often wake up in the middle of the night and rush into my parents' room. I wouldn't be able to fall back to sleep unless I was beside my dad. He always slept on the same side, closest to the door. I'd sit next to him on the bed, too light for him to notice. I'd watch him breathe, his chest rising and falling with a baritone snore. It wasn't peaceful. My father was never a great sleeper, which is a trait he passed on to me. He'd go to bed late and get up early. Rest seemed like labour to him. But I'd watch him take several breaths before giving him a light nudge.

"Dad?"

He'd stir and half open his eyes.

"Can't sleep," I'd say.

"Okay, buddy."

And he'd shift over in bed, never fully waking, while I curled into him, safe from the wild beasts of my mind.

My father does not look peaceful here. This sleep is not rest. I know that somewhere beyond his closed eyes, he's working hard to make it home.

We last spoke—really spoke—a few days ago. He was at the airport, on his way to meetings in Calgary. He was calling to check in, as we always did. He knew I was working towards a book deadline—as well as my regular job as a sportswriter, I write biographies of figures in the field—and that I was stressed. He could hear it in my voice. I wasn't really paying attention to whatever we were discussing.

"I'll let you go. You're busy," he said. "Don't worry. We'll talk soon."

We hung up and I kept typing. But about ten minutes later, I felt sick. We never did that. We never sped through conversations. All my life, whenever I called, he'd never been too busy to talk. He'd step out of a meeting to answer the call. And here I was, thirty-one years old, facing a little stress and brushing him off.

I called him back and he seemed happy to hear my voice. We spoke for about ten minutes while he waited at his gate to catch his plane. I told him I was worried that I wasn't going to be able to pull off the book I was writing in time. It felt like my world was going to collapse. He'd always been the person I called when I needed to be held up. There was something about the connection we had and the way I viewed him. I'd called him back that day because I wanted him to know that I'd never be too busy to chat. But it was a call that I needed much more than he did.

"I don't know how you'll do it," he said. "But you will. You always do."

He knew nothing about writing books, but I knew that his belief in me was real. It always had been, despite me. And even though the confidence he had might have been uninformed, it lifted me the way he always did. We hung up, and Dad took his flight. And I took a deep breath and wrote and wrote and wrote, feeling that confidence too.

We had one more conversation, a couple of days later. It was quick. He was still in Calgary, driving back to the airport. There had been a big construction contract on the line with a major gas company that the engineering firm he worked for desperately needed. He didn't want to talk about that, though. He asked how the book was coming. I told him it was getting there. The call was cut short as he drove by a car wreck on the opposite side of the highway, just a few minutes outside the city. It looked pretty bad, he told me. There were several ambulances.

"I hate seeing that," he said—and then he said something about people's lives being affected forever in a moment.

He had to go. Traffic was heavy. He'd call me when he got back to Toronto.

"Love you, buddy," he said.

"Love you too, Dad."

I walk to the side of the hospital bed and watch him work through sleep. I know he'll wake up soon. That's all we're waiting for; then we can figure out how to overcome whatever comes next, together.

I sit on the edge of the bed and lean towards him.

"Dad. It's me," I say. "I'm here."

I take his left hand in mine.

"It's Dan, Dad," I say. "Can you feel my hand?"

He squeezes, twice.

Two times.

Love you, buddy.

He knows I'm here. He knows.

We just have to wait.

There's a chair in the corner of the room. I decide that I should sit there, take out my laptop, and work on the book until my father wakes up. He would be coming back, after all. He squeezed my hand to tell me.

And when he did wake up, he'd see me there—working on the book beside him, getting the job done, just as he believed I would. He'd shake his head at the commotion he'd caused and tell me to get back home to work. I'd smile and he'd smile and life would move on, and we'd all be better for this reminder of how fragile it all is.

But I can't type a word.

Waiting consumes everything. We wait, and wait. We call family and friends, and reassure them that we're just waiting.

"It looks like he'll be okay," I tell Andrew, a best friend who lives in San Francisco. "We're just waiting."

He's already booked a flight home.

Everyone is on the way to us. The waiting room fills up with all the people we know. They sit quietly, making small talk and trying not to look nervous. My uncle, Dad's younger brother by a dozen years, plans to drive in from two hours away. I tell him we'll call when Dad wakes up so that he won't have to drive the whole way. My aunt, Dad's only sister, arrives with my ninety-three-year-old grandmother, who almost never leaves the house.

When I go down through the lobby to meet them, I see the hospital's lead neurosurgeon standing in line at the coffee shop. I give him a nod and he smiles softly back. I want to tell him how much I appreciate his saving my father's life, but the man's just trying to get a coffee. No need to embarrass him, I decide. Be cool.

Hours pass.

I don't know how. But I still don't type a single word, and soon it's almost night. We're still waiting. Some friends from my parents' church come in to Dad's room to say a prayer, hoping for healing. Everyone around us looks sadder and sadder. It annoys me. Their discomfort makes me anxious. They don't know: he squeezed my hand. Dad just needs to rest.

I leave to sit in the waiting room for a while. But I'm there for only a few minutes when I see Mom through the window into the hallway. Her face is white. She's walking fast. Jai and Jenna follow quickly behind.

My aunt asks first: "What's wrong?"

The doctor did a routine check on Dad while their friends were in the room to pray. His eyes didn't respond, Mom says. They're rushing him down into a CAT scan.

No one speaks.

It's just a test, I tell myself, and I want to believe it. I sit there, numb and blurry.

I don't know how we arrived at the glass doors to the ICU, but the four of us are there now—some indefinable time after the scan to find out where my father has gone.

A doctor opens the glass door. He's new. *Where did the old guy go?* This guy has just started a shift. He's young—probably younger than me. He couldn't be more than a couple years out of med school. He has a stubbly beard. He has a clipboard.

"Is this just the family?" he asks.

It is.

He wants to talk to us privately.

We follow the doctor down a hallway, outside of the ICU. He stops when he can see that no one else is within earshot. Through the window behind him, I can see Dad's hospital room across a small courtyard.

The doctor looks down at his chart and then back up at us, and begins to speak. He says something about the previous doctor and something about the size of the stroke. It was massive.

"All we could do was wait," he says.

All we could do . . .

"The swelling . . ." he says.

Wait.

"In our opinion, there is no chance for any quality of life."

Wait.

And it hits.

Jenna first. Jai follows. Mom folds over. A sharp, rising cry. I float above my body, watching them fall to the floor, watching myself stand still, staring at the doctor, hearing his words on loop, trying to process this moment—the moment I know my father will die.

I've thought of this moment many times before, ever since I first learned about death—when both of my grandfathers passed away, when I was old enough to know what it meant that they were never coming back. I'd dealt with bouts of severe anxiety in the years after, unable to spend nights away from my parents, worrying when they left us with a sitter, watching the clock if they took an evening walk. It was the kind of electric anxiety you can feel in your entire body. I overcame it with age and reason, but it's always lived inside of me. That old current jolts through me now as I float, watching myself stare at the doctor.

The rage follows. I feel it in my lungs. *What were we doing all this time? Watching him die? This man let my father die. Did you even try? Is there nothing else we can do? Why are you here—why aren't you trying?*

Then it all falls away, like a crashed wave. I am back in my body and my mind. Seconds have passed. My mother and sisters are sobbing on the floor and I don't know where my father is. I'm a boy standing beside his bed in the dark of a haunted night, but he's not there. I can't speak. I can't move. I can't cry.

I stare at the doctor.

Then I hear my voice asking, "What do we do now?"

"We wait," he says.

But he doesn't mean we're waiting for a second opinion, or even for some kind of miracle. He's saying it's only a matter of time; the clock is running down. We're waiting for him to die.

It's seven-thirty p.m. The doors at the end of the hall open. My aunt comes through first. My uncle follows behind, pushing my grandmother in a wheelchair. And I'm floating again, watching. I meet them before they reach my sisters and mom.

"He's not going to make it." I hear myself saying it—and again it's some automatic version of me, operating while I'm weightless.

They melt beneath me. I've never seen my uncle weep. He folds over like the others. My grandmother's head falls forward as she cries. She's lived for more than eight decades and I've never seen her unhappy. It's the most horrible, unsettling sight. I get down on my knees and hug her. I feel her tears on my cheek.

"Rick," she says. My father's name.

I don't cry, still. I feel everything and nothing.

I don't know how we get to the room, but now we're standing outside of it and I hug my sisters and say something about how it's okay, it's going to be all right—something that Dad would say. I hold them hard, as he would too. But I don't believe it's true. Nothing is all right.

We agree to go in alone to say goodbye.

In my younger days when I thought about my father dying, I'd picture myself standing beside his bed and speaking to him one last time while he looked up at me and we shared a proper goodbye. But it was always sometime in the faraway future, like when you imagine what it will be like to be an old man looking back on your life. It was something that time tells you will come but that always seems so impossibly far off, until it isn't.

There would be no final conversation, because there never really is. I walk in, floating still. He looks like he's sleeping. I kneel down beside him and kiss his forehead. It's warm and damp. He breathes softly, through a machine. I stare at his closed eyes, trying to will them open, begging him to come back from the faraway place where he's drifted.

I hold his hand and squeeze it.

"I love you, Dad."

He doesn't squeeze back.

We wait fourteen more hours, watching him die.

More waves crash and I finally cry, several times through the night. I weep on his chest—deep, heaving sobs. I can't hold it in. Dozens of family friends have come through the night to say goodbye, though I won't remember who. Some pray for a miracle. Some weep, too.

Dad snores through much of it, restless and working to the end. I don't know where his last dreams take him, but mine stay there, on the rise and fall of his chest—breathing and breathing. Breathing, forever.

2

The tool bag sits on the laundry room floor, exactly where he always left it. It lies beneath a row of old winter coats hanging from a rack nailed to walls painted a shade of peach that went out of style two decades ago. I'm soaked right through. Outside, it's pouring. Thin legs of rain drip down the small window above the utility sink, lightning flashing through the downpour.

It's the middle of the afternoon on the day my father died.

Dad exhaled for the last time at nine-thirty a.m. I watched his breath leave. We sat there, waiting for his chest to rise again, until it hit us one by one. This was the long pause that becomes the end. I watched his face go pale and harden. I cried hard then too. Probably the hardest I would.

And it was done.

I left the room quickly, because I couldn't see him like that. But I'd left my bag behind, and had to go back a few minutes later. From the door, I saw my two grandmothers, both in their nineties, sitting on chairs beside his body. They held hands but didn't speak. They were more familiar with the pause than any of us could be, but nothing in their long lives had prepared them for an endless gap as hollow and wide as this.

I walked in behind them, to the corner where I'd planned to write thousands of words but couldn't come up with one. Dad's body lay impossibly still, like a model of his image—but it wasn't him. Standing next to my grandmothers, I took one last long look at his face, trying to memorize the shape of him before he became a ghost.

And now we're back in the house where I grew up, and I don't remember how I got here. I can hear a muted crowd just beyond the laundry room door. The voices are soft and sad, an incoherent hum. They've brought lasagnas, small sandwiches, and flowers—offered with mourning smiles and here-for-you hugs. I should be out there, in the hall, greeting them, thanking them. I should frown with them, and return their hugs and firm handshakes, and thank them for taking the time, for showing that they care. Because they do. I'm sure of it.

But I can't take my eyes off my father's tool bag.

It is black and grey, its soft case still thick and rough and sturdy. Quality before everything, he'd say. He'd buy one to last forever, but forever has come and gone. Now it's filled with all the tools he'd accumulated over the decades, made of steel and meant to serve a lasting purpose, but stripped of all utility without the one person in this house who knew how to use them.

The old hammer with its brown leather grip, so worn and slick it was a marvel it didn't go flying on every back swing; the small metal level that ensured no picture or shelf ever hung crooked; the chalk reel that laid out perfect lines; a screwdriver for every head.

These were the tools he'd employed with skill and purpose through every stage of his life. He replaced only the ones that went missing after he'd reluctantly lent them out—each with his *R.R.* initials or

Robson signed neatly with a black Sharpie, a permanent reminder that it was *his* tool, one that had a specific role among the dozens of other absolutely necessary instruments living inside the bag with it. The Unreturned Tool was one of life's greatest crimes. If you didn't know that, you likely weren't the kind of person adept at using them anyway, because in this world there are people who know tools and people who don't. The moment you swing a hammer, grip a drill, or angle a saw leaves no doubt. There are masters and then there are amateurs. Masters know the code. They stand in a construction job with confident ease. They know of a tool for every problem. Their *hands* know. They reach in the bag and their brain sorts through the mess of steel instruments as reflexively as a goalie reacting to a shot. They grab the precise one and execute the task. It's clinical, like a surgeon repairing a broken heart or a mechanic beneath the hood of a dying car. It is serious, precise work.

Amateurs, in contrast, are easy to spot. They fumble and second-guess. They strike out on nail heads. They measure once and cut twice, then thrice—with odd angles and rough edges. They drill too deep, with a wobbly, unsure hand. They hover around employees at Home Depot and ask for help.

A craftsman just knows where things are. The trip is always quick. Ideally, it's to the local mom-and-pop hardware shop they've frequented for decades. But if the Henry's Hardware has been devoured by a monster big box store, the tool master still knows exactly where to find what they need. It's instinctual. Ideally, they make the trip only if they absolutely need to—if, say, some rookie has borrowed a tool and forgotten to return it. God that annoyed him.

The tools that sit in my father's bag, that line the workshop in our garage and his workbench in the basement, always signified something deeply inherent about the kind of person he was. There was, in him, a confident self-reliance. And because of that, a reliance on my father by those who surrounded him. We rely on those who rely on themselves.

These weren't tools he'd dreamed of mastering. Rather, these were tools of survival and necessity. Tools that made him reliable and exact—tools that made sure every angle was perfect, every screw was secure, every foundation held. These were the tools that made him. Tools he used to mould a life that allowed me to find a different set of tools and a different life entirely.

He'd learned how to use his father's tools as a boy. It was just assumed that he'd become equally adept with them. Being handy, in his world, was just a part of life.

It wasn't only that there was value in understanding the mechanical function of tools; it was considered to be a fundamental skill set. A teenager who saved up to buy a new car didn't just learn how to drive it; he also learned how the machine came to life. As a young man my father turned the oil-stained driveway of his parents' modest suburban bungalow into his own mechanic shop, taking apart the engine of his tiny yellow Volkswagen Beetle, then later the hulking army-green Toyota Land Cruiser, then upgrading to a roaring blue Firebird.

It was a time when our hands knew the working of the machines in the world around us. They had an essential role in the homes we lived in, the cars we drove. Handiness was still a function of being, at least in the life of the working class.

Today, beyond hobby-making, it seems a lost art. Yet we're not that far removed from a time when many families actually *built* their own homes. At the turn of the twentieth century, prairie homesteaders looking for a new beginning were granted land with the expectation that they'd build a house capable of withstanding the notoriously windy, frigid winters of the open plains. Likewise, many of the now million-dollar houses that line the streets of Toronto's formerly working-class neighbourhoods were constructed, maintained, and repaired by their original owners. A friend's basement renovation in the west-end community of Roncesvalles recently revealed that a tree stump had been used as a corner foundation. There was a resourceful ingenuity to the art of building. And it wasn't just a hobby; it was a fundamental part of life.

But there remains something about craftsmanship and handiness—about being able to construct and maintain—that still feels essential. Not necessarily the actual constructing of a home from scratch, but the ability to hold something up and to keep it standing.

There's an inherent independence that comes with a proficiency with tools. I often think about an Amish family I lived with for a time as part of a university project. They were a family of dairy farmers who lived entirely off the grid, virtually disconnected from the world beyond them. The parents had built the house and two large barns on their property near Kitchener, Ontario, with the help of the local community. Decades later, one of their sons built his house on the same property, adjacent to his parents. The family and their friends helped piece it all together, from the foundation to the roof. They even carved a wide tunnel that connected the basements of the two houses so that through winter nights they could reach each other without facing the snowy winds that ripped across the fields. They lived without electricity. They farmed the land together. They were completely self-sufficient in the function of their home. Anything that needed to be fixed or built was done by them.

By necessity, this family was masterful with their tools. And having been invited into their home for a brief time, fumbling along as I helped in the barn, I witnessed something I lacked: an intimate relationship with the tools and machinery that kept my world functioning in the most basic ways. I wasn't alone in this. Handiness was an art that had long been devalued in the culture that framed my youth. Ontario's education system pushed skilled labour to the bottom of the class hierarchy, viewing it as an option for "remedial" students who were unlikely to attend university. Shop class was quietly understood as a place where you wound up rather than a place you aspired to be.

I've often wondered about the outcome of that underlying attitude. What have we lost with the increasing expectation that broken things are meant to be discarded and replaced—or, if absolutely necessary, repaired by someone else?

Previous generations of my family had an intimate relationship with tools and handiness. There was pride in repairing your own engine, in building your own fence. It was much more than a do-it-yourself hobby; resourcefulness was part of who we were. It was always that way, until me.

I'd always admired my father for being a master craftsman. Our house was filled with wooden cabinets and dressers he'd built. Our home and yard had been transformed by his skill as a renovator and a contractor. He had assembled the world we lived in and he, quite literally, held it together.

But now?

There is a small puddle at my feet, pooling on the linoleum, and my socks are soaked. I pull my rain jacket over my damp head and hang it on top of several other coats clinging to a single hook. The tool bag is nearly full to the top with the instruments of my father's wizardry, very few of which I could properly name even though I'd seen him use each one hundreds of times before.

I've never seen it zipped closed. It was always wide open, wherever he brought it—sitting in the backseat of his Ford pickup, hauled into my dilapidated university apartment or around the block to his boyhood home to fix up the place where his mother still lived. He'd reach into his bag with a quick glance, or, sifting blindly, he'd feel the shape and weight of the instruments to pull out the perfect one for the job.

The bag sits on top of a solid red case holding a Milwaukee hammer drill that pounds through concrete. A drill for big jobs. A mother of a machine. It kicks back and waywardly if you don't press with enough confident force. I learned that the hard way, when he tried to show me how.

"Hold it steady, buddy, straight—and push," he said patiently as the piercing whine of steel-on-concrete ripped through my apartment, a modern concrete shoebox built to have an "industrial" look. Some concrete powder fell to the floor, but the bit went in only a millimetre at most.

"Try again," he said.

Another horrible, piercing whine. Concrete dust. Another millimetre.

"Hold it steady, and push with all your weight," he said.

Same result.

"Okay, slow—and make sure it's not on an angle . . . Yep, got it."

I sighed. Horrible whine, concrete dust, nothing.

"It's okay," he said. "I'll do it."

He took the drill. And done, first try, with no effort. His hands knew something mine didn't. Screw drilled. Painting hung.

The sight of the drill's red box brings a burst of anxiety—the kind I used to feel as a kid whenever Dad was taking too long to get home or was late picking me up from an after-school practice. It rises from my chest and shoots through each nerve to the tips of my fingers and toes. My teeth clench, biting hard to hold it in. I take a few deep breaths as it passes through me, the scene playing out in my mind again and again: that stupid drill, useless in my hands.

"Try again."

It's impossible.

"Hold it steady, buddy."

God.

"Push with all your weight."

Noise and dust . . . and nothing.

"It's okay, I'll do it."

Done.

When I was two years old he gave me a little tape measure on which he'd inscribed *Danny Robson, 1985*. I'd follow him around in a tiny blue hard hat, mimicking his moves as he measured up the wood beams for the family deck he built in the backyard. As he sawed the pieces precisely I'd gather the discarded ends and use them as building blocks—pretending to measure, saw, and hammer together my own creation while he completed the project in real life.

For my father, it was probably just another task that needed to get done. I don't know that he took particular pride in what he was able to accomplish, although he was always adamant that it be done to perfection, no corners cut. But he never pushed me to learn about tools the same way his father had with him, and he never became frustrated when I wasn't as adept or if I showed little interest. My father didn't have a university degree, and that always seemed to be a point of quiet shame for him. So in his own home he'd push me away from the workbench and the tool bag—away from skills that didn't seem to be valued the same way they once had been. Skills I'm not certain that he ever fully valued in himself.

Standing in this puddle, staring at the bag of tools my father once wielded, I realize how useless they are absent the mastery of his hands. These instruments were part of him; they'd built my vision of who and what my father was. Now they're pieces of steel that, without him, hold no magic.

I feel another wave of anxiety hammer my core again, this time kicking the breath out from my stomach before settling in my throat. It throbs, expanding. It hurts like hell. In the past the anxiety would burst to my edges then recede, settle, and slowly fade— because everything, ultimately, was always okay. I was lucky that way. In the end, nothing bad ever actually happened. Dad would pull up in his truck, having been caught in traffic on his way from a worksite. I'd feel the tightness in my chest release and the tension in my shoulders relax, followed by a flash of embarrassment for having let myself get so worked up. I'd open the back door, toss my knapsack in next to his workboots and hard hat, then climb up into the front seat to his smile and his questions about how practice had gone and what we'd talked about in class that day. I longed to feel that release again. But this time the anxiety wasn't going away. All those years of irrational fear had been realized. Dad wasn't pulling up. There would be no common-sense answer to soothe it, no deep-breath moment to dispel the panic. His calm voice wouldn't say "Hey, buddy, it's okay."

So the panic doesn't fully subside. This is real and final.

I imagine the squeal of the garage door opening beside me and the scratch of our dog's paws on the hardwood as she scampers to greet him. He wears jeans and a plaid shirt. He holds blueprints under his right arm and a white hard hat in his left hand. His steel-toe boots are caked in mud. He smells like sawdust. We have to leave quickly, he says, because he'd run late at the site and the game starts soon.

"You should have had your baseball uniform on by now," he chides. "Hurry, buddy."

And I charge up the stairs to get changed, excited, because it is Thursday in the summer and that means baseball at dusk.

We inhale some tortellini Mom had on the stove, and I spill a little tomato sauce on my bleach-white pants. But who cares, because soon I'll be sliding through the dirt into second base . . . and from the dugout, Dad in his blue and white coach's uniform will yell for me to run for third, because the catcher overthrows the bag . . . and, *oh my god*, the ball's in the outfield! I'll catch my breath on the corner—and he'll smile and clap. On the next hit, I'll run home.

But he didn't open the door.

I did.

And I wasn't ten years old. I was thirty-one.

I stare into the dark garage, fumbling for the light switch. The bulb casts a beam through the dust, across more tools piled on the workbench and the landscaping gear on the hooks he screwed to the walls. The lawn mower, the weed whacker, the Skilsaw, the compressor, the drills—so many different drills—everything old and new: jars of nails, jars of screws, scraps of wood left over from years of household projects, hard hats, a couple of levels, a pair of old workboots, a row of hockey sticks from every year of my minor hockey life, baseball bats, tennis rackets from the 1980s, a deflated basketball, a few old cans of outdated paint, one half-filled bucket of bromine for the pool. All these old pieces of junk scattered across the garage feel connected to him, like points of entry to distant memories. They tell the story of who he was and why that mattered—the essence of my father, which I can't quite grasp.

His name is sketched on the wall in white chalk, the big, perfectly even letters unmistakably his: *Rick*. In all these years I'd never noticed it before. He could have written it a decade ago or last week. I have no idea why he thought to tag his own space. Maybe he just felt the need to make it known that he was here.

And I forget why I am.

Was it Perrier?

I open the fridge by the door and grab the bottle my mother asked for.

Rain patters on the roof and there's another crack of thunder. It smells like damp spring. I flick off the light, head back to the laundry room. The garage door squeaks and thuds shut behind me, just as it always has. I can hear the scrape of my Goldendoodle puppy's paws on the hardwood in the hallway as he leaps with glee on sombre guests.

The anxiety hasn't left. It's stuck in my throat, still expanding.

There is no way that this house, or this family, will survive without him. It feels like the biggest failure of my life.

I should have been ready. I should have been able.

He's passed the responsibility on to me, and I'm not even close to being man enough for the job. He built it, he fixed it—he held it all together. I should have paid more attention, I should have asked more questions, I should have learned more skills. I should have learned to hammer, to saw, to measure twice and cut once.

I shouldn't have relied on him as I did—and he shouldn't have let me.

He should have been harder on me. He should have told me to rely on myself. He should have forced me to be the kind of man who knows how to build things well, and how to keep them standing.

But he didn't. And I didn't. So now I'm a grown man who doesn't know how to build or fix a thing. I am an amateur.

I look down, again, and stare at my father's tools, lost in the tangled maze of steel.

Everything he built is about to fall down.

"What are we going to do without you?"

3

The funeral is held in the large church where we went as children. It was where my father and mother were married, and where they brought us every Sunday—a Pentecostal congregation in the heart of Brampton, a sprawling suburb north of Toronto. Kennedy Road Tabernacle, built in the seventies, is a local landmark. Everyone knows it for the large cross atop a long, narrow tower that slopes down like an Olympic ski jump to a round sanctuary that looks like the Roman Colosseum; for years it was one of the highest structures around. We'd dress in our best each week and drive to the church, sitting in the same spot in the balcony in the second section from the doors. Always about fifteen minutes late, arriving in the middle of the pre-sermon worship fuelled by a lively Southern Baptist–style choir that rocked and danced as they sang and were always the best part.

But this time we're early. We've been waiting downstairs as people filled the seats, first the bottom, then the second level. Then we're given our signal to make our grand entrance, walking slowly to the front row as everyone watches us. It's been a while since I was last here, a place that once felt as familiar as our home. I show up only once a year for Christmas Eve services now, but my parents were still regulars. Dad was a member of the church board, a role my mother had before him.

Today, the place is packed. There are *so many* people, many I've never seen or met before. When I was much younger, I remember thinking that my dad didn't seem to have very many friends. It wasn't that he wasn't likable; it was more that he was just so busy with our life that he didn't have time to go out and be a regular guy. As far as I knew, he wasn't in touch with any of his old boyhood pals. He didn't have a group of guys he'd gather with every once in a while to play softball, catch a game, grab a drink. We had become both the centre and the edges of his life.

But I was wrong. Very wrong. Sitting next to my mother in the front row, I look around the rotunda and scan the crowd as they sing along to Christian worship songs. It's remarkable, seeing the people who've come to mourn and remember my father.

He was never the centre of attention. He'd hate this, I tell myself.

We're holding the funeral on the Saturday that was supposed to be his sixtieth birthday party. Initially we'd planned something grand to mark the milestone, but he'd shut us down. Forcefully. All he wanted, he said, was a barbecue in the backyard with a few friends and family. Then he went and died—and now hundreds of people have come to say goodbye. I picture his frustrated grin as I jab him with the irony, and as another Christian song that sounds like every other Christian song begins, I manage to smile.

Several people take turns speaking on the purple-carpeted stage where we used to listen to weekly sermons. One of them is a former pastor of the church, Jamie Stewart, a close friend of my father's in recent years. They'd cried together when Jamie lost his fifteen-year-old daughter, Emma Grace, a couple of years earlier after a terrible battle with cancer. If this hurt, I couldn't imagine what Jamie and his family were still enduring. He'd since left to lead a different congregation, but he's come back to lead the service to honour my father and say goodbye. It would have meant a lot to Dad, so it means a lot to me.

One of the other speakers is our family friend Jerry Agyemang. An enormous, hulking man, Jerry has recently gained local fame as the security guard and assistant to embattled Toronto mayor Rob Ford, whom he supported vehemently. Jayme, my partner, is an investigative reporter at the *Toronto Star* and was on the team that exposed a tape of the mayor smoking crack and his association with an illicit gang. It was a bizarre collision of my worlds. But Jerry was one of many friends from the church who'd spent summer days and weekends at our house growing up, playing basketball on the driveway and swimming in the pool. He was the eldest in a family of six kids and modest means. When he was a teenager his dad returned to Ghana, and Jerry was left to be, as he told me, the "man of the house."

His voice quavers as he speaks about the father figure mine had been to him, and to many other young men in our community who didn't have the same kind of family structure we had. Several came to the hospital that night as news spread through our friends that Dad would soon die.

At Jerry's wedding my father hugged him hard, with eyes full of happy tears, and told him how proud he was of the man he'd become.

A slide show, the standard funeral staple, follows Jerry. It's accompanied by a soundtrack of songs we've selected that Dad always used to sing: "Jeremiah Was a Bullfrog" . . . "Who'll Stop the Rain" . . . "House at Pooh Corner." In the middle of the photographs we dug up from old stacks in our basement—between pictures of his childhood and then as our father—there's a section from a part of his life I don't recognize. There's this young guy in short white shorts and gold aviators, standing in a group that looks like the cast of *Dazed and Confused* at some cottage I've never seen before. I've heard some stories of those past days—of the late seventies and early eighties—when my parents were regular young people who had much different lives. All these years together, and there was still so much about him that I didn't know.

I clutch the memorial program. It carries a photo of Dad as a child with blond curly hair, smiling wide and bright, using his entire face. Next to it is a photo of him with the same grin, but this time as a young man with long mid-1970s hair down to his shoulders. It's almost the exact same smile he wears in the photograph of him in his mid-fifties, the one that appears at the top of the obituary we've had printed in the *Star* and then reprinted on the back page of the program.

I wrote it while sitting in his chair at the head of the dining room table at our house at three a.m.. I couldn't recall whether I'd ever sat in that chair before. It felt like an unnatural place to be, looking out at the room from his vantage point—this place where we'd shared birthday, Thanksgiving, and Christmas dinners.

As the chorus of another worship song rises, I read over the story of his life as I knew it.

RICK ROBSON

June 8, 1955–May 30, 2015

Rick Robson, a builder and a fixer, spent his life making things work for other people.

He grew up in Brampton and became a carpenter. He fell madly in love with a beautiful nurse from Tavistock, married her, and started a family. He built houses and high-rises, just as he built their lives. Firm foundations, every brick and beam placed with care. He had two daughters and a son, and showed them how to love and dream. He taught them to have faith that this life was part of a grand blueprint. He followed it passionately. Rick showed love and grace to everyone he met. He mastered those tools. He used them to build others up and to fix whatever they needed.

He excelled professionally, starting his own successful business, creating a reputation for skill and integrity, before becoming a leader in a national engineering and construction firm. His work is everywhere—rows of houses, tall buildings, service stations. It is in the school he constructed, where his children grew up. And in the church where he praised and prayed, humbly, thanking God for this beautiful life.

Rick Robson was a pancake maker, a barbecuer, a photographer, an astronomer, a storyteller, a fan, a friend, a rock. He was a husband, strong and steady. A loving father to his own kids—and many more. He was a laugher. A singer.

A crier. A dreamer. He was a pillar that held everything up, and nothing seems secure without him.

Ever efficient, Rick built and fixed all he could in just six decades. There were no regrets. No words left unsaid when he fell asleep, and with his family beside him, he slipped quietly away.

He leaves behind his resilient wife Sharon. And his ever-grateful kids, Jaime, Dan, and Jenna. His mother, Peggy, sister, Debbie, and younger brother, Larry (Tracey) and nephews Noah and Jacob. He leaves them and count-less friends with broken hearts.

But he'll be sure to fix those too, in time.

LUM.

LUM. It means "Love you much." I'm not sure where it came from or why, exactly. But it was one of those family things, something our parents would say whenever we were heading away somewhere. We'd write it in cards, and later in e-mails. It was a family signature.

After the service I shake hands in a fog of people, familiar faces blending together. They'll all be lost in the haze of memory, except for one man I've never seen before. He is young—probably in his late twenties—with warm eyes and a soft, apologetic smile.

"Excuse me," he says, pulling me aside. "You don't know me, but I've heard all about you. My name is Ajith."

He was the store manager at the Starbucks my father would stop at on his way to work, he tells me. Every morning he'd watch Dad's dark-blue Ford F-150 park in front of the store, in an old police station on Queen Street in downtown Brampton, and he'd get started on the grande non-fat, no-sugar latte he always ordered. And every morning my father would greet him with a smile.

"It was an unforgettable smile," Ajith says.

He tells me they developed a friendship through the daily ritual. My father knew all about Ajith's family, how they'd moved to Canada from Dubai, where he'd managed a five-star hotel. Dad had told him everything about me and my two sisters. He'd told Ajith about my book. He knew all about it.

But last week Ajith noticed that the blue F-150 hadn't pulled up in front of the store for several mornings in a row. Then he recognized a smile while flipping through the *Toronto Star*.

"My heart sank," he says.

He felt he needed to come to the memorial to say goodbye. I'm not sure how he knew where or when it was. I don't recall putting those details in the obituary, but to be honest I don't recall many specifics. Regardless, Ajith found it and showed up.

I smile. I don't know why I'm so moved. It was unexpected. The idea that Dad had connected so simply, so briefly—but so deeply— with someone who could have so easily remained a stranger. It was a small, astounding thing. I thank Ajith for coming, because really what a lovely thing to do. I ask him if we can speak again and he pulls his Starbucks manager card out from his wallet. I tell him I'll call, and I mean it. It's the only conversation I'll remember having that day.

After the memorial, we hold a celebration up at the church's high school, on the edge of the city, where new subdivisions now push up against farmers' fields. My sisters and I went to that evangelical school, right from kindergarten through secondary.

Dad managed the construction of its high school wing in the mid-nineties. He had a temporary trailer office in the parking lot, where he laid out the project's blueprints. I'd visit him during lunch breaks from my grade six class. Sometimes we'd eat our sandwiches together and he'd try to explain what all the blue ink on the large white sheets that rolled up like treasure maps meant. That fall, during recess in the afternoons, my friends and I in the schoolyard watched as the wooden frame of the new two-storey building rose up beyond the original one-level school. It looked like Noah's ark being built in one of the Christian cartoons we were sometimes shown in class. I bragged about how my dad was building it, about how I'd seen the blueprints.

At the memorial celebration, I sneak away from the gym, filled with giant balloons and dozens of faces I don't recognize lining up to offer condolences to my mother, and walk through the dimly lit hallway of the wing I'd watched my father build. It now holds the school's junior high, with artwork and announcements from the ending of another semester decorating the walls between the same grey lockers into which my classmates and I had once stuffed our gym bags, assignments, and notes to crushes.

It all feels familiar to me, reaching back through the years I spent there as a student to the day Dad first took me through it—still unfinished, but with red bricks lining the exterior and the spaces between the frames filled in with drywall. It was a masterpiece, I'd thought, as we walked with our hard hats on, inspecting the first floor and the second floor, looking inside each classroom. The giant hole in the grass had grown into this entirely new, permanent thing. My father had followed the course laid out on those blue-inked pages that would give shape and meaning to an empty space.

Dad could build anything. I remembered that feeling as I stood in the small lobby between the two floors, looking out the window to where his portable office once sat. And I was a boy again, knocking carefully on the brown door to make sure he wasn't in the middle of one of his essential, top-secret construction meetings. He'd open the door and greet me with his big smile, and we'd sit there looking over the sketches as he let me in on the amazing plans that would turn nothing into something.

My favourite book as a boy was Roald Dahl's *Danny, the Champion of the World*, about a young boy who lives in a trailer with his father, next to the mechanic shop he runs. The story follows the father and son as they embark on a scheme to poach pheasants from a rich villain who owns the land around them. In Dahl's tale, Danny is enthralled by his dad's imaginative stories and enchanting personality. I devoured Dahl's adventure, captivated by the journey Danny and his father took together. He viewed his father as a larger-than-life hero, even though he was just an impoverished widower, trying to hold the world together for his son. Even with his father's flaws, the son saw the man guiding him as a heroic figure.

"What I have been trying so hard to tell you all along is simply that my father, without the slightest doubt, was the most marvellous and exciting father any boy ever had," Danny tells the reader in the last chapter of the book.

Even though it had been years since I'd sat down and read about the champion of the world, those words rushed back.

I wasn't able, or perhaps ready, to grasp the lore I'd built up around my dad when I was young, beyond this feeling that he too did marvellous things. Even as an adult it was hard to place the appreciation. But within those first days after he was gone, within the constant ache of that finality, it became clear. In my mind, he'd created magical works of art. From houses to high-rises and from gas stations to schools. My father built things that are so indispensable we don't even see them.

I'd hear his clock beeping every day at five a.m. and the thud of his hand hushing it. After his alarm woke me, I'd hear the creak when his feet hit the floor and the soft squeak of the bedsprings as he pushed himself up from the bed. He must have been exhausted all those dark, lonely mornings while the world was still. He seemed to walk softly across the carpet and into the bathroom, because the next thing I'd hear was the water rushing through the pipes and then a quick, sharp squeal as it hit the shower head. He'd pull the pin and I could almost feel the warmth of the hot water. He'd removed the water saver that came with the shower, because there is nothing more disappointing than weak pressure when it's five a.m.

I'd felt some sort of comfort lying there in the dark, listening to Dad's day begin.

After about five minutes of melody in the rushing water, crackling on the shower floor, it'd stop with an abrupt thud—and the metallic scratch of the shower curtains opening and his footsteps on the linoleum. At some point I'd drift back to sleep, until a quiet creak in my bedroom door woke me again. He'd peek his head in to each of our rooms, just for a few seconds. I don't know his motivation behind that morning glimpse, but I can guess it was a quick check to make sure we were still there, or still breathing, or perhaps just for a quick reminder of why on earth he had to lug himself out of bed before the sun every day.

He'd creak down the stairs, followed by the scratch of paws as our golden retriever leapt off the couch at the sound of him. From my room at the top of the stairs I could hear the *clack-clack-clack* of the garage door opening. And he'd drive off to build the world as I knew it.

This was how I'd viewed the second half of the man.

The other, first half was still unknown, and rarely considered. He was that young man standing with friends I'd never known, in white shorts and aviators at a distant cottage in the past. I'd seen other versions of him in old photographs. Standing proudly beside his Land Cruiser. Or sitting at the kitchen table in his parents' house with his long seventies rock hair. Photos of him looking very much like an alternative, cooler version of me.

He'd told me some stories about that guy. While his path to practical employment remained in construction, here on earth his dreams were up in the sky. When he was young he'd wanted to become an airline pilot, flying above the clouds; he was enamoured with the physics of flight. So in his early twenties he saved up his money and joined the Brampton Flying Club, just a few kilometres north of where the school he'd one day build would be. After long days as a crew member on construction sites, he'd drive out to the flying club to climb into a Cessna and log some extra time in the clouds. He needed to put in the hours towards advancing in his flight training.

It's near dusk on the day of the memorial, and I walk out the back doors of the old school to take a moment away from the crowd still gathering inside. I find a basketball that's fallen into a ditch by the playground and swings. A net hangs next to the red-brick wall of the school. Still wearing my suit and tie, I dribble over to take a shot. As I raise the ball, I notice the roof of the wing he constructed peeking out just behind the gym where he'd show up for every high school basketball game I played. I think about standing in the same spot way back when it was still just a wooden frame I bragged about to my middle-school friends.

As my jumpshot arcs towards the rim I spot a small plane flying low beneath pink clouds. I think of time folding over, of my father gliding through a blue sky with everything yet undone. I see him weaving between the scattered clouds, looking down through his gold aviators on what would be the rest of his life. He wouldn't know what lay ahead of him then. He wouldn't know that he'd soon meet a girl, settle down, and have three kids who'd adore him. And as he flew, he wouldn't yet know that those kids would grow up at the red-brick school in one of those fields beneath him. He'd take a deep breath. Admire the view. And when it was finally time for him to come in from the clouds, he'd navigate the wind and glide back to earth, softly, to live it all again.

4

As a boy, I had this recurring dream that my family and I lived inside an invincible vehicle on an endless journey to everywhere and nowhere in particular.

The truck was made of impenetrable steel and had special guards that lowered to the ground to cover the wheels and any other external vulnerabilities that our enemies might use to blow us up. With a push of a button, steel panels would also cover the windows and the windshield. We'd monitor the outside threat—usually some sort of angry evil gang with immense weapons—through a camera we dispatched overhead so that it would hover above us.

In real life, by day, my father's truck seemed like our spaceship. For all the indestructible, impossible technology my mind ascribed to the vehicle of my dreams, we could as well have been beaming through the galaxies on those long road trips we took. But we were here, on earth, driving through the days and nights of our lives together.

I remember feeling the warmth of our closeness in the cab as we journeyed through the dark. No matter what happened, we were safe inside that vessel. It seemed impenetrable, its hulking metal frame raised high off the ground so that you had to hop up to get inside. We could drive through snow squalls and thunderstorms, and the ship would cut through it all with unwavering ease. It could feel as though the world was crashing in around us, but the truck would refuse to bend or break. It contained and sustained our lives, together, protecting us from whatever untold, unseen evil was trying to tear it all apart.

For so much of my youth, as my dad and I travelled across those long stretches of bland Ontario highways to weeknight hockey games, the true joy—the warmth—wasn't in the thrill of the sport but rather in the time and space between here and there. It was in those hours of nothing but us and the truck and the road. And as we drove, I'd watch the highway recede behind us in the side mirror—fading back into the distance, into the past, until it disappeared. And up ahead the edge of the sky looked just like the shoreline of a wide sea—always way out before us, always unreachable, always in a future we'd never touch. At night stars would shoot across the black sky as the truck carried us through the darkness. I'd close my eyes and wonder whether somewhere out there, somewhere far away, there was another version of us, circling a different sun, travelling a different terrain, on their own infinitesimally small voyage in the universe. My father would hum along to the radio beside me as we drove, glancing over at me and smiling. And I'd wonder if way out there, in that great beyond, fathers and sons journeyed together too.

The truck carried us on, heading home. And it was just my dad and me facing that endless road ahead. And nothing—not bad weather, not space invaders, not life, not death—*no, nothing* could ever stop us.

But now his truck is gone. It's been missing from the spot on the driveway where it always sat. The absence of it makes me feel weak.

Physically incomplete. As though something wasn't whole. I need to find it and bring it back to where it belongs.

I know that the transmission conked out a week before Dad died, and that he'd had it towed to a shop in hopes of having his company cough up the cash for the repair. One of his colleagues suggests I check out a mechanic shop not far from the head office of the engineering firm where my dad worked. Sometimes they had their vehicles serviced there.

I find the extra set of keys hanging on a hook by the front door of my parents' house—or now, my *mom's* house. A friend, Alex, offers to drive me to the shop where I've been told the truck might be. Alex is one of the handful of guys who spent most of their youth at my house, hanging out with my family. Our open-door policy meant that a lot of hungry teenagers wound up at our place, raiding our fridge, even when we weren't home. I'd never known Alex's father. We'd never talked about him. We've rarely discussed serious things, though I know he's seen and dealt with much more in his life than I have. A frequent user of the eggplant emoji, Alex is the kind of guy who's always ready to cut tension with an obscene joke—but also capable of carrying enormous responsibility. He never stops working, often holding several different gigs at a time. He manages first aid protocol for film sets in Toronto and security at local nightclubs. And he is tough as hell. I once watched him throw a guy who'd pulled a knife on him across a sidewalk, through a cluster of trash cans that fell like bowling pins. Dad had been a constant encouragement to Alex throughout his life. He was one of the few men who'd told him that he believed in him. I'd never seen tears in Alex's eyes until he showed up at the hospital the day my father died.

Alex and I cross a highway overpass, next to one of the apartments Dad had let me explore as it was coming to life—riding up the temporary elevator together, passing the concrete floors that had no finished walls or windows, just the bones of what would be. His hard hat sat loose and tilted on my head. He kept me close as we reached our destination, where he'd check some overhead duct work or something else I didn't understand. I looked out from the open edge into the clear blue, the skyline of Toronto laid out in the distance, birds flying by. It was the most exhilarating thing I'd ever seen. I pressed close to him as he chatted with the crew, holding his hand tight as we stood there in the sky.

Moving towards the edge of town, near the international airport, I know we're getting close. I can feel it in my throat. The area near my father's office is a maze of endless industrial complexes that all blend together. I'm not sure what we'll find, if anything at all. But then we turn left off Torbram Road—and there it is. The blue nose peeks out from the edge of a lot at the far end of the block. It's a dark-blue Ford F-150 and there are countless like it on the road. But this one is different. I recognize it right away. I *know* this truck. I've watched it pull up so many times that I've memorized its image—the crack in the windshield, the rust around the wheel well. But it's even deeper, more instinctual than that. It's the way you can spot a loved one in a large crowd. Or your pup in a dog park full of matching Doodles. The identical is decipherable to family.

My heart races as we slow and turn into the lot. I'm flooded with relief—as if I've found something that's been searching for me just as much as I've searched for it. Something that was stolen or lost but is finally back where it belongs.

For a brief moment I expect to see him open the door and climb out with a wide smile, as he's done every time before. But it's just a flash, a twitch in the muscle of my memory. The pain grows in my throat. The truck is dusty. It looks forgotten. Abandoned. As though it's just been left there, waiting to rot away. I get out of Alex's car and he waits as I walk up to the driver's side door. I put my hand on the hot blue metal and brush away the dirt. I run my fingers along the numbered buttons beneath the door handle, ones that carry an unlock code that has been lost with him. I give it a shot—maybe we'd be in sync. I punch in *4-5-1-0*, the first four digits in our home phone number. Nothing. I try *0-6-5-5*, his birthday. Nothing. *5-5-0-6*. No.

I look through the window into the empty cab, still littered with the receipts and papers that recorded his final journeys. I sigh, pushing the unlock button on the spare set of keys I'd found, hoping the battery still works. *Thunk.* The locks unbolt. I pull the door open and feel the sun's heat rush past me with a familiar scent of dry mud and sawdust. I breathe deep, taking it in. The strips of duct tape he'd used to cover a rip in his seat wilt upwards, exposing the yellow foam beneath. The roll of tape in the side console, the cloth work gloves he kept handy, the coins in the cup holders, the screwdriver and tape measure between the seats, his workboots in the backseat—it's all here, waiting for him.

I step up and slide behind the steering wheel, leaning back against the faded grey fabric. Just above the rear-view mirror I find his black Ray-Ban sunglasses and put them on. I rest my arm on the middle console and put my left hand on the steering wheel, the same position he took whenever we drove—left hand on the top of the wheel, right arm resting so that his shoulder leaned back, tilting slightly towards me.

It feels strange, sitting there in his space—in *his* place. The passenger seat is empty. *My seat.*

I turn the key—*click, click, click . . . click, click, click.* Lifeless. I try again, twisting hard, as though a little more force could will it back to life. But again, no reply. This vessel that carried us from adventure to adventure between the edges of sky is now nothing more than a hunk of rusting metal. The jolting halt to what had been the constant forward momentum of our lives.

I shake my head, looking over at my empty seat, and see myself sitting there, looking back through all our years. I picture him looking over at me and smiling softly, the way he always did. I can feel him there with me. I swear it. Ghosts are memories that you feel. And for the first time, it feels like he isn't gone.

I need that feeling again. I want to live in it. There is no way, I think, no way it dies here.

It will cost thousands to fix something that—after more than a decade and some quarter-million kilometres—is barely worth that much alive and running. The rust around the wheels is spreading to the frame beneath the rear doors. The air conditioning conked out years ago.

I can see him telling me to just let it go. "It's just a truck," he'd say. "Don't be ridiculous."

The tow truck I've called arrives a few minutes later. It rigs up the truck, lifting its front wheels off the ground, and then pulls out towards the road. The frame is like a corpse being carted away. Alex and I follow behind in solemn procession until we reach a local mechanic shop where my father always took our cars to be fixed. When I called ahead, Dex, the owner, told me he'd start looking for used transmissions. It was likely going to be a couple thousand dollars. But he'd do his best to keep the costs down, he said, knowing why I was trying to fix it up.

"It's such a shame. Your dad was a good man," he said over the phone. "You just never know."

The shop is closed when we get there, so the driver unhooks the truck in the back lot, next to a row of other dead vehicles awaiting revival—cars with bashed-in doors, shattered windows, and rusted-out frames, on the verge of being sent to the junkyard. Dad's truck sat beside them, still dusty, still lifeless, but taller and prouder than the others.

Dex calls a couple of days later. I hold my breath, waiting for the diagnosis. He's found a decent deal on a transmission that has a little more than ten thousand kilometres on it; it'll cost about $2500. If we dropped it in, the truck would run great, he says. But—the inevitable bad news—the brake pads absolutely need to be replaced too. It'll run me another grand.

After *that*, though, it'll be almost perfect . . . aside from the rust, the cracked windshield, and the balding tires. Otherwise, good as new.

It's been less than two weeks since my father died. The thought that I could bring our spaceship back to life gives me the feeling that I'm in control of something, finally, after being powerless to stop him from leaving. But there is no practical use for this truck in my life. I don't have construction sites to visit. I don't have lumber to pile in the back or tools to cart around. I don't have a son or daughter to spend time with on the road.

It doesn't matter. I want to feel the engine rumble to life beneath me. I want to decide what gets to survive. I want to sit in his seat, take the wheel, and steer our indestructible ride through the next leg of our never-ending journey. Because this is much more than an old truck. In my mangled grief—this twisting wreck of fear and pain— I've convinced myself that I need to fill the space he left behind.

So a few days later, I return to Dex and a massive bill. It's more than I've ever spent to repair anything, but it's the first time spending that much money has ever felt worth it. I pay the bill and take the keys. The truck sits in the parking lot. It seems brighter than it did those few days before. The blue paint sparkles in the sun.

I unlock the door and climb back into the driver's side. I turn the ignition and feel the rumble. The truck's low murmur, its vibration, is like a miracle. This thing was dead but now it is alive. It is defiance. It is resurrection. He's here.

"There you are," I say.

Idling in the mechanic shop parking lot, I run my hands along the steering wheel as my eyes well. On the back side of its faux-leather wrap, near the top left side of ten o'clock, my finger runs across a small divot. It surprises me, but I understand the mark immediately. There he was: his right arm resting on the console, his body tilted slightly towards me in the passenger seat, and his left hand gripping the wheel—always in the exact same spot, on top, to the left, so his wedding ring pushed into the soft wrap, leaving a permanent impression. A trace of him that time had not got around to effacing.

My finger circles the indent again, slowly this time. I close my eyes and lean forward, resting my forehead on the wheel between my hands as the truck trembles beneath me. After a long moment, I sit back in the seat and shift the truck into reverse, ready to bring it home. I grip the wheel with my left hand, holding the memory of his.

5

The wedding hit us a few months after the funeral, pulling us towards it while we tried to hold ourselves in the past. It was going to happen. And it was going to be beautiful, the kind of celebration my little sister Jenna and her fiancé, Tim, deserved.

But it was also going to be brutal.

We'd never had a family celebration like this. Jenna, the youngest by five years, would be the first of us to get hitched. While our parents had been supportive of both me and Jai as we blundered unmarried through adulthood, there was always an underlying—and sometimes overt—hope that we'd just hurry up and settle into our duty as humans to wed and start families of our own. I'd been a terrible disappointment on that front. But not Jenna. She'd been dating Tim, her teenage sweetheart, for years. He was a strong, burly lumberjack of a man, with a soft heart. He was lovely and perfect for her.

Our parents had paid for the venue, even though Dad wasn't keen on the rustic, understated fieldhouse with its sizable downtown price tag. It didn't matter, though. He'd wanted Jenna to have everything exactly as she dreamed it up. He'd told his close friends how proud, how excited he was about the day he'd get to walk her down the aisle. Even that would have been a task. He'd have cried the whole way.

We know he'd want the day to be perfect for Jenna. But as much as we wanted to push past it, the reality was that he wasn't there—and the depth of that hole would be impossible to avoid.

A few days before the wedding I stay up through the night, driving towards another book deadline I'd botched. It's the day of the wedding rehearsal. Everyone in the party is coming over to run through the game plan in our backyard. I lie down a couple hours after sunrise and wake up to the sound of people laughing downstairs. In a daze, for several moments, I'm confused. I've forgotten about the all-nighter and the rehearsal. I just know that I'm lying in bed at our home and that I hear my family downstairs having a wonderful time. For a few brief moments I allow myself to imagine Dad in the kitchen with them, flipping pancakes and frying bacon. I imagine him laughing along while Jai or Jenna fills the room with some wild, exaggerated story. He smiles and shakes his head, listening as they go on and on. It was one of his favourite things to do, he told me several times—just listening to "his girls" laugh and tell tales. He'd have spent his life doing that if he could.

The illusion lingers a few moments longer. I lie there listening as long as I can before the truth of it returns. This is reality now and I have to deal with it. I've tried to push it down for months, but it's back and it's unavoidable. It crashes through me, and I break into a heaving sob.

I feel pathetic. Grief has obliterated me. The bags below my eyes rest on my cheeks, which sag with the weight of my wild, untrimmed beard. In a few months I've aged physically and regressed emotionally. I'm at least a dozen pounds heavier. I've allowed myself to crumble. He'd be so disappointed in what I've let myself become.

We make it through the rehearsal with smiles and laughs, and carry the act through dinner at my parents' favourite Italian restaurant. I force a smile through the next few days leading up to the wedding. I feel terrible about it—about not being able to fight through the cloud that hangs over the celebration. Jenna deserves better than that, although I know she feels it too.

Grief is universal, of course. We all fight with it at some point. Some people live their entire lives constantly facing it down. Some endure such brutal bouts—the death of a child, I can only imagine, being the worst of all. Still, I hadn't expected such a blow to follow my father's death. I'd witnessed good friends go through the exact same thing, and while they each dealt with the pain differently, they each *dealt with it*. But I'm not dealing with anything at all. Part of me doesn't want to because moving forward feels like some kind of betrayal. And what's the point of the coming days and months and years if he's not there to share them with?

I know it's a completely irrational way to think. I'm furious with myself for it, but I still can't break it. During those hours at my father's desk working on the book I'm behind on, I've spent far too much time procrastinating by flipping through the C.S. Lewis anthology he left on top of a stack of old bills. One of the titles in the collection is *A Grief Observed*, Lewis's reflection on the death of his wife, Joy Davidman, in 1960. He'd initially published it under a pseudonym, N.W. Clerk, perhaps because the raw sentiment of his pain and spiritual doubt seemed incongruous with Lewis's great esteem as a writer of faith. Having lived with a similar faith for much of my life, forged through my evangelical upbringing, I appreciated his honesty.

"No one ever told me that grief felt so like fear," Lewis wrote, describing the unexpected emotion that overcame him when he lost his wife. "I am not afraid, but the sensation is like being afraid. The same fluttering in the stomach, the same restlessness, the yawning. I keep on swallowing."

I swallowed hard, reading that.

Lewis's vulnerability gave me comfort. Fear was exactly the feeling. Constant, unabating fear. It's that feeling you get when you just know that something isn't quite right, isn't quite secure, and all that should be safe is exposed. Not fear of something, in particular—but a fear that fills an absence. So maybe what I felt and what Lewis described wasn't really fear so much as it was loneliness. The great, wide, unavoidable absence. I was surrounded by family and friends who loved me. But none of them had been the voice that wrapped around me since I was young. Although I loved them, I didn't rely on them or seek them out. None of them meant what Dad had meant to me. They didn't play the role of supporter or confidant. I didn't think to call them when I was awed by an adventure or faced with some terrible fear. But I did with him. I hadn't realized that we spoke almost every day, for no reason and every reason. We'd shared it all. And now that he was gone, even though I was surrounded by everyone, I had no one. No one like him, anyway. No one who could fill the space he left behind. Yes, that was it: loneliness. That was the feeling of fear that ached in me.

"At other times it feels like being mildly drunk, or concussed," Lewis wrote. "There is a sort of invisible blanket between the world and me. I find it hard to take in what anyone says. Or perhaps, hard to want to take it in. It is so uninteresting."

I was mildly drunk, too. And quite often. Lately I'd found that most things make more sense with tequila. I could feel that blanket separating me from the rest of the world, and I had little desire to rejoin it. That probably should have been the scariest feeling of all. The drinking had become a point of contention between me and Jayme. More than anyone, she knew what I was doing to myself. And I was good at it—meaning, I'm a good drunk. I don't get belligerent or angry. I get louder, but just enough to avoid offence—and I'm never the loudest in the room. Usually I just fold into myself, drowning out everything else around me. Or, with good friends, I melt into innocuous conversation, washed in numbness—having another, and another—until I can feel something like happiness down to my toes. Those are the binges that create the most tension with Jayme, because I stay out late and lose all sense of time. It's irresponsible and sloppy, and a form of self-destruction. But I'm defiant. The world keeps on spinning, and I simply and truly do not care. It is so uninteresting. I'll stay drunk behind the veil, restless and fluttering and swallowing, swallowing—stuck firmly, stubbornly, in this place between then and now.

The night before Jenna's wedding, the four of us meet in a suite near the venue—my mother, sisters, and me. It feels like an odd return to those long-ago days when we'd pack up the van and travel south through the States, where we'd visit family in Georgia and Disney World in Florida. We'd drive through the Appalachians, riding along sweeping tree-lined hills and cutting through long dark tunnels. And at night, when Dad—who always drove—was too tired to keep going, we'd find a roadside motel to settle into for the night. The five of us would snuggle into two beds somewhere in the middle of America. The comfort and safety of home travelled with us. It didn't matter how many hours or days we were from the start; if it was the five of us together, we were home.

Years later, when I was away in Ottawa working on a post-graduate degree in journalism, the four of them came down for a weekend to visit. I'd rented a small bachelor apartment, which Dad had driven five hours to move me into—the two of us hulking up bookshelves, a desk, and bed—before he drove five hours back home that night. When the four of them came down, we didn't even think of renting a hotel room. We all crammed together in my three-hundred-square-foot apartment. It was crowded, but after a day of skating on the Rideau Canal and exploring the capital's ice sculptures, we all just passed out on the couch, futon, and bed. I'd lain on the lumpy loveseat, tossing and turning, trying to find an angle in which to sleep while Dad snored loudly a couple of metres away in my bed. I thought about the many journeys we'd shared on the road, our ship carrying us through the days and nights.

Our last journey together was the winter before he died. For Christmas, we'd surprised our parents with a family trip to a cottage in Muskoka. For years they'd unveil our next "Robson Family Adventure" as we sat around the tree opening presents. We'd been to typical hot spots like Jamaica and Mexico, although in later years we went mostly to the Ontario woods for snowshoe or snowmobile treks—but also just to sit by the fire in a rented cabin, playing board games and sipping hot chocolate. We knew this would be the last with just the five of us, with Jenna getting married the next fall.

A snowstorm hit on that final trip in early January. We sat inside the A-frame cottage overlooking a lake as enormous snowflakes swooped and swirled in the moonlight, landing softly on the white blanket that covered the ice. We played Risk late into the night, with Dad becoming champion of the world. The next morning, before any of us had woken up, he was outside shovelling several feet of snow off the driveway and clearing the cars—even though we had no intention of leaving. It was just an old habit, I guess. I opened the door with a coffee in hand and felt the cold rush in. He stood there smiling with apple-red cheeks, a shovelful of snow, and a clear driveway behind him. He wore a black toque and my blue Brampton Capitals parka from when I'd played junior hockey a dozen years before.

"Need a hand?" I asked.

"Now?" he laughed. "It's already done."

"Yeah," I said. "Perfect timing."

He came in from the cold, and we had a feast of an old-school winter breakfast—cinnamon buns, pancakes, sausages, everything. And afterwards we all went to explore the wonderland. Dad grabbed hold of Mom—who wore a bright-pink one-piece snowsuit she'd had since the eighties—and swung her around playfully in a bank of snow. They both had bigger smiles and laughs than I'd ever remembered, flirting like they were young. We tossed around snowballs, made angels in the drifts, and marched across the white fields, sinking down to our knees. And as the three of us walked ahead down a clearing, Mom and Dad stayed back. He snapped a photo of us moving away from them, up the path between the trees.

Dad was always the one who took the photos while we played in the sand and waves, in autumn leaves, on the ice and in the snow. It was always us looking back at him as he'd pause to capture the moment. I'd searched through hundreds of old photographs when he died, looking for one of us together—but there weren't many with him actually in the frame. We had piles of photos of our world through his eyes. But there were so few of how we saw him.

He did get to see Jenna in her wedding dress, though. The girls sent him a photo of her in it when she went for a fitting that December.

"She's beautiful," he texted. "And I haven't even cried yet."

A few minutes later, he wrote again.

"Okay, now I've shed a few tears."

As my family slept the night before the wedding, I sat on the couch in the hotel suite, thinking about how our lives had been framed by him. Dad was the happiest behind the lens. He'd build the deck, barbecue the food, fix the cars, clear off the snow, take the pictures—he'd build and provide everything we needed for those small moments of our lives. He'd take it in from the sidelines, finding his joy in watching ours. So it was terribly fitting that it was the four of us left without him. Dad had to be the first to fade away, because as difficult as it was for the rest of us, a world with one of us missing would have been unlivable for him. This was always how it had to be.

It's a bitter morning, with rain on the way. Guests are given blankets in the courtyard to keep them warm. Jai and I stand at the front, just ahead of Tim. Then Jenna emerges. I can't imagine what she feels not having her father there to walk her down the aisle. But my little sister is brave and tough and makes the long walk alongside my mother, the two of them the perfect picture of strength and grace. The dress is beautiful, and the girl in it, just as Dad said. All eyes turn to her. She smiles at Tim, her lumberjack prince.

They are married just before the sky opens.

It is the most beautiful day our family has had. And it's the worst since May. Every smile hurts because our lives are moving on without him.

Jai and I went to Dad's office to clear out all his things a couple of weeks after the memorial. Everyone stopped in their cubicles and stared at us as we walked by to unseal the tomb marked Rick Robson, with a key from human resources. A whiteboard near the front desk lined with employees' names still had his name up, with a circle magnet marking him "In."

His desk was untouched since the last time he'd been there, a week before he died. It was cluttered and messy. It looked like he'd been in a rush to leave. There wasn't much to the space—a modest rectangle on the second floor with a wall of windows that looked out over the parking lot. A dusty fake plant standing in the corner by the frosted glass wall and door to the hallway. A half-empty jar of cashews. One of those old calculators that print answers on a roll of paper. Photos of his wife and kids. A version of us, as seen by strangers.

There were at least a decade of documents and notebooks stored in the shelves in and above his standard-issue faux-mahogany desk, and rolls of old blueprints stacked in the corner. It looked as though he'd kept a record of every project he'd ever worked on. A water main and sanitary sewer on Dixie Road in 2010. A 7-Eleven at Spadina and College. A contract for a Shell gas station in Fort McMurray, dated May 13—the project he went out West for, when I spoke to him last. The brochure for Paramount Design Build, the company he'd started in the mid-1990s and sold to a bigger company that led to this office and his magnet marked eternally "In."

I couldn't picture Dad enjoying his time there, although several of the solemn onlookers stopped to tell us how happy he'd made them and how shocked and sad they were that he was gone. I could tell they meant it. The receptionist started to cry. We nodded and said thank you, because no one ever really knows what to say in moments like that.

We were told we could take only personal items, but it all seemed personal to me. I quickly filled a dozen bankers boxes with his old files, as though I were securing state secrets. The language of contracts, work orders, and blueprints was all foreign code to me—but it still felt like part of him, and I resented the notion of having to leave any part of him behind. On his desk I found a pad of graph paper—the only kind he ever wrote on—with notes he'd written to himself, the letters perfectly proportioned within the squares even though they'd been written quickly.

"Remember," he wrote at the top of the page. "Don't rely on our understanding. Proverbs 3:5."

It's a Bible verse I'd learned by heart as a child and was still lodged deep in my memory, like an old tune you can't forget. *Trust in the Lord with all your heart, and lean not on your own understanding. In all your ways acknowledge him, and he shall direct your path.*

I wondered why Dad had written that and why he'd left it on his desk. Years before I probably would have read it as a divine sign. I took a picture of it with my phone and slid the notebook into a box along with all the other coded messages I vowed to decipher later.

Those boxes are now stacked in Jai's old bedroom—the room where we used to say our prayers as a family each night, the room he'd turned into a home office when we all left for school. It's been six months since we packed them up and brought them here. None are opened.

For me, it's been half a year of falling apart.

I've finished writing two books in that time, written almost entirely in my father's home office, at the black-brown Ikea desk next to the stack of boxes filled with his career. My mind and body worked, co-operating with the spinning world—but my heart has remained stuck in the past. I learned that I can function well enough on autopilot, especially when there's no alternative. Deadlines have to be hit. Bills have to be paid. But the fear of failing was the only thing that kept me going.

Everything on the desk is just as he had it. The whiteboard above still has all his notes and the papers he'd clipped to it with magnets. His briefcase sits at the bottom left of the desk, where he'd placed it the last night he came home. And I wrote and wrote each day, and each night I readjusted the jar with his pens and pencils and moved his ruler back into place.

I've spent very little time at the place in Toronto that Jayme and I share. She knew I was broken, so she mostly accepted my absence— but I know it hurt her. I've put the life we promised to build together on pause. I haven't been able to feel the excitement of the dreams we shared. I haven't been able to feel much at all, besides anger and exhaustion. I worked from morning to night, writing and writing— losing myself in other people's stories, unwilling to face my own. Because when I did face it, it felt as though the walls were caving in.

So I pushed forward, thinking it was what I was supposed to do, because if you keep moving you can't fall. And when I looked in the mirror and saw my sagging eyes and the weight in my face, I didn't recognize myself. When I realized that the scotch bottle on the shelf was near empty again, I told myself it was only for the buzz. When I heard Jayme's voice breaking on the phone, asking if I could just come home, I told myself that she didn't understand. And I let myself resent her for it.

Death is a flame. It doesn't stop with the last breath. It flickers and jumps, and spreads to all the edges of the lives of those left behind, withering them. Death burns and keeps burning, if you let it. It burns until you fall apart.

Half a year has gone like that, and I'm no closer to closure than I was the day the phone woke me from my sleep. Deep inside, I know it. Deep inside, I feel ashamed. I can feel the part of me that is screaming at me to stop this ridiculous cycle of grief. To get up and move forward—to live my life the way my father would want me to. Part of me knows that the flame has reached my future. That if I don't stop this now, I'll lose Jayme—I'll lose everything.

But I don't go back, because I need to fill the void he left. I think about my mother living there, alone, without him—and the thought feels like abandonment. I think about the house, crumbling without his hands, and it is betrayal. I stay to fight those feelings, even though I know they are my own illusions.

When I was young, sleeping in these rooms, I had a recurring nightmare. It haunted me for years. I'd dream that I was awake and alert, but alone. I'd be in a bedroom, or the living room, and suddenly I'd feel something grab hold of my arms and begin to pull me further into the room. I couldn't move. I'd try to scream, but I'd have no voice. No one was coming to save me. The unseen force was holding me, taking my breath away. I was stuck, until I'd wake up in a panicked sweat and run into my parents' room and climb into their bed to hide beside my father.

I think about those haunting dreams and wonder if that's how he felt as he lay on the floor beside that same bed, unable to move or speak, dying. I feel that way now. And somewhere in the depths of me I know that the real reason I'm stuck here, in this place, in this state, is that the grip of guilt and grief won't stop until I force myself to wake up.

The house has gone untouched since the day he died, aside from the inevitable accumulation of things. The problem of it is inescapable. In our house, every task had fallen to him, from tightening the smallest loose screw to tearing down walls.

And he loved it. Whenever he received a call from me or my sisters while we were away at school, wondering how to fix this or that—really, asking him to come down and fix it for us—he always seemed eager to get in his truck and drive over, as though he was happy we'd found yet another thing we needed him for. Fixing was a kind of love for him. I think he found joy not only in the work but also in the outcome. In a practical sense, there was very little in our lives that Dad couldn't fix with his tools. I can't remember a single time when he had to call on someone else to get a job done. And he was often the person whom people we knew called when they needed help. If it was something they didn't know how to do, Rick would know. They relied on him. I think knowing that enriched him.

The house he fixed is our biggest problem now. We refuse to just sell it. It feels too much like quitting—and besides, Mom isn't ready to leave it behind, she tells us. I wasn't either, so even if she'd wanted to move she'd have felt too much pressure to stay.

But if we wouldn't let it go, we'd have to find a solution to the matter of Mom living here alone. That thought plagues me more than anything.

Renovating the basement is her idea. Years ago, Dad roughed in plans to put in a full bathroom and bedroom, but there was never time to get it done. Why not finish the job now? There are always people at the church looking for a place to stay. And the addition would help cover the cost of maintaining the place, and potentially fill it with life again.

It was a good idea, but actually carrying it out presents another problem entirely.

Through the near dozen times Dad had moved me between cities and condos throughout my twenties he had, without fail, managed to find a construction flaw in each of them. Most were blamed on the work of lazy, rushed contractors who just wanted to get the job done. He'd check out a door that wouldn't shut cleanly, a towel rack barely clinging to drywall, or a light switch that appeared to have no purpose, and he'd shake his head at the state of the world today.

His handiness was just a wonderful convenience then. And I shrugged off my father's attention to detail as an idiosyncrasy. I'd never considered the philosophy behind his disgust for cutting corners. If you started a job, you needed to finish it right. That was one very clear lesson he'd taught me. To always do your best work, because that is how you will be remembered.

I knew that if this was a job Dad could take on, he wouldn't seek outside help. It was a simple renovation, after all—put up a few walls, add a tub and a toilet, slap on some paint, and call it a day. So the idea of bringing in an outside contractor to finish Dad's job felt wrong. It was a skill set that had been close to me my entire life, and yet one I'd never sought to master, let alone show any real interest in. But I'd wanted to. I'd planned to. I'd told myself that one day, when life slowed down and maybe I had a son of my own, Dad and I would take the time to build something together.

It was always someday, though. Never today. And today never came, and so we never did.

Guilt is a twisted cousin of grief. Sometimes they seem almost identical, tangled up in each other. But grief is understandable. It's the agony of absence. That knowledge deep in your consciousness that no matter what you believe—no matter what faith you carry, what hope you possess—it is a near certainty that you will never see the person you love again. Maybe that feeling is wrong (and wouldn't that be wonderful), but we all recognize it. Grief is the endless good-bye. But guilt, after death, is different. It's the pain of memory. It's the realization that there are no more chances to make right what you should have in life. People leave forever, but their ghosts linger, at least for a time, in the constant haunting of our minds.

As much as my father's tools and the things he built carry his memory, they carry my guilt. In my adult life, I'd focused entirely on my own journey. I never took a Saturday to sit in the garage and work with my father on the car or help him construct a new shelf for the laundry room. I never asked him to show me how to use his new table saw without chopping off a finger, or how to sink a nail on the first swing. It just wasn't useful information to me, then. I didn't know what it meant to be square, plumb, and level—even though he'd been showing me his entire life.

And let's just lay out the metaphor here. This guilt isn't just about the physical tools I didn't learn how to use while he was here. It's about the life of a man I loved deeply but never took the time to understand. It's about hearing the words spoken at his packed memorial—seeing that he touched people's lives in meaningful ways—and not knowing why or how he'd done that. And realizing that I'm not equipped to do the same.

This pain is about the feeling that I've failed him as well as the need to keep learning from him and from his life, because he left me incomplete. That's what I see in a bag of tools that I don't know how to use and in a house that's falling down.

There is a belief in Japanese folklore that tools acquire souls through use. I'm not an expert on *tsukumogami*, but the idea that objects carry life when they're properly used resonates with me. When I grasp the smooth, worn leather grip on my father's oldest hammer, it feels like so much more than a piece of steel. Dad brought this hammer to life. He gave all these tools purpose—he gave them a soul.

So when Mom suggests the renovation, I see it as a way to find him again. A way to spend time with his ghost and the tools he animated. A way to give them purpose again. This is my chance to keep that part of him alive.

"I'll do it," I tell Mom. "I'll renovate the basement."

She looks up, trying to find a soft way to say the obvious.

"Well, maybe you can help someone?"

She means hire someone else to do it. The thought is unconscionable. But I also know she's right. If I tried to renovate the basement alone, it would end badly. Very badly. I don't know the slightest thing about what I've proposed. The truth is, I don't even know the difference between a Phillips and a Robertson screwdriver. I don't know how to lock in a drill bit or operate a circular saw. I certainly have no concept of how to put up studs and drywall a room. Every interaction I've had with tools has been beside Dad, watching Dad, admiring Dad—but never actually emulating him. Never learning the same way he had from his father.

If I don't know how to replace one of the rotting pieces of wood on the deck, how can I possibly think I can figure out how to frame, wire, drywall, plumb, or tile on my own?

There is one possible way around this, though. One of my closest friends, Andrew Lockhart, is one of four brothers who grew up in an endlessly creative and wildly rambunctious household. Their mother, Claire, is a colourfully talented art teacher, and their father, John, a sharp, logical personal injury lawyer. The boys inherited both of their parents' traits. Sleepovers at the Lockhart house regularly included a vigorous debate about religion or politics, the completion by at least one of the brothers of a self-directed art project, and a fist fight. Without any brothers of my own, I viewed the Lockhart boys as a mystifying model for the competitive chaos of brotherhood. They were gifted, erudite, wild things. And I loved them dearly. Andrew completed an MBA at Stanford and now runs his own start-up in Silicon Valley. Luke, the eldest, also has an MBA and works in marketing. Tim, the third, is a lawyer. Matthew, the youngest, is the most creative—and struggled to find the right fit for those talents until embarking on a series of do-it-yourself projects and realizing a remarkable skill for renovations and carpentry. He's recently finished the Lockhart basement, one that once served as a dank, unfinished arena for those heated debates, art shows, and bloody brawls. He's also built a large deck in their backyard, which my father had stood on, inspected casually, and approved of overwhelmingly. Now, after flipping a couple of houses, Matthew and his wife, Rachael, have launched a design and renovation company.

It was Andrew who first suggested that I chat with his little brother about my family's intentions for the basement and my unreasonable plan to complete them by myself.

"Why not hire Matt?" he says. "Do the job with him."

It's a decent idea. I knew Matt well enough to know that he'd understand my obsession with being part of the teardown and resurrection. He was close enough that he might tolerate my bumbling presence as we worked side by side.

The Lockhart boys grew up within a devoutly Christian household and Matt had come to a profound experience with faith in adulthood. He was one of the many who came to visit us at the hospital after we'd been told there was nothing that could be done to save Dad. He stood next to the bed where Dad lay, connected to tubes and wires and a bunch of beeping machines, and he prayed. It was deep and earnest, with his full heart, with every last ounce of faith that I knew he truly, deeply believed in. I was grateful.

Matt was excited when I called to ask him about doing the basement. He's the kind of guy who *always* sounds thrilled, but I could tell the concept had connected with him. He happily agreed.

With him on board, I've tweaked Dad's original plans just enough to gain Mom's approval. Matt and Rachael come over to discuss the project. Rachael is the grounded, professional mind in the operation—the perfect balance to Matt's scattered, creative genes. He's sketched out a rough outline for the basement while she's prepared a "lookbook" of potential tiles, flooring, paints, and designs my mother might want to use in the new basement. I'd thought the process would weigh heavily on my mom, but she seems energized—eager for the improvement.

It's comforting to see Mom's keen interest as she sits at the dining room table flipping through the colour schemes and design options Rachael has brought along. She seemed refreshed and recharged—excited to push forward, after these hard months, with a future she'll have to design on her own.

Part II
Foundations

6

When I was nearing fourteen and he was past forty, Dad and I renovated the main floor of our house by removing a wall between the
kitchen and the family room. I say "Dad and I" because that was how
he framed it—as if I were part of the project, a member of the crew.

My specific job was to help him knock down the wall by smashing a hammer through the drywall between the studs, punching out
holes wherever I could. It was destructive and deeply satisfying work.
We bashed the wall to bits, exposing the unseen space between. We
toppled old studs that had held up the wall, and I helped Dad carry
them out to the garage. Later we ripped up the linoleum in the
kitchen and the beige carpet in the living room. We replaced these
with hardwood, connecting the rooms together.

There was something in the demolition and the rebuild that I
found exciting. You don't often get permission to whack through a
wall with a hammer. I was astonished to discover that our house had
its own skeleton, these old bones, that held everything together. It
was part of the structure and shape of our place. I'd never considered
that many of the walls between us could just come down—but there

we were, smashing through the drywall, moving the duct work, and cutting out the wooden frame.

With the wall down, from the kitchen sink you could see over the table and all the way to the fireplace in what had been the living room. The transformation of two rooms into one seemed remarkable to me. The wall had appeared so permanent, but nothing really is. That's just how we see it. Two unique spaces, each carrying its own collection of moments and memories, merging into something familiar but entirely new. And by our own hands.

Before we finished the renovation, we decided to put together a time capsule to explain who we were to whoever might find it long after we were gone.

I typed out the details: that we were a family of five—Mom, Dad, me, and my slightly older sister Jaime, and our younger sister Jenna. We had a cat and a dog, our dad worked in construction, and our mom was a nurse. I planned to be a goalie in the NHL. Jean Chrétien was prime minister. Each of us included something we cherished, something that would help show the future exactly who the Robsons were. (My artifact was a Patrick Roy hockey card, the Montreal Canadiens goalie who was my boyhood idol.)

We placed it all in a Ziploc bag inside an old shoebox and wrapped it with tape. Then I laid it on the floor, just inside an opening between two studs. Dad put up the drywall, sealing in the story of us.

Later we embarked on another home improvement project. Dad sketched out the plan on a napkin at the Family Restaurant, an old greasy spoon where we'd often go after church. We were all getting older and it was apparent that more space was badly needed. The basement was no longer usable in its unfinished state. We'd outgrown the blank canvas that the concrete floors and wooden rafters provided. We had no more use for the old toys, the playhouse, the chalkboard, or the easel. Imagination alone wasn't enough. We were teenagers and needed a space to entertain our friends—to navigate the complicated social scene of adolescence.

Dad's plans included a large open rec room with a tiled drop ceiling and a carpeted floor. And at the bottom of the stairs that led into it he planned to add a new bathroom and bedroom.

I poured syrup over my pigs-in-a-blanket as we considered Dad's rough sketch.

A basement is the most honest space in a house. And ours was much more authentic than the tidy halls and rooms of the main floor hastily cleaned whenever visitors arrived. The polished veneer of the entrance, the tidied living room, the sparkling kitchen always felt like a family fib that smelled of Pledge and freshly placed potpourri. The basement held the scattered, messy truth that lay beneath us.

It was the starting and ending point for so many childhood adventures. It was where we spent our rainy days in the summer and our evenings when it was too dark to play outside. It was where the cardboard box our refrigerator was delivered in became a small plane that took us around the world. The basement was where our painted masterpieces came to life on the wooden easel Dad built for us, literally painting the wood when we ran out of paper. It was where Teenage Mutant Turtles went to war with Batman and the Joker, where we practised the cursive we'd learned in school on a chalkboard drilled into the concrete, where we pretended to be grown-ups in a two-storey wooden playhouse that soared from the floor to the ceiling.

The basement was hockey cards, Slinkys, Play-Doh, Nerf guns, My Little Pony, and My Little Monster. It was Christmas mornings and birthday parties. It was the Secret Garden; it was Narnia.

It was popsicles and ice cream cake. It was kids who had it all, and exhausted parents fretting over adult things to keep it that way. It was fist fights and tantrums and tears.

Under the plans Dad proposed, the basement's cold concrete would be hidden beneath a warm layer of carpet and the marked-up grey walls and yellow insulation would be boxed in by a layer of smooth, painted drywall. The wooden rafters would be hidden by ceiling tiles.

And we'd do it all ourselves.

I went with Dad to the hardware store to pick up the wood for framing. Later, I watched as he meticulously measured each piece with the pencil he kept behind his ear. He cut each one with his mitre saw, filling the basement with clouds of sawdust. I picked up the pieces as they fell and stacked them to the side.

Dad would wear an old T-shirt and faded dad jeans, loose through the thighs and tapering in at the ankle, tucked into his clunky brown steel-toe boots. He kept his measuring tape in a brown leather tool belt slung around his waist. His forehead always carried the slight sheen of sweat as he worked. It was serious, focused business. Each squealing press to the wood with the spinning blade was exacting. It was cut clean and quick. He never missed the mark. I remember collecting the fallen ends and seeing the perfect symmetry with which the blade had erased the thin pencil line Dad had drawn. It had become dust.

The Great Basement Cleanout happens on a rainy spring afternoon. We're all there: Jai, Jenna, Mom, and me.

Before we can start the new renovation, we have to clear out the old completely. Dad would never have believed it could happen.

It's never been done. Since the day we moved in way back in the summer of 1988—when I turned five—this place has been accumulating the remnants of our family. But now a large metal garbage bin sits in our driveway and there is no avoiding it.

We stare at the boxes stacked on the shelves Dad built when we first moved in. An overflow piles up in front of them, along the wall and down the unfinished side of the basement—running the entire width of our house. It spills out into the finished part of the basement, too, from terracotta wall to terracotta wall, covering the carpeted floor with boxes, books, and gift-wrapping paper left out months before.

Where did it all come from? And why had we kept it?

As we added layer upon layer to the great collection of our lives, we had, of course, become something approaching hoarders. Dad always fought this. He wanted to clear out as much as possible. He was the least sentimental when it came to this collection of "stuff." I'm certain that one of his deepest desires was to live a clutter-free life, but his family had refused him that one perfectly reasonable wish. Even when he successfully managed to bring some order to things we'd accumulated by clearing out some of the most useless pieces and making a trip to the dump or to Goodwill, there'd just be a new box of something else to take its place. Tidiness was always fleeting in our home. It was not the natural order of things—especially in the basement.

The boxes had started to fill since my parents' wedding day, with things like the casserole dishes they never unpacked and the fondue set they brought out once or twice in the eighties when dipping forked food in hot oil was cool. We all knew that none of us would ever use the blue-and-white cross-country skis that had leaned against the wall by the furnace since the early nineties. Or the wooden tennis racquet that hadn't been used since the seventies, or the set of golf clubs from that long-ago time when woods were made of actual wood. We clung to them anyway.

The end of each school semester or new move to an apartment brought crates of barely cracked, hundred-dollar textbooks and notebooks filled with illegible scribble. Because you never know when you'll need to read that 1342-page brick of a text known as *Introduction to Contemporary Civilization in the West*, Third Edition, Volume I.

There are two old fridges along the wall next to Dad's workbench and the shelves he put up for storage. A large "Robson Renovations" magnet—with its brown-and-orange font—is stuck to the side of one of them. He put the decal on his truck when he ran his own renovation company, back around the time we were born.

There is an artificial Christmas tree and boxes of decorations that haven't been touched in two decades. There are old tea cups and candlesticks. A punch bowl on top of one of the fridges. There are bankers boxes of old bills and legal documents. And tools piled in milk crates on top and below the workbench. There are paintbrushes and hammers. Sandpaper. Wrenches. Boxes of screws, nails, and used light bulbs. Coils of electrical wire. Caulking guns. The chalkboard we used as kids leans against the wall on top of the workbench, with *Merry Christmas* scrawled in my father's handwriting in chalk. There is an open bottle of pest control poison. Half-used cans of paint, labelled in his rigid, precise print: *Jai's Old Room*—just in case cotton-candy pink comes back in style. Eggshell enamel. Semi-transparent wood stain.

"Look, Jai," I say to my sister, pointing at the easel Dad made for us, long since covered in the splashed-on paint and scribbled designs from our childhood creative art sessions.

"That's in pretty poor condition," she says.

"We're not getting rid of it," I say.

"But we could repaint it—maybe white?"

"It has all your artwork on it," I point out. "No."

There are three slim brown boxes filled with plastic cases holding old photo slides. Jai reads out the labels: "Andrew and Marion's cottage, 1980 . . . 1979 . . ."

"We should get those slides into something we can watch them on," Jenna says.

She's clearly not aware that such devices have existed as long as slides have.

Jai laughs. "Ladies and gentlemen, our sister . . ."

Jenna rolls her eyes.

Jai fiddles with the lid before she pries open another set of slides.

"Cross-country skiing—1982," she says. "I was there. I was one month old. Dad tucked me in the front of his jacket and skied with me. For real, this happened."

She flips through a few more.

"Randy and Lynn's wedding, in Georgia, 1979—Baseball!—John and Brenda—Monica and John."

Evidence of a time before us.

We shift to the stacks of *National Geographic* magazines that I used to flip through, learning about faraway places where I might travel. They sit in a box beneath my father's old drafting table, where he'd lay out the blueprints for the projects he was working on. A couple dozen of those blueprints lean in the corner and others are rolled up in a long plastic bin. All the pages have started to turn light brown and are curling at the edges like a trove of ancient treasure maps.

Slowly, the shelves begin to clear.

We open a box of colourful plush animals.

"What are these things called?" Jai asks.

"Jelly Bellies?" I say from the other side of the room.

"No. Jenna, what are these called?"

"What?" She walks down the stairs.

"Oh!" she says, in the overly excited voice that can properly be described as an exclamation, which we've mocked her for since she was young. "My Beanie Babies!"

She was once a Beanie Baby aficionado. There are dozens of these little stuffed creatures. Some are in glass cases, special edition collector's items.

"We can't get rid of these," she says.

"We have to," I say. "Or take them to your house. You live somewhere else now."

She ignores me and picks up a booklet inside the box. It's a Beanie Babies price guide.

"Market value," she says, flipping through.

Jenna sets the box in the pile of things we plan to keep, which has grown much larger than we intended.

The sun is falling and a golden light shines through the tiny basement window above the spare fridge. Beside it, an electrical panel holds a maze of intertwining wires. It looks like an elaborate bomb from the movies, when it's impossible to guess which wire to cut. We avoid it entirely.

We've spent an entire day at it. The blue garbage bin on the driveway is nearly full. Most of the shelves are bare, exposing the yellow insulation behind the warped plywood.

Jai notes the doorway into the storage area that Dad had framed in place in order to add the extra bedroom and bathroom during that initial renovation. Instead, there are two side-by-side doors to the same unfinished place. Reminders of past intentions to use the space for something practical. We all know that we're more sifting through the past than preparing for a renovation. We're bringing memories back to life before letting them go. And we're returning to those past intentions because for the past year everything has felt unfinished. We're completing the job for him now.

We take a quick break for dinner upstairs. Sitting at the kitchen table, Mom starts a conversation we've tried hard to delay.

It's April. Next month is the anniversary of our father's death. It's a cliché to say that something feels like it was yesterday, but my head spins trying to put together a year without him. So much has happened, but nothing at all. It's an unsettling feeling to understand what that means. Time has never felt this blurry before.

A week after that, it will be his birthday. We've already pushed through so many difficult moments without him—all our birthdays, the wedding, Christmas.

What will we do on the anniversary of his death?

It's not a day I'm eager to remember, I say. Jai agrees—she wants to "avoid being crippled by it," she says. But what's the right thing to do? What are you *supposed* to do? Is there protocol for this kind of thing?

And what about Dad's birthday? We seem more interested in celebrating that, even though he never was. That's something we can handle, we all agree—but we're just nodding, making no specific plans. And we move on.

His ashes are upstairs in their bedroom. Mom's bedroom, now. We haven't decided what to do with them yet. That decision feels too final. This is the first time we've spoken of it at any length.

"I don't know what Dad wanted," Mom says. "We never talked about it."

But she wants to bury his ashes in the ground. She wants a place she can visit—something permanent, a place that says he was here, that he existed, and that he mattered.

That seems too morbid to us. A cemetery? We couldn't imagine Dad wanting his ashes placed in another row of dead people.

"Who likes a cemetery?" Jai says.

A long pause.

"Some people do," Mom says. "Old women do."

Meaning her, I think.

We move on quickly, again. Because, again, no one wants to talk about it.

7

Thick black dress socks, folded once over—lined in perfect rows. White athletic socks, cut just above the ankle, each pair rolled into a tidy ball. Beside them, a pill container filled with spare change.

That's how he left them, and that's how they remain.

I open the drawer in the closet, beneath the shelf where he kept his Dolce & Gabbana cologne (a gift from Mom) and his watches (an aluminum Swiss Army one, and one with a black leather band and a rectangular gold-rimmed face, likely from Costco).

As with the items on his desk, I've tried to keep everything in place. It's an act of preservation, as though if we just kept waiting, keeping everything as it was, Dad will eventually come back. His dress shirts and sweaters hang from the rack beside the drawers. Beside the bed are his reading glasses, a Swiss Army knife, and his prescription hydrocortisone cream, all still tucked in a table that his alarm clock sat on.

I'm irritated when anyone else moves something that belongs to him. I've watched over his tools in the garage to make sure none go missing. When one of his closest friends asked to use the driver from his golf bag for an upcoming tournament they were supposed to play in together, I handed it over reluctantly—and then made up a lie about playing the next week and needing it back right away.

So, the socks—I pick out a pair of white ones.

It's early Monday morning. I've slept over at the house, again, knowing that Matt wants to get an early start on the basement. But I forgot to bring socks, so Dad's will have to do. I pull the neatly tucked ball apart and put them on carefully. They feel too thick for athletic socks. The band ends an inch above my ankle. As far as socks go, they're terrible. They're "dad socks." I'll never wear them in public, but this morning they feel right.

Next to his tool bag in the laundry room I find his workboots, which have also not moved since the day he died. I slide into them. They're too wide on the sides and I can wiggle my toes freely, although I can't feel how far they reach because of the steel toe. I tug the laces as tight as I can and tie them. The leather work belt sits on top of the tools in the tool bag. I pick it up and wrap it around my waist. It's rough and faded. I remember Dad wearing it when I was young; I figure it's the only one he'd ever owned. I clip the clasp and spin the belt around so the pouches hang at my side, as I imagine a carpenter would. It fits a little too well—better than it would have a year ago. I fill it with the things I imagine will be useful: the old hammer with its worn leather strap, a few screwdrivers with different heads, a big silver tape measure, a flat orange carpenter pencil that I sharpen with a metal retracting knife. Then I pull on a pair of black work gloves I'd found tucked inside a pocket in the front of the tool bag, completing my look.

I'm dressed the part when Matt arrives at seven-thirty a.m. The bed of his mint-green pickup truck holds a garbage can, a ladder, and a roll of insulation stacked on top of two-by-fours that have been piled several feet above the lip, everything tied down by a single strap. A large tool box teeters on one side of the bed and an air compressor angles off the other.

He parks behind my old silver Honda Civic (a landmark since its battery failed years ago), next to the dumpster.

We've made it this far.

Jonathan Jacobs, Matt's partner and apprentice, looks the part too. He's in his early twenties and tall, probably six three, with light black skin, glasses, a blue fleece, faded jeans, and workboots. As he starts to unload the truck he looks over and nods, balancing several long pieces of wood on his shoulder.

Tim arrives a few minutes later, after dropping Jenna off at the community outreach centre she helps run in downtown Brampton. If Jonathan's construction superpower is his height, Tim's is his Hulk strength. He's a fitness expert, with an affinity for wearing a disproportionate amount of plaid. He also wears brown, worn-out Sperry boat shoes everywhere he goes, from the gym to, apparently, construction sites.

Matt's in skinny jeans and a white T layered over a grey long-sleeved shirt. He's the slimmest of the bunch but also the operation's alpha, chipper and eager to get moving. He seems to be a few coffees deep as he heads downstairs, telling me how job one is to figure out how to get the long two-by-fours into the basement with the least amount of collateral damage.

We decide to pass the wood through a small basement window on the side of the house in the backyard—one of the single sources of natural light on either side of the house that isn't covered by the deck. I'm not sure that window has ever been opened. But with a couple of tugs it squeaks back—an opening wide enough to pass a couple of two-by-fours through at a time. Tim stays in the basement to pull in the lumber we pass down to him.

Pulling the wood off the bed of Matt's truck feels like a life-sized game of Jenga. I have no idea how he managed to get to our house without leaving a trail of lumber in his wake. We fumble with as many pieces of wood as we can, carrying them to the side of the house and then sliding them down through the window to Tim, who stacks the rows neatly, each the same height, perfectly aligned.

When all of the wood is unloaded, we get started with the unfinished portion of the basement—where the new bedroom and bathroom will go. The area that Dad didn't manage to complete. It's a dusty grey canvas now. Matt lays out the plans, which, it turns out, are more of a mental map than a blueprint.

This feels wrong. It's not the way my father would approach a project like this. The endless files he's left behind are enough evidence of that. I don't mean to dismiss Matt's approach, or that of any other contractor—but I just know that Dad would have started from a plan and stuck to that plan. It has a sobering impact on the spirit in which I entered this project. I set out to walk in my father's boots, to use his tools the way he did, but already I feel like a boy pretending.

First we'll mark the location of the studs (the vertical lengths of wood extending from floor to ceiling) that will make up our walls, Matt tells us. He crouches down and lays out his tape measure just off the wall where the fridge used to be.

"A two-by-four is three and a half inches, and there's a half-inch of drywall on each side," he says, making a mark with his pencil. "So it's four and half inches."

"Yep," I say, as though it's something I already know.

He scratches parallel lines with his orange carpenter's pencil and stands up.

"So," he says, pointing to the pencil markings on the floor. "There's a wall right there."

I look at the lines. It takes me a moment to realize that he's marked the start of a wall that will divide the bedroom from the bathroom, four and a half inches wide.

"All right," I say.

"And then a bathtub is five feet," Matt says.

He zips out his tape measure with practised skill and lays down a five-foot measurement from the edge of the last pencil mark he made.

"And then our wall, here—four and a half inches." He scribbles another line just beyond the last.

He keeps moving.

"There's our tub." Matt steps a few feet over to the other side of the room. "And then the toilet's going to be right here."

But the imaginary toilet seems way too close to the door Dad had installed. You'd bump right into the toilet as soon as you walked in. I keep my own counsel as Matt mumbles to himself, gesturing to the other side of the imaginary room, waving his hand as though moving the pieces around. We're half an hour in and already editing on the fly.

After brief deliberations, we keep moving without—I think—a real solution. We use a laser level to mark out the remaining bathroom walls. It shoots a straight red line across the room.

"Now, off this laser line, let's mark another one out at five feet," Matt says, but I'm not really sure why.

Tim helps Matt lay out the tape measure. I mark a line at five feet.

"Here we go," I say, with some enthusiasm.

After a few more measurements, we can see the beginning of what will become the bathroom overlaid on the battered concrete floor.

"It's going to be tight here," Matthew warns.

"Should we factor that into what we get in a vanity, then?" I say. "Like get something as narrow as we can?"

"Yeah. Not something that's too deep," Matt agrees.

I note the word "deep" as the right descriptor for vanity talk.

"Okay," I say. "We'll get like a not-deep rectangular sink kind of thing."

Matt zips in his tape measure, which I take as agreement.

"What about the tub?" I ask. "Should we revisit having a shower, or is the tub still the plan? Does it make a difference?"

I sniff, casually.

"I don't think it should matter too much," Matt says. "What I'm thinking is, let's start getting these walls up. We'll get the bedroom framed out and let things sink in a little bit..."

We're not just making edits on the fly. We're *building* on the fly. Whatever will be, will be—and it seems we have no idea what shape this place is going to take when we're done.

When we're sure of where the wall between the bathroom and bedroom will go, I pull a line covered in chalk along the laser we've shot across the room leaving a straight layer of blue dust. Matt marks another four and a half inches off the wall on one side of the open space where the bathroom will be—and Tim does it at the other. We repeat the process in the space that will become the bedroom.

We end up with a chalk outline of where our walls will stand. The idea is that, having made our marks, we've effectively created a 1:1 scale architectural drawing. We can understand the space in two dimensions. Now we push on to a third. And I can actually see the shape of things. The concern in my stomach begins to fade.

Outside in the rec area, Jonathan and I set up a workstation with sawhorses I found in the garage and lay a couple of the two-by-fours on top. Matt plugs in a red circular saw and gives me a quick tutorial on how to avoid cutting off a finger.

He begins by placing the circular saw across a piece of lumber which he grips with his right hand, and bracing the guide at the tip of the saw against the wood. With his left hand, he holds the wood in place, a few inches from the round jagged blade. Matt tells me that you have to follow the guide forward as you push through the wood so that you always cut square.

"Some guys will use a speed square," Matt smiles. "But they're not as cool as we are."

He gives the trigger on the saw a tug and it whirls briefly, making a small cut in the wood.

"You can make a little mark and see where your blade is," he says, pointing to an opening in the guide where the mark is visible.

"And then just go for it . . ."

I've watched Dad do this many times. He often coupled it with the dadest of dad jokes—bending his index finger and pretending that he'd accidentally chopped it off at the joint. That bit must have received a strong reaction at least once, because he went back to it continually.

After the lesson, Matt and Tim mark out measurements for the first "plates"—long pieces of wood that are hammered into the floor to support the studs. These plates are the next step in laying out the bedroom and the bathroom.

While they do that, Jonathan and I begin to rip up the old beige carpet in the rec room, next to the workstation. Starting behind the stairs, we cut rectangular sections and then pull each one up with a few tough tugs. Beneath the carpet is a green underlay we put down when we first finished the space. Jonathan and I tear into that as well, exposing the cold grey concrete I used to play on back when we were young and the basement was unfinished. We move quickly down the side of the room where the trophies and plaques and photos from my minor hockey life used to sit on shelves and hang on the wall. The baseboard pops off as we rip up the carpet—revealing some previously unknown water damage that has browned the old drywall.

Jonathan works more quickly than I do, and I hustle to catch up to him. Soon we're at the far corner of the basement where the TV and couch used to be. Then, when we pull up a piece of carpet beneath the little window, we uncover a thick red line on the concrete.

I'd forgotten.

Another tug reveals the rest of the rectangle Dad had carefully measured out and painted red when I was seven years old. It was my first year in organized hockey—and I'd begged him to let me play goal.

I remember the tryout for the select team. It was at Century Gardens, a rink in Brampton. I lay on my stomach as Dad strapped on the brown leather pads the team had provided. He made them too tight; I could barely bend my legs. Neither of us knew what we were doing. I wobbled around the ice and then settled into the net, which felt enormous behind me. Then I crouched, just as I'd seen the goalies on TV do. I kicked aside almost every shot I faced, flopping to my knees and pushing at the puck with an oversized stick. None of the kids could raise the puck off the ice, but I felt like a human wall.

I can still remember hearing his whistle. I looked up, and there was Dad in the stands with his pinky fingers in his mouth. He clapped and cheered. I smiled at him—then crouched and kicked away another shot.

It was after I'd made the select team as a goalie that Dad brought my road hockey net downstairs and laid out the crease on the basement floor. It was the best way to practise, he said. If I wanted to play hockey, I had to put in the work.

So I'd strap on my equipment and Dad would shoot tennis balls at me. We worked on my glove side and my blocker side. We ran through my butterfly save and my pad save. We perfected my angles—and my reaction time whenever he deflected a shot off the wall beside me.

We spent hours down in that basement. Dad didn't know anything about being a goalie; he'd never had much of a chance to play the game himself. After he died, though, I found a photo tucked away at my grandmother's house of him with a hockey team he played on as a kid. My grandfather, who was a team coach, stands at one end of the back row. I wondered why he'd never told me about that.

What Dad and I didn't know about the game, we taught ourselves. We'd read goalie technique books, and he'd watch the weekly lessons I took with the minor hockey program. We worked on the details in the basement rink together.

Take another step out.

Stick flat.

Bend your knees.

Hold your glove higher.

As I got older, I spent years on the Brampton AA travel team—the one below the top-level AAA squad. I was so frustrated that I couldn't make that top team. Once, after I played poorly in Georgetown, I threw my gear angrily in the back of Dad's truck and slammed the door when I got in. I'd cost my team the game on a terrible goal in the third period, after letting in several before that, and was furious at myself for it. It was shame and rage balled up in one. I'd failed. I bit my lip and started to cry.

Dad pulled out of the parking lot and headed for home, not saying a thing. I could tell he was angry. His nose always flared a bit when he was pissed off. The silence had told me something was wrong, but his widening nostrils confirmed it. Then, when he finally spoke, his voice was steady and firm—which is how he spoke when he was angry. He never yelled. I have no memory of him ever raising his voice. Instead it just got slower and stronger. Deliberate. He'd measured his thoughts, taking the time to consider them, which I think is what gave them such weight. His words were so heavy that they've remained stuck in my mind for decades.

"If you ever do that again, you won't play anymore."

I looked over at him, eyes red.

"It's a game," he said, softly. "It's just a game. Don't ever let it do that to you again."

I tried not to. He kept shooting and I kept learning. We kept driving to practices and games. He kept whistling from the stands. Each fall we'd go back to the rink for AAA tryouts, where I'd make it all the way to last cut. I'd walk out, disappointed. But we'd go down to the basement and practise all over again.

Then, one fall at the end of AAA tryouts, the coach called me into the locker room after practice and told me I'd made the team.

Dad saw it on my face as I walked into the lobby, lugging my enormous equipment bag over one shoulder and my pads over the other. He smiled wide—the big Dad smile that reached the edges of his cheeks and made his eyes squint. He hugged me.

"You did it, buddy," he said.

The weight of those words never left me either. We celebrated with a root beer from the concession stand.

I give the carpet another tug, ripping it up from the edge of the wall. Jonathan bats out the dust. By nine-thirty, just two hours after we started, the carpet is completely pulled up. And with a lot of its grey paint having come away with the layer of insulation, the floor looks like rough marble.

In the other room, Tim's measuring tape cracks as he retracts it. It sounds like a wooden blade snapping against the concrete floor.

Bend your knees . . .

Hold your glove higher . . .

Another step out . . .

8

I've dreamt of Dad often since he's been gone. It's always in different stages of his life, usually distinguished by the amount of hair he has on his head or the colour and pattern of a shirt I must have stored away in memory from a specific time. The pink oxford he wore in the early nineties. The red plaid from that family photo in the forest in the fall.

And once a yellow polo shirt I didn't recall. In that dream I was a kid. When we were young, children were always called down after the worship songs and before the sermons to be prayed for by the minister. Then we'd all go to the gymnasium to sing songs about Jesus, colour in pictures of David and Goliath and other Bible stories, and snack on digestive cookies and fruit punch. It would be a party. Anyway, in my dream I was standing with my sisters and mom, talking about something I wouldn't be able to recall when I woke. But I would remember feeling Dad's hand on my shoulder. I turned into him and gave him a hug. I stepped back and saw that he wore a yellow polo shirt. And then, still in the gym, I was grown—and we were standing close, looking at each other. My sisters and my mother couldn't see him. They didn't know he was there. Jai asked me who I was talking to. And Dad and I thought it was funny. We were just looking at each other, smiling and laughing—because no one else in the world knew we could.

"They wouldn't understand," he said.

I hugged him again. I could feel him; I could smell him. I hugged him tighter and could feel the muscles in his back. I wasn't yet aware of its being a dream; it was real to me, until that sinking feeling started to set in. I felt that pain that hits your throat before you cry. I looked at him and he looked at me, smiling sadly—as though he knew something that I was about to learn. I was going to wake up, and he would be gone. I hugged him again and opened my eyes in the dark.

I told Mom about the dream a few days later. She was sad because she hadn't been able to dream about him yet, and I could see in her eyes how deeply she wanted to.

I told her about the yellow shirt he wore.

She smiled.

"He wore a yellow polo shirt on our first date," she said. He went out and bought it with his sister, my aunt. He wanted to make sure he impressed her. He wore it with jeans and beige desert boots. It worked, because she never forgot it.

Mom didn't recall his yellow shirt as though it was just a coincidence that I'd dreamed it, nor did it seem to come as a shock. It was just a matter of fact—as though of course he'd appear in *my* dream wearing a shirt *she* remembered. She believes in God and in miracles. She believes in heaven and angels. I used to, too. Maybe that kind of belief, ingrained in your being as a young person, can never really escape you. Even after I'd grown out of faith in my mid-twenties and become self-righteous about my enlightenment, I still found myself praying whenever I was scared. I still do.

I'm not sure if I believe in heaven or angels, but I believe in the ghosts who live in our dreams.

After that first visit I tried to dream of him all the time. But I could never control when or why he'd show up. Sometimes, I think, we spent hours together. I remember fragments of what felt like long conversations in our own world. It was as if we'd figured out a way to be together, one that was possible only if I couldn't remember it fully in the other world. I tried to write down these dreams as soon as I'd wake up, but each time I could feel the moments receding as I typed out whatever details I could recall. The memory would start to feel more and more ridiculous as the seconds passed—until, finally, lying in bed and staring at the glow of the notes on my phone, I knew he was gone again.

The few I did manage to capture read like snapshots of a memory. Dad was fixing a table for Jai, planning to cut a right angle off an end so that it would fit into an odd groove in a new apartment she was moving into. I was helping him. I picked up his Skilsaw and cut into the table with it, sawdust flying. It was the first of the two cuts that have to meet.

"I know how to use all your tools now," I bragged to him.

Dad smiled and put his hands on top of mine, holding the saw to the table. I could feel his grip.

"You have to do it like *this*," he said, pressing down.

But when I woke up, I couldn't remember what he'd shown me.

A puff of sawdust hits my nose and I let out a wild sneeze. An expendable end of lumber topples to the floor. I sneeze again, followed by a few more with increasing violence. The whine of the saw whirls down. Matt turns as the blade slows.

"Better get some Reactine," he says.

I sniff hard.

"I live my life like this," I say, as though functioning through allergies is a sign of bravery.

A dozen two-by-fours lie in a neat pile nearby, the studs for the new bedroom walls. Now we have to piece the skeleton together, nailing the studs to the plates, which trace the floor and ceiling like the lines on Matt's plans.

But there are a few complications to account for, Matt tells me. For one thing, a large duct runs across the left edge of the ceiling, meaning we'll need to work out where to position the studs around it. He begins by laying a long flat two-by-four on the floor across the width of the wall—the plate, as I now know to call it. Then he lays down the laser level in the middle of the room, lining up the red beam that shoots along the floor and up the wall—meeting the edge of the duct that hangs from the ceiling. We'll need to place a stud that reaches from the floor to the ceiling along that mark. All the subsequent studs to the right of it will need to be cut shorter so that they reach only to the bottom of the duct, Matt says.

Seems simple enough. From the stud that lines up with the edge of the duct, we'll place the other studs every sixteen inches to the end edge of the wall. But we need to be exact, Matt says. It's sixteen inches—"on the centre"—no more or less. The bottom of the stud has to be right on the mark, he says.

"Why sixteen inches exactly?" I ask. "Why not a foot?"

Sometimes it is a foot, Matt explains. Sometimes it's two feet. It depends on what the plans call for. Floor joists—the support beams in floors and ceilings—are spaced according to both the span and the material you're using. And studs should sit directly under joists if they're bearing weight. But our partitions aren't bearing weight, and sixteen-inch centres are just close enough to keep the drywall nice and flat, he says. Later I do a little research and discover that the long-standing sixteen-inch rule became almost unbreakable after advances in machinery allowed for the development of plywood and drywall—which come in sheets measuring ninety-six by forty-eight inches. So whatever your centres are, they have to be a factor of ninety-six.

"On every tape measure you'll see the feet marked off, of course, but also the *sixteens*—a red sixteen, thirty-two, forty-eight, and so on," Matt explains. He points to the clearly marked red squares along the tape. "It makes it easy for carpenters." There's also a black diamond every three-sixteenth of an inch to help them measure out the proper distance for engineered joists, which are stronger than the usual spruce lumber and so can be spaced farther apart. That is, ninety-six divided by five rather than six.

It seems like the kind of math problem I spent my high school years daydreaming through. I don't have a mind for numbers and this all feels embarrassingly complicated. I'd never noticed the diamonds, or the red squares, or a lot of the other things built into a tape measure. The nail holder in the end hook, for example. The fact that the end hook has a bit of play in it—the exact thickness of the hook—to ensure that you get a true reading whether you're pushing or pulling the tape. The fact that the case has the length of the tape inside printed on the back so that you can keep the tape flat and add that number to the reading to get an accurate measurement.

My introduction to the mysteries of the measuring tape gives me a sense of just how much I have to learn. Surely this was the safest, least complicated tool I'd have to master? What the compound mitre saw and the Hilti drill have in store for me I can only guess. The tape cracks as Matt snaps it back into its metallic case.

There is work to do.

A wall (or "partition," as carpenters say) is assembled on the floor. Although it won't actually partition a space; instead it will stand against the concrete along the existing back wall. (Later, Matt tells me, we will be constructing the wall that'll divide the bathroom and bedroom.) I lay out the plates side by side on their edges and mark off sixteen-inch centres (using the red marks on the tape). Next, Tim and I measure out the height between the floor and the ceiling and between the floor and the duct, where the ceiling will drop. Then, with the Skilsaw, we cut the studs we'll use to make up the wall (subtracting three inches—an inch and a half for each plate; I am reminded that two-by-fours are actually an inch and a half by three and a half). Finally we line up the studs between the top and bottom plates, aligning their ends with each mark. It looks like the bars of a jail cell.

Now Matt unveils his prized Home Depot rental: a nail gun powered by an air compressor.

"Just get your hands at a safe distance," he says, crouching over the top plate and placing the edge of the nail gun against its bottom, right in the middle of the stud that extends vertically above it. He grips the stud with his right hand.

"And push in."

Thwack.

The nail shoots through the top plate and straight up into the stud, securing the two at a right angle. It's a startling sound—harsh and final. There is no taking this bolt back.

"And that's it."

He lines up the next stud on the floor and gives two quick, confident punches with the gun into the plate: *thwack, thwack.*

When the frame is complete, Matt and Tim lift it off the floor together, looking like homesteaders raising the walls of a barn. When they nearly smash into the ceiling light bulb I shout to warn them, fulfilling my duty as the frame-raising bystander.

After some jostling, the bottom of the partition bumps into place on top of the chalk line we laid on the floor. If you've never felt the satisfaction of seeing a partition line up with a chalk line—the moment when a plan turns into a wall—you might be surprised by the joy such a seemingly simple moment can yield.

For us, the moment is brief. As we try to slide the top of the partition into place, it doesn't take.

The top plate leans back towards us, because it's a fraction too tall. Matt takes a hammer and gives it a smack at several points to see if he can knock it in. The frame bounces with each smack, uncooperatively.

It's the first time we realize that one of the ceiling joists hangs slightly lower than the others, preventing the partition from slipping under. (This also explains the squeaky floor upstairs: there's a gap between the hardwood and the plywood where the joist sags, and the weight of each passing step bends the hardwood down to close the gap, forcing the wood to squeak along the nails that hold it down. Now I know.) We try to bash the joist up with the hammer. No luck. We try to knock the top of the frame at the joist, hoping to force it in. It doesn't move.

There's only one solution. I grab the red Skilsaw sitting on the floor in the other room. Matt plugs it in and sets the stepladder beneath the rebellious joist. We need to shave off less than an inch.

Matt revs the saw twice, then twists it sideways and lines up the blade against the bottom of the joist. The saw squeals as he cuts into the wood, making a small, wobbly incision that creates a large splinter. Then he pulls the severed wood down and back, snapping off the sliver.

But the surgery fails. He can't cut out deep enough with the circular saw and so has to switch to the Sawzall with its long, narrow blade. Matt takes it to the joist, carving off a good inch and creating a new wobbly edge. It's not a model of precision, but this time when we lift it, the frame fits snugly in place.

Now Tim holds a level to the side of one of the studs. It's plumb. We'll take the small victory, though I'm not convinced the now compromised joist would pass a building inspection.

Matt leaves the room and comes back carrying what looks like a small model of a tower, with an orange base, a long frame, and a narrow peak.

"What is it?" I ask.

"It's like a hammer punch," Tim says, recognizing it. "It's *awesome*."

"It's a Ramset. It's like a twenty-two-calibre little thing you load in—kind of like a bullet," Matt says. He's holding a metallic cylinder, which actually looks exactly like a bullet. He loads it into the barrel.

"If you manage to do it right you look like a badass," Matt adds. He pulls the handle back, which opens the barrel where the bolt was loaded. "The casing goes flying. You feel pretty cool. Let's see if we can do it . . ."

He places the end of the barrel on the bottom plate supporting the frame and whacks the punch with his hammer. There's a spark and a crack, like a muted gunshot. A bolt drives through the wood into the concrete.

Matt pulls back the barrel quickly and the casing drops to the floor.

"Ah, that was all right," he says.

He hands it to Tim, showing him how to load a new bolt in the front of the barrel. Tim then presses the mouth of the Ramset to the stud and gives it a whack—followed by a clanking metallic echo. He wasn't holding it strongly enough to keep it pressed against the wood.

He tries again.

Pop! The bolt drives in effortlessly.

"That's awesome," he confirms.

I note that this is precisely the kind of tool that can get the wrong kind of person into trouble. And Matt has a story about that, of course.

He used to have a captive bolt pistol that had a trigger on it, he says. One day he went out with a couple of his friends, guys I know, and was goofing around at a Fall Fair in town. Naturally, he brought the pistol along. They decided to see how far they could launch the bolt, so one friend held back the mechanism at the end of the barrel, as though it was being compressed against a piece of wood, while the other pulled the trigger. It fired, and the bolt disappeared somewhere into the sky. The guy holding the barrel felt his fingers vibrating for the rest of the day. They don't know where the bolt landed, but thankfully they never heard about it again.

"That was funny," Matt concludes.

"You're a bunch of idiots," I say.

But Matt doesn't hear me. He laughs to himself.

"That was hilarious," he says.

In the middle of the partition we use the hammer gun to bolt smaller pieces of two-by-four to the insulation next to the studs.

Then we attach another small piece of two-by-four, this one extending from the wood affixed to the insulation to the stud, adding extra support to the partition. It creates an extended arm from the centre stud to the concrete wall behind the old insulation.

Tim and I use the level to check that the first frame is still plumb. It's not—it's off the mark in several spots. I groan.

But we all agree to leave close enough alone.

For the next wall, I'm tasked with marking every sixteen inches on the two-by-fours that will be the plates for a fourteen-foot wall that runs from one of the doors to the back of the room. It's probably the same job Dad would have given me when I was a toddler stumbling around behind him, but I'm much more adept at it now—especially armed with the useful tip that sixteen-inch distances are already indicated on my measuring tape.

We have the second partition cut, nailed, and standing in place in less than half the time it took us to do the first. But the opposite wall won't be as easy. We have to work around the fuse boxes and the narrow window at the ceiling that brings in light from the backyard.

Matt says the solution is to build two "headers," another term I'm not familiar with. Basically, he explains, a header is a support beam that runs horizontally over the top of a door or a window opening in order to support the weight of the joists above. It's supported by two studs on each side—a "king stud" and a "jack stud." The king stud is full length, meaning it reaches from the floor to the ceiling. The jack stud is shorter, holding up the ends of the header and nailed flush with the king stud that extends beyond.

After building the headers, Matt explains that we'll carry on with a regular frame all the way down the wall, past the bedroom to the far end of where the bathroom will be. And to do that, we have to take down a long narrow fluorescent light that hangs from the ceiling above where the new bathtub will go—a light that Dad had hung above his old workbench back when we first moved in.

The table was really just a rough-edged piece of plywood whose corners, for some reason, Dad had taken care to mark with an *A*, *B*, *C*, and *D* to match the legs he'd cut. The workbench that held all his old tools in milk crates, because even though he had newer ones, he just might find a use for the retired ones. He always did. The bench is in the garage now, taken apart and stored away, one of the many items I've refused to part with. I plan to put it back together one day in a place of my own, where I can hang his tools around it and build dollhouses and easels for my kids to use, just as he did.

As the guys work around me, I stop and think about what this process really means. The space where the workbench sat will now hold a bathtub in a new bathroom, and I know that no one but me will remember that it was ever there. The table he built and the tools it held, will be forgotten. We're building over him.

I know it's weird and it's wrong—but as they work I feel some resentment towards Matt, Jonathan, and Tim for being here. I resent them for doing what I think no one but Dad should do. To them, this is just a job to get done. And I understand that, of course. They didn't know him like I do. They can't see him like I do. They don't see a man standing at the workbench while we mark out plans for a bathtub around him. And for a moment I wish they weren't here, not because of anything they've done, but simply because they're not him. This is not their job to complete. It's Dad's. It's mine.

I want to close my eyes and go to sleep. I want to find him again and ask him how it's done.

9

Matt has sketched out a rough plan with pencil on a piece of plywood that sits on the kitchen table. The scribbled design seems more like a suggestion than an actual guide. The crew stands over it, munching on pizza and sipping beer during our first break, examining it as if we were explorers journeying into a new land.

He's drawn in the doors that sit at the bottom of the stairs, the ones that Dad put in long ago. Our initial idea was to keep the current wall and door frames in place. But the doors sit about a foot and a half back from the bottom of the stairs, creating a rectangular alcove of useless space. And with the wall Dad put up, there isn't enough room to fit a toilet, a tub, and a sink.

"The problem is there's not enough room to walk here," Matt says, circling the tiny gap between the crude sketches of a toilet, a vanity, and a tub along the back wall. If the completely not-to-scale drawing on the piece of plywood in front of us was close to correct, a regular-sized thirty-inch door would bang into the toilet every time it was opened, he explains, confirming something I'd worried about earlier.

"So we need to move this wall back as far as possible," Matt says, pointing to the original doors.

I remember that wall going up. I remember the plans to finish the job we'd started years ago—plans that kept getting pushed back until they were forgotten entirely. I'd viewed those two doors that sat uselessly to the right of the stairs as a sort of tribute—a heritage centrepiece at the heart of our rebuild. The edit will mean taking down a wall that Dad had put in place.

This wasn't something I'd agreed to. We were supposed to build on what Dad had started, not tear it down.

I stare at the plywood blueprint. It's clear that we'd gain several feet this way. There really isn't a choice. But the boys have to wait for me to say it. It takes me a few moments.

"I'm concerned that we'll have tried to fit a bathroom into space that isn't there," I say. "This gives it more room. It will feel more natural."

Tear Dad's work down, in other words.

They each nod dutifully. And we shift from framing something new to demolishing a piece of the past.

For years I'd watched Dad sketch out plans in his exact, careful hand. If he drew a line, he'd use a ruler. If he drew a circle, he'd use a compass. *Always.* If he messed up he'd erase the pencil marks, and if he used a pen he'd make corrections with Wite-Out. It was meticulous. His handwriting was impeccable, too. It hadn't always been. But in his early twenties, when one of his first bosses told him that neat handwriting was a sign of professionalism, he worked on it. It was the kind of thing people noticed, like always showing up on time.

I remember him telling me that: It's about the impression you leave.

I'd found his old green notebook from junior high in one of the boxes in the basement. It was from an algebra class. His writing was young, then. Shaky and uneven, drifting off course, aimless. In other words, it was like mine. When I was seven my parents brought me to a special tutor because I kept scoring poorly on penmanship. This lady made me draw circles, over and over. She made me connect the lines of triangles and squares and print out every letter of the alphabet one by one, pages at a time. And because I kept trying to hold my pencil with every finger but my pinky, I was given a special grip for my pencils that held my fingers and thumb in place. It was like wearing braces for spelling class.

I never really got the hang of it.

My parents must have thought I was hopeless, and were probably legitimately concerned about my prospects in school. Teachers constantly commented on how messy my writing was. Often, I couldn't even read it myself. My sentences drifted off the line, taking their own angles—following their own course. Even today, it's mostly illegible. Unlike my father, I never took the time to slow down and perfect the craft.

Dad's handwriting was not only flawless, it was beautiful. He'd practised it until it was measured and symmetrical, with perfectly straight lines and elegant ribbons that curled gracefully from the end of his R's and bowed down the shaft of each D. Even when he was in a rush and scribbled, the slant would increase without sacrificing symmetry. He used the boxes of the graph paper he always wrote on as absolute bounds—taking up a single row, or stretching over two, but always, *always*, the same throughout that entry.

And there are many entries. He kept notes daily. Meetings he took, calls he made, tasks he needed to accomplish, sermons he enjoyed, points he might need to recall.

He left stacks of black notebooks—dozens—many of which I read by lamplight, sitting at his desk, line by line. Dad's notes went back more than a decade. Every sentence became a riddle I felt I needed to decipher. There had to be some message in there, I thought—some final letter telling me all the things he needed to say in case he died before he could.

I even looked for some sort of code in his construction jargon. But as hard as I tried, his perfect cursive told only the story of job sites. Measurements I didn't understand. Dimensions noted on sketches with little context. Names of people he'd called and people he needed to call. Lists of things he had to get done. The sermon notes offered the most potential—he had to have been thinking inwardly then. But he'd written out only the pastor's points that had flashed on the screen above the pulpit. He underlined some and made note of a few verses. I read them all, but couldn't connect.

It was something he'd said he admired in me—the practice of putting feelings into words. When I was a teenager I spent a couple weeks' worth of our road trips to hockey games typing out on his laptop what I thought would be a small book as a gift for my girlfriend. I was sixteen and felt something like love for the first time. It was insatiable. I was captive to the scent of her Tommy Girl perfume and her cigarettes and to the maze of making out on her bed to Chantal Kreviazuk songs. I just *had* to write about it. I had to get it out, on paper, to let her know—and so I wrote her that little book, which was probably about twenty pages long, called *My Everything*. It would be dreadful to see it now, though fascinating if I could endure it. But she had the only copy and I expect she tossed it a year later, when she dumped me, and when I wrote bad poetry about heartache for the first time. Anyway, Dad knew what I was doing and said that it amazed him, because he'd never written out a story before—he'd never recorded how he really felt about anything, really. He didn't know how. He wrote words that conveyed facts, not feelings.

When he was on the road, driving between the different construction sites he managed, he used to record voice memos on an old pocket tape recorder he kept in the console between the seats of his truck. It was the kind that used tiny tapes. I had a vague memory of seeing a bag full of those old mini cassettes in the basement years before.

I'd searched for them when we cleared it out, hoping to listen to his voice as he read out the things he still needed to accomplish before sunset. I wanted to pull my headphones on and fall asleep hearing him in the background just as I used to ... *Tony needs to review the blueprints for the Sunoco station ... Have Steve look into the AC unit at the Belvedere ... We'll need to have the Mavis Road site cleared out before the safety inspector comes in on Wednesday ...* I'd have given anything to have hours and hours of those daily whispers. And maybe, somewhere in the static, I'd find a message that time, folded over, had compelled him to record years ago for a son who would search for him in the future ... *Hey, buddy, it's Dad ... I'm sorry that I can't be there now. But I'm proud of you. Keep your head up. And remember, it's never as bad as you think it is. Now, take care of your mom and sisters ... I love you.*

I hunted through every dusty old box we had. It seemed a lost hope. He must have tossed the tapes out years ago, forgetting that one day in the future I'd need to hear his voice.

All I had was the voicemail message he'd kept on the house phone: *"You've reached the Robson family, I'm sorry we're unavailable to take your call right now, but leave your name, phone number, and a detailed message and we'll return your call as soon as possible. Thank you."*

That, and the last phone call I missed: *"Hey, son, it's your dad calling. It's about five-thirty. Give me a call when you get this message, okay? Talk to you later. Love you. Bye."*

There was no other recording of his voice. No message of wisdom or guidance; nothing like you read about in stories. I was angry with him for that. I hadn't realized how badly I'd needed it until I searched and found nothing.

I played the call over and over, trying to satisfy that longing by lingering on the sound of his voice and hoping it would never fade.

Later, I set up the old VCR and hunted through two boxes of VHS tapes until I found the one in the yellow Kodak case labelled *Maple Leaf Gardens*. I'd known exactly what I was looking for: the video from my first year in hockey, when I was seven and my team played at the Gardens in an Easter Seals tournament. A parent had brought their camcorder into the dressing room before we chased the puck around the ice, barely able to skate, and before I wobbled in goal, flopping every time the puck got close. It was an enormous moment. In the video our parents are helping us get ready to go on, since we're still much too young to handle the medieval armour of hockey gear on our own. I'd hoped we had the sense to have spoken to the camera together, Dad and seven-year-old me.

I recognize his burgundy jacket with green sleeves as soon as the camera pans to the corner. He's facing away from it, wrestling with a sweater he's trying to pull over my chest protector as I stick my arms in the air, trying to help. After a brief jostle, my shaggy blond hair pops through the opening and I smile at the camera with a missing tooth. Dad turns and looks at the camera. He is thirty-five years old, his hair just starting to recede and his face still slim with youth. He smiles too. The camera pans across us and away.

One day, shortly after I'd given up searching, I opened the drawer in the side table next to Dad's bed. It was filled with old keys and reading glasses and other odd items he'd tucked away. And in the back, I found a silver recorder. It was newer than the one I remembered. Fully digital, with an SD card. It couldn't have been more than a decade old. I felt a rush of excitement—and hope. Maybe it was the voice I was searching for.

I waited several hours, until later that night, to sit alone and play whatever the recorder had captured. The screen lit up. There was only one file. It was more than an hour long.

I pressed play.

It took a few moments to realize that the static was the sound of a moving car. There was a slow hum, almost a rumble, rising and falling with traffic.

I closed my eyes and listened to the world pass by as we drove, not knowing where the road would lead. Him in the driver's seat, and me beside.

Neither of us said a word.

My fingers thin in Dad's work gloves, I gently grip the reciprocating saw by its handle and its neck, my finger twitching nervously on the trigger—the jagged blade anxious but ready to begin the demolition.

I'm standing in front of the wall Dad put up and that we're now taking down. A perfectly straight red laser line runs from floor to ceiling along the drywall beside the door frame, carefully marking the first cut, a couple of inches from the concrete wall it meets at the corner.

Matt offers some instruction. "You always want to keep the guard up against whatever you're sawing," he says. "Because if you don't it will bounce around."

He takes the saw from me and places it loosely against the wall as he pulls the trigger. It whirls to life—and the blade jolts back quickly.

"But if you keep it nice and tight . . ." He presses in, pushing near the guard and carving horizontally from the edge of the wall to the laser line. It makes a perfect incision.

Then he hands the saw back to me.

I set the blade on the line on an angle the way Matt has instructed. A lip beneath the blade presses against the wall to exact the carnage.

The saw shakes to life in my hand when I press the trigger. The blade jumps back, startling me—until Matt yells for me to push down. I do, this time. The saw sends out a high-pitched squeal until the drywall grumbles as it splits apart.

I stop near the floor as the cut gets lower, uneasy with how quickly it's all coming apart, and step back in a cloud of drywall dust. My hands are numb.

Matt takes over, finishing the first incision down to the bottom, until the white baseboard pops off. I stand back as he repeats the same cut a few inches over, and then again next to the edge of the steel stud (along with wood, the metal is the other material commonly used for framing). There are now three long cuts through the drywall from the ceiling to the floor, crumbling white innards of the structure lining each gash. Wounded and weak, it's ready to fall.

I line up to start the demolition but feel weighted with guilt. My first kick with Dad's steel toe is soft and apprehensive. The wall bulges but doesn't break. I take a deep breath and deliver another kick, harder this time—and there's an audible crack. A small buckle folds out, opening along the line we cut.

It feels good. I picture myself standing next to Dad as a thirteen-year-old, taking out the wall between the kitchen and the family room. Side by side, swinging hammers.

The guilt shifts to anger. I step back and throw all my weight into the next drive, connecting with my heel. A three-foot piece of drywall punches out and the steel frame bends with the blow.

The crew stands on the other side, filming the spectacle. They can't see me bite my lip and take another deep, long breath.

Everything falls apart, eventually.

I punch the wall hard with a left, at eye level. It buckles a bit, but it takes the right of the one-two to break through, knocking out a rough rectangle.

That sets off a flurry of punches and kicks as fragments scatter across the floor.

I move across the wall, knocking out the next section with more blows. I throw everything into the last piece, reaching from the floor to the ceiling. The drywall falls back, stumbling like a beaten boxer before collapsing to the floor.

"Oh, hey there," Matt says, as I'm suddenly visible to the others.

I'm breathing fast, standing where the wall had been, my fists still clenched.

I give two more violent kicks to a final piece that clings to the bottom of the frame. Shattered bits of drywall lie in a dusty pile on the floor. I let out a long, deep sigh.

"Well," I say, catching my breath. "That was fun."

The job is far from over, though. We still have to bring down the steel studs and a bulkhead that sits just above the door, which Dad built in the original reno to cover a large air vent that runs across the length of the ceiling to the furnace. We have to be careful here, because several live wires run through the bulkhead too.

We decide it's best to make a small incision a couple inches in from the edge of the bulkhead and to pull down the drywall from the opposite side so that we don't damage the outside edge, which we can still use to help frame the new doorway.

The laser level on the floor shoots up the wall and backwards across the ceiling, creating a straight line. Matt takes the reciprocating saw and raises it above his head, cutting in to the ceiling across the red line from one edge to the middle—then he flips it around and starts at the other edge, bracing the saw with his opposite hand so that he can make a precise cut from end to end.

With the old steel frame, he takes a less precise approach—revving up the saw and cutting into the spine in the middle of the opening I'd kicked out. Then he slices quickly through the other two vertical frames, the bottom half of each falling to the floor, leaving the other half dangling from the top.

Matt laughs maniacally.

"Okay," I say. "Was not prepared for that."

He turns and takes the saw to the other corner of the old doorway. The metal studs hit the floor with a crash. A couple of the top pieces cling to the ceiling for a moment and then fall down too.

"Demolition man," I say, slowly clapping my work gloves together.

Matt grins. Destruction is catharsis.

He reaches up and yanks on the back end of the drywalled ceiling, which is now held up only by the edge we'd cut the incision through. He yanks hard and pulls down a large rectangular piece. We crack off the remaining bits of drywall clinging to the severed edge.

The result is impressively precise, considering the violence of the procedure. Matt breaks off one last piece of drywall hanging from the corner.

The old wall and door frames are a shambles of terracotta-coloured rubble, steel bones, and drywall dust. We stand back, surveying our conquest.

"*Sweet,*" Matt says.

By the middle of the afternoon we have the wooden skeleton of three walls up. And I'm exhausted.

We built the remaining partitions on the floor, just as we had the first. The far partition with the window and the fuse box area takes the longest, but Jonathan and Tim manage to work out the measurements and piece the headers together. I fire the bolts through the bottom studs into the concrete, starting to feel the violent rush of construction. And that's what it is: force and violence. The act of taking wood and dismembering it, hammering it into a structure, drilling it, compelling metal and wood to do what you want them to do—including their own demolition. I was struck by the physical satisfaction of the process.

While Tim and Jonathan finish the far wall, Matt and I build the partition that will divide the bedroom and the bathroom. The space is starting to take shape.

After Matt removes the lights from the ceiling and unwires the fixtures, I head up to the garage to get Dad's work lights, two big rectangular lamps behind a cage that hangs off a yellow stand. The set has been around since I was a teenager, when I'd pull the lights out of the garage and place them at the end of the driveway, attached by a couple of extension cords, so that my friends and I could see the basketball court our driveway had become. We'd play two-on-two out there until our neighbour, Bill, would come out and remind me that he had to go to work at six a.m. That was the only time I'd ever plugged them in—and I'd found them fantastically useful—but now I hauled them out for their real purpose: to illuminate the work area until we were ready to put up the new lights.

There's only one section left to frame in the new bedroom. We need to take it to the edge of the stairs, building in the two doors that will lead to the new bathroom and bedroom. A duct runs across the top corner of that wall, so we'll have to build a bulkhead to hide it.

I have no concept of how to do this, but Jonathan and I are given the task.

We cut twelve-inch blocks and push them up next to the long, wide duct that runs along the wall above the doorway, spacing them out so they hang down a couple of inches below the duct, the wall, opposite the wall, and at every other ceiling joist. Then we shoot a couple of nails diagonally through the top edge to fasten the wood to the joist.

Next, Jonathan and I need to cut a two-by-four into one-and-a-half-foot pieces. These will extend from the joists on the wall to the wood that peeks down beneath the other side of the duct. Without anyone watching, I try my hand at cutting the wood on the sawhorses, using the mitre saw. I'm much more nervous about this than a grown man should be.

First I try to draw a straight line in pencil, using a discarded scrap of wood as a ruler. It seems straight enough, but it's definitely not exact. I hold the saw with my right hand and nervously place my left hand on the side of the two-by-four overhanging the stand. I put some weight into it, holding it in place, and slowly pull the trigger as the saw squeals to life. I'm timid—and don't press down hard enough. The saw bounces and I let go with my left hand, retreating. None of the guys sees me flinch. I take a deep breath, line up the blade again, and hold it firm. This time the blade cuts clean through.

With the pieces to build the bulkhead, I run upstairs to the laundry room, to Dad's tool bag, and fish around for his small red level. I just need to borrow it. I'm careful about mixing Dad's tools with the ones Matt and Jonathan have brought. I'm worried they'll get lost in the chaos downstairs. Any of his tools that don't fit in my belt are quickly returned to his bag.

We'll use the level to make sure each piece is plumb and to check the angle of a joint we need to nail in place for another bulkhead to encase the water pipes that run above the back end of the bathroom.

The bulkheads come together much more quickly than I thought. The pieces of wood that hang down from the ceiling connect perfectly with the pieces set horizontally across the bottom of the duct. The nails that hold them in place are a mess of different angles and depths—but I tell myself that no one will ever see the rough work beneath the drywall.

We want to get all the framing done before the end of the day, so we hurry to build the final wall at the far end of the bathroom, which is set a couple of feet from the furnace to keep within fire regulations.

Jonathan and I think we've measured meticulously and cut the pieces carefully. But when we raise the wall and try to slide it into place, it doesn't fit beneath the bulkhead we built above it. It's too tall, by at least two inches.

Something is *way* off. But we have no clue as to what.

We stand around for several minutes, staring at the wayward frame—remeasuring, again and again—until Jonathan has a breakthrough. We used the wrong length to build the bulkhead, he says. Instead of using eight-and-a-half-inch pieces we used ten-and-a-half-inch ones. And we did that because, after we cut one piece to the right length, I grabbed the discarded end instead of the properly measured one. Then we replicated the wrong length to finish the rest of the bulkhead.

A simple mistake, but a pretty stupid one—and it sets us back. We have to hammer out the pieces, bashing back the wood until the deeply driven nails pop out, and then piece it all back together. But even with the right-sized studs, it's still a tight fit. As Tim and I brace the frame, Jonathan hammers the top beam until it finally nudges into place beneath the joists.

We check it with the laser level, the red light shooting up the concrete wall beside us and across the ceiling in a straight line. Everything is flush. At a quick glance this might appear to have been done by a crew of professionals.

The rec area of the basement looks like a scrap yard. Shards of wood are everywhere; the carpet is ripped up and lies in a folded, dusty pile in one corner. The place smells like sawdust and metal. We start to tidy up, ready to end our first day of construction. I'm exhausted. My muscles feel wobbly. My bones quite literally ache. I'm fully dazed.

The framing is almost complete. And despite the odd angles of our nails and the parts we had to force into place, the studs are nearly level and the walls look like they could stand for decades.

Part III
What Lies Beneath

10

I knew my father for half his life. It was the half in which a man is supposed to have *figured it out*, in the way that a proper human adult should understand how to care for themselves and the people they love. The smarter, better half—I imagine.

I knew that part well.

But I didn't know much about the first half of him, about the life he lived before I was alive. There was his dream to be a pilot. And there were photographs that told fragments of stories. Of his long rock-star hair and hot summer days playing softball near my grandparents' house, sometime way back in the 1970s—years before I was born. I loved to look at those photos, tucked in shoeboxes and dusty albums, because they held hints of a past that seemed familiar—his eyes, his smile, the shape of his face—but also foreign. It was Dad as a boy, as a teenager, as a young man. I always found that hard to comprehend. Not in an entirely self-centred way. In theory, I knew my parents were humans with independent lives before my sisters and I came along. But their lives became so much about our lives that it was hard to gain perspective on the time before us.

One of my regrets after Dad died was not having taken more time to learn about who he was, and why. To ask more questions about what he daydreamed of as he scribbled in that green algebra notebook. Or who he wanted to be when he was young. Or to hear stories about girls he adored and tried to make them adore him back. Or the ones he truly loved. And what it feels like to have one steal your heart and break it.

Maybe it's that, as kids, we don't really understand time or how fleeting it is. We don't know that the people who raised us will be gone one day. I mean, we know it as a fact—in the way we know that space is endless, say—but we can't comprehend it, so we don't try. And besides, we have so much of our own living to do. Life is too exciting to wonder about the people who gave it to you.

One of the realizations that hurt the most was that there was so much more to my father than I knew.

Half his life. That was it.

He told me once about being part of a gang of 1960s kids, riding their single-gear bikes as fast as they could to the edge of a cornfield forest. They charged right into the mystery of it, cutting through the stalks that reached up beyond them—chasing the laughter and shouts of the pack lost in the maze. There was a blue sky above. The grumble of a tractor and the holler of a farmer, shouting at the boys for disturbing his crop.

The boys all lived on the suburban streets that pushed up against the farmer's field. Their lives were a product of the late-1950s urban sprawl, taking over the agricultural roots of the land beyond the city. The paved streets and cropped grass and rows of matching bungalows of Flowertown, the newest subdivision on the western edge of town, consuming that farmer's history, acre by acre.

Eventually the boys would find the edge. The field would open up to a ditch and a dusty country road. They would catch their breath and calm their pumping hearts.

My father, I imagine—his blond hair neatly parted to the left, his collared shirt somehow still tucked in, an itch of eczema on his cheek—would look back at the tall stalks. And he'd have no idea where he stood in time and what the fields around him would become.

Soon the cornfield would be plowed over and the farmer's house torn down. Soon you could see flat across the acres. The land would be sold and divided into new streets and plots. Giant holes excavated and foundations laid. Homes framed. Basements built, then family rooms, dining rooms, kitchens. Bedrooms and attics, all covered by shingled roofs and protected by bricks. Grass would be planted, fences put up, driveways paved, sidewalks hardened with messages drawn in wet cement. Soon the sounds of laughter would fill the blocks and kids would run through that same place, hopping fences and jumping in pools. They'd play road hockey for hours on courts, past dark under the glow of a single streetlight.

That wild, thrilling maze would cradle the stories of our lives. One day, somewhere in those stalks, our father would lay our foundation. And the crunching soil, the rumbling tractor, the shouting old man, the revelry of boyhood—would all become a faint memory, tucked deep in a grown man's mind. A faint memory to share with his son.

I found Billy Plunket on Facebook. He wasn't hard to find. It's the kind of name that sticks out—and one of the few I remember Dad mentioning when I was a kid. We were driving down an old residential street in downtown Brampton, just a few minutes from our house. We passed a man with long hair, sitting on a lawn chair drinking a beer. Dad noticed him but kept driving.

"That was Billy Plunket," he said.

"Who's that?" I asked.

"One of my old friends, from when I was young," he said. "I haven't seen him in years."

They grew up in Flowertown together, he told me. They burned down a barn once and had to go to court.

What?

They went to junior high and high school together too. They were in a band.

Really?

Dad didn't elaborate much further. He smiled and laughed to himself as though he was reliving a happy memory. Flipping through the old photographs in his mind.

And we drove on.

He could have pulled over. He could have reunited with his past. Could have caught up on the decades that separated them. But he kept going, moving forward and away.

I remember feeling sad that day. I can't even recall how old I was at the time, but I clearly remember that conversation—or rather, the lack of it. I had my own neighbourhood friends then. Guys I played street hockey with every day after school on the cul-de-sac we lived on. Or tennis-baseball—a self-pitch game with a tennis racquet and tennis ball, sewer grates serving as bases and the two houses on the other side of the court as the home-run fence, our neighbours' cars constituting a ground rule double. Or Manhunt—where one person sets out to catch the others, running through gardens and hopping fences, with each player caught joining him like a pack of zombies until the final one was left.

I couldn't imagine a life without the kids who lived on my street. Back then, I couldn't comprehend a world where the boys I set out on adventures with every day wouldn't always be my closest friends.

But here was my dad, driving past a friend from his youth and not even stopping to say hello.

I don't know why I remembered the name. I can only specifically recall Dad mentioning him that one time. Billy Plunket—the man with the long hair, drinking a beer on his lawn.

I felt a chill when I found him. Billy went by Bill now, but I knew it was the same Plunket. I typed a quick message on Facebook.

"Hi Bill. We've never met before—you were a friend of my father, Rick Robson, back in high school and Central Peel in Brampton," I wrote.

I told him that I was trying to learn more about his past after his death.

"I was wondering if you have any memories of my dad, and if you'd be willing to chat about him."

Bill replied within the hour.

"I'm so sorry to hear of Rick's passing," he wrote. "I was unaware and a bit taken aback by the news. Of course, I would be more than happy to chat."

Bill Plunket answers the phone as if he's greeting an old friend. He sounds like a boomer who's permanently baked into his hippie days. But he's excited to talk, brimming with memories. Learning about my father's death has sent them flooding back.

"I was devastated to hear that news. My brother died when he was fifty-nine too, and he was a year and nine months younger than me... I end up going to more funerals than weddings now," he says.

Bill lives in Fort Erie, he tells me. He moved out there a long time ago. But he was at my parents' wedding, he says. It was probably the last time they really spoke. He tried to reconnect with my father years back, leaving a message on our phone, but never heard from him. He doesn't know why.

And then he gets a message one day, out of nowhere, to tell him it's too late.

"You've got memories that you want to remember. You've tapped me into remembering the old days," Bill says. "My mother died of Alzheimer's. Well developed. So did my grandfather. There are so many questions I would have asked both of them."

Bill and my father, and their crew of friends, all met at Beatty-Fleming Public School, in a subdivision that was known as Northwood Park at the time. It's the same neighbourhood my grandmother still lives in, just a few minutes from us. She and my grandfather were the first and only owners of the house.

"You're kidding. She still lives in that house?" Bill says. "Holy shit, man. They probably paid around fifteen thousand for it."

That was six decades ago now. They moved there when my father was four and my aunt was eight. There were no fences or trees there at the time. The farmer's field reached right to the edge of their street, but year by year it was swallowed by more bungalows with large lots. My dad's brother was born when he was twelve—which meant he had to move from the main floor of the bungalow down to a tiny room in the basement. Years later, when my father moved out, my grandfather turned it into his workshop. For my entire life there was a Farah Fawcett poster on the wall, and I was never sure if it had belonged to my dad or my grandfather.

Bill tells me that he remembers my grandparents. He remembers how sweet my grandmother always was and that my grandfather had a bulbous red nose.

"He always seemed to have a drink in his hand," he says.

This lined up with what I remembered of him. We called him Pa.

"My dad didn't drink a lot," I say.

"No," says Bill. "He didn't."

All my life I'd only ever seen Dad have a glass of wine, and only if friends came over. He never told me why he didn't drink, probably because I never asked. It was just normal to me. The only time he and I ever shared a beer was in Vancouver, when our jobs brought us there at the same time and we met up for lunch before his flight out. It felt weird when he ordered one after I had.

"It's about time I had a beer with my son," he said.

That was two months before he died.

Dad hadn't told me much about Pa. I was too young to really know him. He was kind to me, but sort of grumpy at the same time. He used to pick up my sisters and me at our bus stop in his white Buick with maroon seats so plush you could write your name on them. He always had hard candies in the console. And when our parents would drop us off at the house we'd watch golf and *I Love Lucy* reruns together. He'd let me roll his cigarettes, putting the filter and paper in place and stuffing the tobacco into the slider. And he'd let me get him a Coors Light from the fridge, or would give me whatever was left over in the can after he poured a rye and Coke. Sometimes we went to the driving range together, where he'd let me play mini golf. For my birthday one year he gave me a jar of peanut butter and a jar of jam because I kept eating all of his.

He was a loving grandfather in a Walter Matthau kind of way.

Dad didn't elaborate on his relationship with Pa, other than saying he always wanted me to know he loved me because it was something he and his father never did.

I knew Pa's father had passed away when he was a boy and that he spent his teenage years helping to take care of his mother and sister. His name was Emmanuel, but he hated that so he changed it to Robert—and everyone called him Bob. He grew up on Pape Avenue in Toronto's east end, but met my grandmother at a dance in Hamilton. He looked like Marlon Brando then, olive skin, handsome eyes, and strong arms. My grandmother, Peggy, had a Bette Davis thing going on. They fell in love and moved to St. Thomas, where they lived for a few years until their house burned down. Then they moved back, closer to Toronto, where he landed his job and bought a house in a brand-new Brampton subdivision.

Pa was an old-school guy who for decades had been a salesman for Consumers Gas. He was a blue-collar man, and proud of it. He worked hard to enjoy a few pints and a game of darts at the Flowertown Pub a few blocks away. Or a rye and Coke at the bar in the basement. Pa was the kind of man who could fix any problem in the house, and spent most of his weekends doing it. With his son right behind him he sealed the leaky shingles, replaced pipes, mended fences, and repaired all mechanical failures—home or auto—that would otherwise leave his family at the mercy of "professional" repairmen. Through Pa's instruction, my dad learned how to do all those things too. By the time he was old enough to swing a hammer, he was expected to use it. The work he did was seldom fun. It wasn't a labour of love; it was duty.

"I was around when Rick's dad died," says Bill. "Your grandpa."

Having heard about the funeral, he stopped in. I was about to turn eleven then. It was June. Grandma and Pa had been on vacation in Hawaii when he fell and broke his hip. In the hospital they discovered that he had cancer in his lungs. Two weeks later he was on a ventilator at the house, sitting in the same reclining chair he always sat in to watch the Blue Jays or the PGA. My parents brought us over to see him. We didn't really know what to say or do. It was hard to see him struggle to breathe. The next morning, when we woke, Mom and Dad were sitting at the kitchen table in our house. They looked tired.

"Pa died last night," Dad said.

My sisters and I cried. We didn't really know what that meant— we just knew he was gone.

But Dad didn't. He seemed sad, but not upset. I remember that he hugged us, and that later that afternoon we went to Costco where he bought me a red, blue, and black soccer ball I'd seen and decided I needed. I didn't even like soccer, so I never really used it—but it would remain in our garage for years, and whenever I saw it I'd always think, That's the ball we got when Pa died.

"Fifteen—that was about the time when everyone went their own ways," Bill is saying over the phone. He lists off the members of their neighbourhood crew. "There was me, Rick, Dale, Stewart, Charlie, and Arthur . . ."

The boys used to rip around the streets, he says, until they'd hear a parent holler from a porch or the streetlights went on. They used to camp in each other's backyards. They had dance parties in the basements of girls they liked. In the middle of the night they'd go hopping from one neighbour's pool to the next. They spent hours riding their bikes and hiking through the fields and forests around the subdivision. They'd go fishing in Fletcher's Creek and then float down the river, riding the current all the way to the edge of the new highway south of town. Sometimes they'd hike along the side of the rail tracks that ran just north of their houses, heading towards Toronto. One day, Bill says, they found a yellow packet on the side of the track. They couldn't open it, so Bill used a railway spike they found to smash it. It exploded in their faces on the first strike. They all stumbled backwards and ran. Bill's face was singed, but he was all right in the end. He found out later that it was a signal used to alert train conductors that a sharp curve lay ahead.

"I was always the person that if there was an injury going to happen it would be me," Bill says. "*Boom!* That's all we heard."

The boys would journey for miles. One spring, when they were about thirteen, the group visited an old tin barn several miles north in an empty field. There was no farmhouse on the property; they could see only the train bridge running over the street that led to the house in the distance. So they turned the barn into their own clubhouse, hiking out to it each day. There, sitting between the hay bales and the steel machinery, they'd do the kinds of things boys do in places they think are exclusively theirs. They'd smoke cigarettes and talk about women, as men do. They'd dare each other to walk across the rafters. They'd tie up ropes so that they could swing between the landings.

The father of one of the boys was a policeman and a hobby marksman who kept his bullets in the garage. One day the boys stole a packet of bullets and brought it out to the barn, where they built a small fire out of twigs and hay. Then, when the flames were high enough, they threw the packet of bullets into the burning pile—and ran for cover behind the hay bales and machinery.

The ammo exploded in a flurry of flames as the boys hid, imagining bullets whizzing past their heads.

The fire was still simmering on the barn floor when they left later that day, though they thought it'd been put out. Someone was supposed to pee on it to make sure. But no one looked back until they reached the fence by the train tracks. It was only when they climbed up over it and spun to drop down that they saw smoke and flames rising from the roof of the barn. They sat on the edge of the fence, frozen in fear, watching it burn. Then the roof caved and they ran like hell.

They vowed silence together, but it lasted only a couple of days. Someone in the group had buckled under the heat and given them all up. The police showed up at each of their houses, lights blaring, and brought them to the police station downtown. (It's a Starbucks now, the place where Dad would stop in to get his grande non-fat, no-sugar latte every morning on his way to work.)

The boys ended up in the local courthouse sitting next to their mortified parents as the judge reamed them out for the damage they'd caused and the danger they'd put themselves in. It turned out that the old barn was supposed to be ripped down soon anyway. They were each given a fine. But what they'd remember would be the smacks and the grounding they received from their parents when they got home.

It was one of those stories that had clearly morphed with time but had held a place in their memories. Dad had mentioned it once when he drove past the field where the barn had stood, although he'd omitted the part about the police and the court.

Bill's stories keep rolling out. Now he's jumped past middle school to their freshman year.

"Did your dad ever tell you about Janice Marks?" he asks.

"No," I say apprehensively.

"Oh man. You know what your dad was like."

I truly have no idea what Dad was like.

"He always had the shoulder-length hair and stuff like that," Bill says. "But your dad always had the eczema outbreak on the corner of his lips or on his elbows or whatever. Somehow, some way he must have been really sort of dashing because he was going out with probably the best-looking girl in high school."

"Really?"

"I think she was a grade older than us," he says. "That's what sort of blew me away. Probably about grade ten."

Dad was terrible at telling me about women. We never really talked about love or lust—about the thrill and agony of being a teenager in either state. We never spoke about sex. It was a minefield I walked alone. I'd always been painfully shy and dreadfully awkward when it came to girls, so if Dad had actually known what he was doing, I'm furious with him now.

"How was my dad with girls?" I ask. "Was he talkative? Was he shy? Was he some sort of player?"

"He wasn't," Bill says. "That's why we couldn't figure out how he could go out with Janice. Because he *wasn't* a particularly suave guy. We were all basically young and naive. Kept it all to himself."

I have no idea how much of this to believe, but I want to believe it all. *Janice Marks, from grade ten!* Dating someone a year older than you in high school is an enormous deal. And the best-looking girl in school at that? Impressive, Dad.

"Yeah. Nobody could figure out how. I don't know what it was, but he was always very guarded with her," Bill says. "He didn't want to answer any questions. And if he was around today, I'd be asking him about it."

"Me too."

I ask Bill if he knew what my father wanted to become back then; if he had any sense of what his dreams for life were.

"I never would have figured your dad for being a construction guy," Bill says. "He never really built anything when we were growing up . . . I thought he might have continued on in music."

"Music?"

When I was young, Dad used to play his acoustic guitar every now and then. He mentioned he'd been in a band as a teenager, but I never really asked him about it. I only remember him playing "Douglas Mountain," a song that Raffi, the Canadian children's performer, sang on his Christmas album. It's a melodic lullaby of a song, and Dad would sing it beautifully as we lay in bed about to fall asleep.

He often put on albums by artists like Simon and Garfunkel, James Taylor, Boston, Chicago, America, Steely Dan, Deep Purple, and The Who. He'd always turn up the volume while cleaning the house or cooking. In the summer, he'd keep the windows open so he could hear the CD player while he worked in the garden.

Music was undoubtedly a big part of Dad's life, but I'd never thought of him as a musician, or as someone who ever dreamed about being one.

The band was together for only three or four years, Bill tells me.

"What did you call yourselves?" I ask.

"I came up with 'Rubber Bacon,'" he says. "But I don't think we had a name."

They started in middle school, back at Beatty-Fleming, he continues. My father wanted to be a guitar player. His good friend Dale Taylor wanted to be a drummer. Charlie Yuhle, another neighbourhood kid, played the bass. Bill played a knock-off Farfisa organ. Sometimes they had a singer named Carol Millen, but other times Dad took the mic, depending on the song.

"I've always been into music," Bill remarks. "It was all about the sound with me."

The band practised in Charlie Yuhle's basement, playing songs like "Walk Don't Run."

They would perform at battle-of-the-bands events and school dances. During one show, Bill says, my dad told him he'd come down with a cold at the last minute and stuck him with singing "House of the Rising Sun." But Dad scribbled down the lyrics for him. "I don't know the words, so he gave me this sheet of paper," Bill says. "And I'm up there singing 'There is a house in New Orleans...'—and it was a fucking disaster."

My dad lost his voice a couple of times before their shows, Bill says. "I'm not sure if it was planned or not."

I have a difficult time imagining my father standing on a stage, belting out a song. He rarely liked attention. Once, when he was running for a position on the board of our church, he nervously practised his speech and even sent it to me for revisions while I was away at university. I worried about him when I knew he was supposed to be up at the podium, speaking to the congregation. So although I didn't like the idea of him balking in front of a crowd right before a gig with his middle-school band, I didn't find it surprising either.

"I was a hacker anyway," Bill says. "Rick was a pretty good guitar player, but probably mostly rhythm. We didn't really have an outstanding guitar player who could play lead or anything. It was mostly Dale and him and Charlie, doing whatever."

I should find those guys too, Bill suggests. They'd have tons to tell me about Rick and the old days.

"I will," I say. "I'll find them."

Bill tells me again that he had tried to reunite, but never heard back from my father. He called the other guys in the band too, but they never reconnected.

I ask Bill why their friendship had waned. It's just a thing that happens in life, he says.

It's true—sometimes people head over the horizon and never look back, as I remember reading in *On the Road* during my obligatory Jack Kerouac phase: "What is that feeling," he wrote, "when you're driving away from people and they recede on the plain till you see their specks dispersing?—It's the too-huge world vaulting us, and it's good-by. But we lean forward to the next crazy venture beneath the skies."

Maybe, for Dad, it was easier to leave the specks dispersed as he grew up and his life became full and busy with a wife, kids, and career. But I wonder if he'd ever longed to return to the past. If he ever dreamed of those summer days running through a farmer's field.

"I would love to talk about my father's life," Bill says. "But who am I going to talk to about it? He's gone . . ."

He pauses.

"I'd rather it was you interviewing *your dad*," he says.

My voice catches.

"Me too."

11

We've started day two a bit later, slowing down after our non-stop first. The crew gathers in the basement to receive their marching orders.

Matt is wearing black and white flannel, a modern take on Al from *Home Improvement*. Tim wears shorts and deck shoes as though he's heading to the Caribbean. Jonathan's also in shorts, but matches them with steel-toe boots and, curiously, a fleece zip-up. I'm rocking old jeans, a Henley, and Dad's boots, which is the proper way for a style-conscious contractor to dress.

Yesterday went a bit slower than planned, Matt says, so we need to be more efficient today.

Considering how exhausted yesterday left me, I'm a bit concerned about what he means by being even *more* efficient today.

"What issues did we come across yesterday?" I ask.

"Well, I wouldn't call them issues," Matt says. "I'd call them challenges."

I get the sense that by "challenges" he means me.

"I think everyone was getting a feel for the, uh, space," he says. "And also to get the design just right. I think we're all pretty happy with how things turned out. But I mean, as a leader"—he puts his hands on his chest—"I always want to see more get done."

"Well, these guys were standing around too much," I say, nodding to Jonathan and Tim.

They both huff.

"So we gotta work faster today," Matt says.

We all nod.

"We made some good progress yesterday. So we're going to finish up the framing and make this all nice," he says, looking around at the bones of what will be the bathroom.

The end walls of the bathroom are almost done, aside from the alcove where the throne will sit. And we still need to frame in a closet for the bedroom, which will align with the bathtub. But the big job today is really the plumbing.

"We're going to break up the floor and tie in the toilet drain. And we'll also break up the floor to put the drain in for the shower—and then break up another trench over here for the vanity."

Supposedly, beneath this very solid concrete, we're going to discover pipes that have been buried since the house was built. The key here seems to be busting up the floor, but I have no idea how we plan to get that done.

Nonetheless . . .

"All right," I say. "Let's do this."

The morning brings my first significant contribution to the renovation, one that comes by way of the toilet.

In a moment of architectural ingenuity, I notice that there's enough space beside the furnace to build out a small alcove into the bathroom, like a closet with no door, where the toilet could fit. It would create a comfortable little space in which one could go about their business without taking up any of the bathroom's existing floor space. It'll take us a bit more time, but everyone agrees that it's as sound a plan as we've made so far. I bask in quiet satisfaction.

Tim and I get started by finishing off the framing. Matt gives us careful instructions on how the studs in the corner we're piecing together need to line up with the concrete wall so that the drywall can be properly fastened on both sides. This process is crucial, Matt says. He marks out the alignment he's looking for on the joists above us with a pencil.

I immediately screw it up. Certain that I've measured twice, I cut the studs at two different lengths, with one standing at least an inch shorter than the other. It doesn't come close to connecting to the frame vertically. Even the longer stud is too short, by about half an inch. I've wasted both time and wood.

I return to the sawhorse, pick up the circular saw, and try again. I'm incredibly nervous about screwing up *twice*. But this time, after obsessively measuring and remeasuring and double-checking, I manage to get it right.

Then I stand the pieces in place—and they seem half an inch too tall. I'm flooded with frustration. Still, it's better to go long than short.

Matt shows me how to give the studs a proper whack with the hammer to smack them into place. "You just kind of feel the swing, right?" he says, lining up the hammer with the bottom of the stud and cocking it back with his wrist. He's bent over, his ankle right behind the wood he plans to whack. Seems dangerous. But he hits the stud with one perfect arc—*thud*—and it shifts right over the lines on the joists he sketched out in pencil. He throws in a couple more whacks at the top and bottom to make sure it's in place.

"That's it, eh," I say. "All right."

On the other side of the room, Jonathan and Tim have run into a problem with the far wall beneath the window. The partition we built wasn't properly checked yesterday, and now they've discovered that the studs aren't plumb. The imperfections will have a domino effect: as soon as one piece of the puzzle isn't exact, it creates future problems that become a huge headache to fix. The stud that's supposed to anchor the door to the closet is particularly off. If we don't take the time to correct it now, the closet will never open correctly.

Everyone is frustrated. Errors like this erase hours of work.

I'm learning that there's much more complexity within the walls around us than I'd ever considered. You can't frame a room without the complete picture in mind. One mistake affects everything. Each move impacts the next. Everything is connected. Carpentry isn't just hammering and sawing—it's *foreseeing*.

"If you guys want to fix this, you take the Sawzall and cut all of these out," Matt says, tapping the top of each stud in the row with the long silver level in his right hand.

"Make all of these plumb and then bang it back in," he continues. "Somewhere along the way it kind of got pulled out. But that's an easy fix for you guys."

"Yeah," Jonathan groans.

He takes the Sawzall to the studs one by one, jamming it into the thin line between the joist and the top edge of each stud to cut away the nails that bind them.

Matt double-checks the frame on the other side of the room, at what will be the entranceway into the bathroom and the bedroom. The studs aren't plumb there, either. We'll have to cut those pieces as well and do it all again.

As Jonathan and Tim redo work that I'm fairly certain I had a hand in messing up, Matt and I frame the new throne room—the little alcove in the space beside the furnace.

The four of us come back together shortly before noon, eager to move on from all our framing visions and revisions. It's time to smash up the floor.

On his way to the house this morning, Matt dropped into Home Depot and rented us a jackhammer. It's a Bosch. It looks like an oversized drill with a massive steel drill bit—probably a foot and a half long. I've never come close to using a tool built for nothing but destruction. It seems like the kind of thing you should need a licence to operate. But apparently all it takes is a driver's licence and a credit card deposit.

Under the yellow work lights, one of which has burned out, we've measured out the rough area where the toilet is going to go. There's no real precision involved. Now Tim, Jonathan, and I stand in a circle around Matt, who presses the pneumatic drill to the concrete floor. It blasts to life, quaking the ground beneath us. Small cracks break into pieces that shake away from the epicentre. Even with the orange plugs stuffed in our ears, the metallic *rat-tat-tat* sounds like a machine gun. It continues for nearly a minute as Matt moves the bit all around the area, tilting at different angles and smashing out the grey rubble.

The violence echoes in my head as Matt relents and we assess the damage. Despite the mess of concrete bits scattered around, it doesn't look as though he's gotten very far.

"Lucky for us this floor is pretty thin," he says.

It seems pretty thick to me.

Jonathan is holding a pickaxe. Tim has a sledgehammer. I'm not sure where they got them—and I wonder where the hell they were yesterday when I had to use my fists and feet to take down the wall.

"If you just start whaling you can make a nice hole," Matt says to Jonathan. "Just imagine where the toilet bowl is going to be."

Jonathan steps in. He centres himself in his workboots and bends his bare knees, readying the pickaxe in his polar-fleeced arms. The first strike is timid, bouncing back with a sad *clank*. The second chips away a few loose pieces, but gets us nowhere.

"*Give 'er,*" Matt says.

Now Jonathan raises the pickaxe high above his head and slams the blade with force.

This time there's a muted thud. He strikes again and again, gaining strength each time.

After a few blows, the hole seems to sink down and break wider.

Jonathan steps back, huffing. Now Tim moves in, clearing out the debris with his boot as we take a few steps back. He crouches, turning his feet inward to find a grip in his old boat shoes. Then he raises the hammer and smashes it down repeatedly, getting off five swings in ten seconds, which seems like a pretty pro pace. His blows make a considerable impact. The concrete breaks away easily and the hole starts to widen beneath a cloud of dust.

It settles while Tim stops to catch his breath. A rough hole has opened in the floor, exposing layers of what seems to be gravel that rests beneath our house. We step in with a giant broom to sweep the debris aside.

"How do we know when to stop?" Tim asks.

A good question.

Matt's on the other side of the room, where the tub will sit, marking out the spot that will become the drain. He comes over to survey the situation.

"Here's the stack," he says, bending down and pointing to the big black pipe that extends vertically up the side of the wall that runs along the stairs beside us, parallel to the hole we've started.

I've never even noticed it before. It seems as if it's appeared out of nowhere. Matt explains how it allows air into the waste pipe through the vent, which prevents a vacuum from being created in the pipe.

"We'll tee off this guy," he says, making a motion from the pipe to the hole. Then he pulls out his measuring tape, extending it from the back stud in the alcove to the hole.

"The centre of the toilet is fourteen inches off the wall," he tells us. "So get, like, a nice big hole here." He makes a wide, entirely unspecific circle with his finger.

"And then kind of work your way over." He brushes a line with his foot and then kicks in the hole a bit.

"Once you break up around here, it will start getting easier and easier. And then take away as much dirt as you can. Just get a big hole like this"—he draws another wide circle with his finger—"and work it this way. Because once this is big enough, we're going to have to dig out underneath the floor."

"That's the plan?" I ask.

"We'll see how it goes . . ."

Tim hands me the sledgehammer. It's my turn to swing. I grip the handle too tightly on the first crack and don't lean into it enough. It barely makes a dent. It takes a few more swings to get the feel of it, sliding my leading hand down the handle as the velocity of the hammer takes over. My pace is much slower than Tim's, but the rhythm comes. The floor breaks with each long, deliberate swing. The crumbling concrete is wildly satisfying. It feels as if I could swing all day, but there are much more efficient ways to get this job done.

When the toilet hole is wide enough, I start to hammer out a small path to the stack that rises up beside us. Bashing apart the untouched concrete floor feels even better than widening the loose pieces that were already broken off in the hole. The smooth surface cracks with each blow, one after the other in a line, like a river stretching out from a lake.

But while the destruction wrought by the sledgehammer has been rewarding, it's nothing compared to the obliterating force of the jackhammer. After I push the bit into the hole and press the trigger, the bit jumps and dances on the uneven bits, exploding them in a metallic staccato. It's obscenely loud, the vibration so strong that minutes later I can still feel it in my hands.

When the hole is about a foot deep, muddy water starts to seep through the layer of exposed dirt that sits beneath the concrete.

This strikes me as concerning, but Matt doesn't look worried. "That's why, as you can imagine, water can easily come up through your floor," he remarks, sloshing the water with his shovel.

"Right," I say. "Right . . ."

"But this house seems pretty well built," he continues. "With older houses it's more of an issue because of drainage and stuff, and over the years they've maybe changed the slope of the land—they've done landscaping, say—so then you have problems with water running underneath the house. At my house in Orangeville, I opened up the floor and there was, like, this much space underneath." He makes about a two-foot gap with his hands.

"And there was tons of water. And the foundation, they had actually extended it even lower than what would be to code. So they must have dug down and had serious water problems, and had to pump out water—and then lay the foundation probably six to eight feet below grade. Four feet below grade is normal—it's the frost line; frost doesn't reach under your house at four feet . . ."

He trails off, digging into the hole with the shovel.

"So when you found all the water under the house, what did you do?" I ask.

"Oh, I just filled it with as much aggregate as I could and closed it back up," Matt says. (Aggregate is what contractors call gravel, instead of just calling it gravel.) "Because it hadn't been a problem for twenty or thirty years."

By now, after a couple of inches, the water in the hole seems to have stopped rising. It doesn't look as though it's going to flood into the basement, as I first thought. I decide to put my faith in Matt's lack of concern.

We've marked out a thick line from the drain to the toilet hole. The plan is to drill directly along the line, digging out a trench so that we can lay a new pipe beneath the floor. We'll use the jackhammer along each edge of the line, pushing the bit inward and pulling up the concrete as the trench begins to form.

For the next hour we work like a production line—one person drilling down with the jackhammer, the next working behind him to break up the concrete with the sledgehammer, the one behind him digging deeper with a shovel, and the fourth sweeping up the debris. We rotate through the roles every ten minutes or so.

Tim is easily our best concrete buster. He is Thor in loafers. When the trench swerves to cut across to the vanity on the other side of the room, he skips his turn with the jackhammer and instead uses the sledgehammer to bash up the concrete all the way to the other side. The rest of us stand back and watch. Tim lands a blow pretty much every other second—connecting, then winding up and hammering again. The wooden frames of the walls around us shake with each thud that echoes through the basement like thunder.

"Whoa!" I say appreciatively as Tim pauses for a moment. Then he starts hammering back in the other direction, double time.

Finally he stops and takes a deep breath. "Whew . . ." he says.

"How you feeling?" I ask, laughing.

The sledgehammer drops to the floor.

"Tired," he huffs.

"You can skip that workout today, eh?"

"Heh, yeah," he says, still catching his breath.

He slams the hammer down one more time, shaking the thick membrane between the damp earth beneath us and the dry warmth of our home. Each crack in the concrete exposes this place to the hidden elements. The foundation feels less steady—penetrable. As though the house is vulnerable to the mud and trash that my father had always kept out.

The brown water rises over the edge and spreads across the floor.

12

It's a strange thing to track down your father's ex-girlfriend. It's not something I ever imagined myself doing. And it's stranger still when his old best friend is sitting at the kitchen table beside her. But this is where the search for Dad-before-me has led.

Carol Taylor knows a lot about my life. She's still good friends with my aunt Debbie (who we've always called Auntie B because we pronounced her name as *Aunt-De-Bee* when we were kids). She's kept her up to date on all my life's developments. My aunt is the kind of person who stays connected to the past. I find it endearing. Hearing Carol tell me stories about myself feels like the relaying of Auntie B's love.

Carol was my father's teenage sweetheart. She must have arrived sometime after whoever it was Bill Plunket remembers him dating. But she's the only girlfriend of his I'd ever heard about from his past life. Her name was Carol Sheppard back then.

Dad's best friend was Dale Taylor. He was part of the crew who'd met at Beatty-Fleming Public School and would go camping in backyards and pool hopping in the middle of the night. He was one of the kids who burned the barn down. Probably one of the ones who ran through the cornfield, although he can't recall. Dale was the drummer in the band—and the only one to actually stick with it. He still plays in a band today.

Carol and Dale came to Dad's funeral together, even though they've been divorced for several years now. (I didn't know them, so I didn't see them there.) They have two grown sons, one of whom plays in a band, just like his dad. They're the kind of divorced couple that still sits in the kitchen together. That's where they are when Carol answers the phone and tells me about the first time she saw Rick Robson.

It was at Central Peel Secondary. She was in grade nine and he was in grade ten. It was the first day of school.

"I was at the top of the stairs and he and his friends were at the bottom. And he had this striped shirt with purple in it," Carol says. "He had the blondish hair. He was so nice looking."

They went to either a dance or a concert together, she says, though she can't remember much about it. Dale assures me that it was indeed a dance, because he was there.

"Carol says she liked Rick because of his blond hair. Or whatever," Dale says. "And of course, it's no secret that I liked Carol too."

Dad and Carol started dating soon after that, and would be together for nearly decade, through all those magnified years of adolescence.

"He was like . . . oh, you know what he was like," Carol says. "He was the sweetest guy ever."

She tells me about coming over to my father's house as a teenager, at first too afraid to go up the stairs from the front-door landing. But soon she was there all the time. She remembers my uncle, who was about three at the time. And my grandmother, who was sweet, like Rick, and made the best roast pork with cauliflower. They had dinner at the Robsons every Sunday. And she remembers my grandfather, who seemed intimidating at first but was always sweet to her.

At the end of that first year they dated, my grandfather decided he wanted to take the above-ground pool they had in the backyard and put it below ground. Much of that task fell to my father, who was not very happy about it. He spent most of the summer digging out an enormous hole.

"A couple of times we'd want to see each other, but he'd say, 'My dad is making me dig the pool,'" Carol tells me. "I think his dad had him do a lot of work, and he didn't quite like that."

Dale remembers that part too. He helped dig the hole. (When it was finally done they even scrawled their names in paint on the metalwork around the edge.) It was the only way Dale could really hang out with Rick that summer. My grandfather had given him a task, and he expected it to be finished.

"He always used to put Rick to work and he wanted to come out and play with us," Dale says. "His dad would always have him doing something."

Dale helped my dad build the little bedroom he used throughout his teenage years—the one with the swinging saloon doors at the back of the basement rec room. And he used to get in trouble for drumming on top of the bar my grandfather had built out of an old bowling alley floor whenever the band used their basement to practise.

"The biggest memory I have of your grandfather is him with his glass of rum or whatever he drank. And he'd have his shirt off," Dale says. "And he had the big nose. And sweat would be dripping off his nose, and he'd be working—saying, 'Don't do that! You, get over here!' He'd always be trying to boss us around, but not really, just because we didn't know what we were doing."

"He was a curmudgeon," I suggest.

"Don't get me wrong," Dale says. "He was a really nice man."

"I remember that glass of rum too," I tell him. "He liked to drink a bit."

"Oh yeah." Dale agrees. "Yeah, for sure."

When he wasn't stuck helping my grandfather repair things around the house—or digging out a hole big enough to fit a pool—Dad loved two things: music and cars. He wasn't really into sports, even though so much of my time with him had been spent on the road to hockey games. For him, as a boy, the spark never caught. Instead, he saved up his money and bought guitars and cars. His first guitar was a Rickenbacker.

"You know the black one that John Lennon plays for the Beatles?" Dale says. "It was the same as that, except it was sunburst . . . I don't know how he got it, but that was his first guitar. It was an amazing guitar."

After graduating from the basics that Plunket mentioned, they moved on to cover bands like Creedence Clearwater Revival and Steppenwolf.

"Back then, to learn you had to put the needle on the record and put it on slow speed," Dale says. They'd rent an amp from a music store downtown to make sure they could rock each song as loud as it was meant to be played.

The band managed to cut a deal with the owner of a laundromat at the strip mall a few blocks away, where they'd play every weekend in an unfinished space beneath the storefront. At first they invited just a few friends—but more and more showed up until it became a regular party and the owner finally shut it down.

And along with the music was Dad's affinity for cars. His first was a powder-blue 1966 Volkswagen Beetle.

"We used to boot around in his little bug," Carol says. "And I shouldn't tell you this, but one time we fit a bizarre amount of people—it was beyond belief. We must have fit nine or ten people. I don't think there was an inch to spare in that car. It was ridiculous. Rick was driving."

From the Volkswagen, Dad upgraded to a green Toyota Land Cruiser. Then he traded that for a '72 or '73 Mach 1 Mustang, Dale says. It was also green. They'd spend hours together fixing cars on the driveway, listening to their favourite songs rocking through the AM radio.

Dad and I almost never worked on cars together. I don't really know why, but it probably had to do with the fact that we only ever had his pickup truck or a family SUV or van, none of which carried much intrigue. But I remember one summer when he was buying a new Honda Civic and I begged him to get a standard transmission so that I could learn how to drive one. We picked up the silver two-door at the dealership. Mom must have dropped us there, because we drove it off the lot together.

Or rather, Dad made *me* drive it off the lot. Having never driven stick before, I stalled at least half a dozen times in the dealership parking lot as he tried to teach me how to release the clutch and hit the gas together. I felt like a fool. It must have taken us an hour to get home. I stalled again in the middle of a busy intersection, barely getting the engine back on before the traffic lights switched. We took an odd route that afternoon, one that brought us past the old laundromat where Dad would have played his Rickenbacker and up to the intersection of Cumbrian Court and Flowertown Road, where the bungalow he grew up in sat just off the corner.

I remember it distinctly because of the horn that raged behind us for at least ten seconds while we sat motionless at the stop sign, clutch and gears grinding as I tried to make the car move. The other car eventually swerved abruptly and roared past us in a rage. I was flustered and angry. I just couldn't get the hang of it and wanted to quit.

"Don't worry about them," Dad said. "Just take your time. You'll get it."

Another car drove around us. And another.

Looking past me from the passenger seat, Dad would have been able to see the driveway where he'd worked on all those cars he cared for in decades past. He might have heard those old songs drifting through the open windows of the tiny blue Beetle he tried to cram a dozen people into. He might have, but I don't know. He never told me.

The car jumped forward as I finally found the balance, and we jolted on.

That memory came back as Dale told me about the cars Dad loved and the music he played. I wondered why he'd never let me be a part of that. Was it because I didn't seem to have any interest? Was it because I didn't ask? Maybe he wanted to tell me all about it but thought I wouldn't care.

That same silver Honda still sat in the driveway at the house, next to the garbage bin where we were carting the basement junk away. The battery was dead. Rust inched across the wheel well. I hadn't driven the car in years.

13

Matt leans against a stud, pondering the delicate intricacies of moving shit from point A to point B.

We've drilled another hole in the floor about a foot in front of the stack, exposing the thick black pipe at a junction where it turns left, towards the other side of the house. It's the main sewage line, Matt explains. Our objective is to tie our new drains into it.

"It might get jammed up in one place," Matt says, referring to the course of excrement. "So it has to actually be a perfect ratio, a perfect slope."

He kneels next to the hole where the toilet will eventually sit.

"The toilet is going to flow down this way." He motions to the left, towards the hole we've drilled out to view the sewage pipe.

He explains that we'll put in a "four-inch T," which will connect both the tub and the vanity to the main pipe, following the trench we're smashing into the floor. We'll lay the drain pipes on a slight slope.

"I have to look it up on the internet, I forget the exact rise," he says. "But I think it's a quarter inch over two feet or something. The optimal level for solids to flow through—not too fast and not too slow. If it's too flat you'll get clogs, but if it's too sloped it can be a problem as well."

Tim, Jonathan, and I lean on the studs beside him, listening and nodding as though being bestowed with a great wisdom. I imagine this as some kind of Greek mathematical breakthrough—Pythagoras in his toga, squatting over the aqueducts and working out the consummate theory of how waste will flow through millennia to come.

Matt moves over to the trench where the tub will sit. "By the time you get around here, this pipe will probably be about two inches or so below," he explains.

Now he turns to address his students.

"So that's the story. That's the game plan," he says. "Keep working. While Jonathan is opening up this hole where our T is going to be, we'll start working on this line right here." He points to an imaginary line from the trench across the floor to where the vanity will go.

"Perfect."

"All right."

"Perfect."

We have a plan.

But we become less and less meticulous as we go. Matt eyeballs a path for the line to tie into the vanity. Then he blasts out the sides of the trench with the jackhammer, running it along the path and breaking up the floor. The trench zigs and zags like the kind of straight line I drew back when I needed a tutor to make a connection between two points.

I'm surprised to realized that the ground beneath the house is just crumbled bits of concrete stones. A light brown mud cakes the floor around us as groundwater creeps through the foundation. While I'm digging out the unearthed pieces with a shovel behind Matt, I hit something metallic. I kneel down, brush away the stones, and find a yellow can of Canada Dry. I pick it up gently, pinching it between my finger and thumb like an archeologist uncovering an artifact from a lost civilization.

The can is crushed and faded. It's narrow, unlike the stubby pop cans I know. A construction worker must have tossed it in the rubble while laying the foundation decades ago. It's not exactly a treasure. It's trash, actually. But still, I'm fascinated to find a piece of the past beneath us. It invades an illusion I hadn't realized I held: that *we* were the first. That this house just always *was*. It reminds me of the stories Dad told about running through these fields as a boy, and the corn that grew in this place. It reminds me that our lives here are just a fraction of what was and will be.

Our house was built by people who disappeared but left something behind. A house, a pop can—in whatever form, something that says they were here.

Near the waste pipe, the dig goes deeper. We're probably at a couple of feet down when more water seeps through the damp dirt around the exposed black tube. The recent spring thaw left it there. Jonathan slops the water and stones up and onto the basement floor.

When Matt is done carving out his jagged trench and I've concluded my treasure hunt, Tim picks up the sledgehammer. He twists his stance into the sloppy mud puddle that's engulfed the floor and, once again, hammers the path to pieces. He takes more than a dozen swings, each one smashing the concrete apart without any loss of speed or force.

"Keep it straight!" Matt yells when Tim is three-quarters of the way across.

"Almost there," Jonathan says encouragingly.

Tim is determined. He's breathing fast and hard—but he won't slow down. A little more than a foot from the edge he finally lets up and lets out a long, red-faced sigh . . . And then he strikes again. He takes two more swings before Matt intervenes.

"Stop right there! Stop right there!" he shouts, sweeping his foot across the space where the new trench will connect with the existing one. A foot-long crack has spread between the two canyons. "You'll break up a big chunk of rock right here and that will mean more patching for us."

Tim puts the sledgehammer down and takes another deep breath.

"Whoo!" I shout, oddly jacked up about what should be my brother-in-law's strongman audition tape.

"That was beautiful," Matt says. "Look at how straight it is!"

It's a near perfect line of crushed concrete, obliterating all the earlier zigs and zags.

Tim rests his hands on his hips. "All right, that's enough for me."

After another lunch of pizza and beer, the traditional meal of Reno Titans, Matt is back teaching us Plumbing 101. He's on his knees, looking down at the toilet hole.

"We have ninety, forty-five, and twenty-two and half degrees—that's all you have to work with," he says. "So if I'm coming straight off this toilet, this degree is something like a twenty-two-degree fitting."

He makes the motion of a curved fitting in the open space with his hands.

"But then we have to fit a T in here as well," he adds. "So really what we can do is just go and buy a bunch of different fittings all at once and use the ones that work—and take back the rest. We'll figure it out. It's going to be drain day tomorrow."

Matt looks down into the toilet hole as he taps the stack beside him. "The thing about this is, I don't think we'll have to do a vent because it's so close to this vent here. Because usually you have to come off with a vent and tie it back in here." He looks up and down at the stack. "Yeah," he says to himself. "Right on."

Tim, Jonathan, and I stand around him, holding beers. It sounds like Matt is up to something, but I'm not sure if that's a good or bad thing.

I sigh. "Good work," I say, nodding.

Matt takes a long, slow sip of his beer.

Then he walks over to the wall between the rafters where the tub will sit. "We need to find a place to pop a fan vent through," he tells us. "We'll have to go out to the side of the house with the rotary hammer. And we'll just pop a hole through here."

This surprises me. Does he mean we're going to drill an actual hole through the house? "What?" I ask, with clear concern.

"We'll want to make sure nothing is in the way," Matt continues, ignoring the question.

Nothing as in *what*, exactly, I wonder. Just the brick walls that hold up our house?

"Let's go outside," Matt says. "We'll check it out."

Minutes later, I'm standing next to the house holding a rotary hammer. It's a sunny afternoon. I'm wearing a blue T-shirt and a dust mask pulled up on my forehead. I've also got on Dad's tool belt, Dad's boots and socks, a pair of his old jogging pants, and his black work gloves. The rotary hammer is huge and green. It looks like a normal drill, but is at least five times the size. It's a drill for giants.

We set up to the right of the bay window that looks out from the dining room, next to our air-conditioning system. Our neighbour, Pete, watches over the fence. Matt has marked a spot on the brick wall that we intend to bore a hole into, breaking through to the basement. He offers me the honours. But I'm uneasy about driving this enormous drill bit through the side of our house. It seems a little too trial-and-error to be drilling through a perfectly fine brick wall.

I move to hand Matt the drill, but he objects.

"No, no—*you've* got to put a hole in this house," he says.

I know he's right.

"How *do* you put a hole in a house?" I ask. I'm holding the drill at my hip with two hands, like a flame thrower in an action movie.

Matt puts his hand on mine, on top of the trigger. "You just aim and . . ." He squeezes and the rotary hammer screams to life.

"Start going straight!" Matt yells.

I'm not sure I've even started in the right spot. "Did you mark it off?" I shout.

He doesn't hear me. But it feels like this is an important detail. I'm holding the bit about an inch from the wall.

"Did you mark it off!?" I shout again. Then I let go of the trigger and step back as the bit slows.

"It's here," Matt says, pointing to an unmarked spot on a brick that I'm certain is random.

I crouch down with the hammer drill in place. We're beyond questions now.

I push the bit softly against the brick, where it rips to life and bounces right back, just as the jackhammer had.

Tim and Jonathan stand by the fence next to where Pete is peering over, each of them laughing at the spectacle.

I try to focus.

"Here," Matt says. He grabs the hammer bit, pushes it against the wall, and backs away.

"And then I start pushing?" I ask.

"It'll do the work," Matt assures me. "You don't have to put a lot of pressure on it."

I shake my head and pull the trigger again.

The bit whirls for a moment, and then it gets high-pitched—almost a metallic squeal. The drill jumps back, drops, and then hits the wall again lower down. And I jump back and stand up, retreating.

The crew laughs again—and I let out a laughing huff too. But I'm angry at this stupid wall. I crouch back down immediately, like a boxer bouncing back after taking a punch.

"More pressure than that?" I ask Matt—putting the blame on his directions.

I line up the drill bit again. "Right here?"

Matt adjusts it, raising it several inches. "Yeah, right there," he says.

This time I'll be ready, I tell myself. The bit sticks with a bit of pressure as I hold the drill steady, my right hand on the handle and my left at the base. It whines and grinds, but it doesn't scream. As I press in gently it disappears into the light brown brick.

Then it stops. I push harder and it doesn't move. I let go of the trigger and turn back to Matt. "Yeah, stopped going anywhere."

"Do a bunch all around it," Matt offers.

"A bunch all around it? How big *is* this hole?"

"We're going to need about a four-inch hole."

"Four inches?" That seems enormous.

"Maybe five," Matt says.

When the drill roars back to life I press it just beneath the small hole I made. It jumps off the brick with the same metallic retort.

I'd lost focus. I'd doubted, and now I was sinking. It takes me a few seconds to find my concentration again.

Now I move up and to the left of the hole, leaning into the pressure. The bit sinks through the brick once more, the holes now breaking in pieces together. So I keep the rhythm, starting another hole above the one I've just made.

Easy.

Matt taps me on the shoulder and I turn off the drill.

"All right, let's start chipping it," he says.

He holds what looks like a giant flat spatula in his hand. I put the drill on the ground and he hands it to me.

I press it against the hole, holding it like an actual utensil. "And I'm just supposed to chip away?" I ask.

As he picks up the drill, Matt looks over just as I start scraping the debris out of the hole.

"No," he corrects—kindly, considering the laughter that's rising near the fence. He pulls the long concrete bit out of the drill and then takes the spoon implement and twists it into place.

"Oh, we're going to use that thing?" I say, trying to rush past my embarrassment. "I was going to say, 'You want me to use my hand? Are you crazy?'"

Matt just nods.

"It looks like a giant cake mixer," I add.

He doesn't respond. He flips a switch on the side of the drill, moving it from "rotary hammer" mode to "strict hammer" mode.

"Right," I say. "*Strict* hammer."

I take the drill back, bend down, and press the new bit into the mess of the three holes I've made. "Okay, so what's going to happen here?"

"I don't know," Matt says. He steps back. "We'll find out. I'm really curious to see myself."

I pull the trigger. It sounds like the quick burst of a motorcycle engine, then comes the previous whine and grind. I push in with my weight as the blade hammers back and forth, cutting into the brick and ripping apart the holes. It bores into a larger, narrow slit in the wall. I press the drill into it for a good twenty seconds, moving deeper and deeper. It's all a bit much, so I let go of the trigger and the bit spins to a halt. I pull back to get the bit out, but it won't move. I wiggle it a few times. No give. It's stuck.

I give the drill another tug, then look at Matt, clearly frustrated. He takes it from me and angles it downward, above the hole I've made. Then he turns the drill on, it shakes and a good-sized piece of brick pops out.

"A nice four-inch hole," he says.

It's a perfectly symmetrical rectangle. How did he manage to do that with the mess I'd started?

Matt hands the drill to me and I jump back in, trying to do the exact same thing he had, tilting the bit down on an angle. But the bit jumps back and so do I.

"So, you want me to go above it?" I ask, as though I'm just double-checking and haven't already screwed it up.

"Wherever. You can go above or below," he says. "No problem."

Up to me, then.

I jab at the hole with the drill in short spurts from all different directions. The drill sounds as though it's sputtering. I'm making very little progress, it seems, with only small pieces of brick starting to fall out as I go.

Matt moves in and clears out the hole.

"More?" I ask.

"Yeah. Yeah . . ." he says, digging out the debris.

I peer into the hole.

"Where else am I going here?"

"That's only about three-by-three or something," he says, and tells me to drill into the brick beneath the hole to widen it out and make it bigger.

I have very little luck with this. I try to push down from above, but nothing moves. The solid brick repels every attempt. For about thirty seconds I move this way and that way, trying to find an angle—but the wall keeps rejecting me.

Eventually, though, a triangular crack breaks in the brick beside the hole, causing the corner to fall away.

"It's wide enough," Matt says. "Knock out the brick beneath it now."

Jonathan has gone down to the basement to monitor our progress from inside. Through the window several feet away he shouts something about wood, but I have no idea what he's talking about.

Matt translates. "This is plywood—and this is a moisture barrier," he says, digging into the hole, pulling out the bits. "We still have to get through here. We can probably just do that with a wood bit and then finish it off with a Sawzall. So try not to take out the full brick," he adds, as though I'm in control. "Maybe about halfway down."

I give it another whirl. The drill is a touch steadier in my hand now. The final pieces of brick break away, exposing the wood that was hidden behind it. I step back confidently. Matt pulls out the final debris and measures the hole. It's four inches high and four inches wide.

Perfect.

"Tomorrow we'll just pop through all that wood there and then that's it," Matt says. "And that'll be the vent for the bathroom."

"Beauty," I say.

And we call it a day. The sun sinks in the backyard. My old faded Fisher-Price basketball net sits on the concrete base of a shed we never got around to building. The anchor bolts for the diving board jut out from the patio stones. The pool is unopened, a foot of dark winter water resting in the bottom of its black tarp cover. The bushes and trees are still bare, but the air is cool and it smells like spring.

The anniversary of my father's death is creeping closer, and I don't know what's on the other side. But this grief-tinged fiction can't go on forever. What am I really trying to accomplish? Why am I here? Why am I doing this, really?

Dad lived his life through blueprints, I think. He always had a plan for what he was building. And he always had a tool to fix any problem that arose within them. Now his plans need to carry on, even though he's gone. I can't shake that feeling. It's what lies beneath everything. His tools need to be used, even though he can't. Maybe none of it was ever really his. Tools build and shape our lives, but then outlive us. They are passed on. My grandfather gave his to my father. Now they belong to me. One day it will be my job to build a life for a child of my own. But I'm struggling read the plans and understand the tools Dad left behind—and it feels as though there's nobody left in this world to really show me.

So I keep searching for him.

14

Carol's father died in the parking lot of the strip mall with the laundromat that Dad's band used to play in.

Dale found him slumped over in his car. He hadn't felt well that day and a friend had agreed to take him to the hospital. On the way, the friend stopped to grab cigarettes while Carol's dad waited in the car. Dale was walking by and saw him hunched over in the front seat. He ran down the street to tell Carol that he thought her dad was drunk.

It was a heart attack. Carol was only fourteen at the time.

"I was dating Rick then," she tells me. "And my dad actually said to me one time, 'I really like this guy—he's a good guy.'...I met him in the fall. And my dad died the following May."

From that moment on, my father—who would have been only fifteen—became a constant in the Sheppard house. Carol's mother was sick at the time. She'd caught polio when she was younger, and its complications eventually put her in a wheelchair. She ended up with epilepsy, too.

My father took care of everything around the house, doing all the repairs whenever they needed to be done. He made sure it stayed standing.

"It meant everything," Carol says. "The only way I can really say it is that he was part of our family. Like he really was so close to everybody and so good to everybody. Rick didn't have a mean bone in his body."

Carol's brother, Carson, had had serious kidney problems since he was a toddler and was often in the hospital. He was a year and a half older, the same age as my dad; they were close friends. Carson was a musician too, and they shared their love for that. And when Carson wasn't well enough to drive, my dad would often chauffeur him around from place to place. He loved to help him out.

Carol and my father's adolescent lives were intertwined with the mess of teenage love. They became inseparable.

One Christmas Eve, Dad threw Carol a surprise party in the rec room with the bowling alley bar because her birthday was on Christmas Day and she never got to celebrate. And for *his* birthday Carol bought him a puppy—a collie they named Sheena—because Dad had never had any pets growing up. My grandfather was away at the time. "Bob won't like this," my grandmother objected when Carol brought the puppy over. "He's *not* going to like this." But Sheena stayed with my grandparents for fifteen years, long after my father had moved away.

Carol and Dad took long road trips with my aunt Deb and her boyfriend, she tells me. One day they all decided to drive through the States to Georgia, where my father's cousins lived. They drove straight through a blizzard—and Carol was certain they would die.

They'd watch *Saturday Night Live* every weekend. And on Sunday mornings they'd drive to the Country Style café downtown and have a coffee and doughnut, like an old retired couple.

Sometimes the group of friends they hung out with did psychedelic drugs on the weekends—and mostly at the Sheppard house, which had become the go-to party spot after their father died. Carson and his friends were heavily into it too. My father was always there but never partook, Carol says, because he didn't want to disappoint his parents. I wonder if that's true, or if it's just something you tell the son of a dead man. It's not hard to believe Dad didn't take drugs—I couldn't imagine him on psychedelics—but because of *his parents*? That seemed unlikely. I can only speculate, but I wondered if maybe it was the weight of the gap he was filling in a house that was spiralling around him. Someone had to be in control, making sure the place didn't burn down. That seemed more likely. It wasn't so much what his parents thought as that he was already thinking like a parent himself.

Dad had also become close with Carol's younger sister, Cindy. She was very shy, but she trusted him. "Rick was kind of like a father to her, even though he was just a bit older," Carol says. Several years later, when Cindy was twenty-one, he'd walk her down the aisle at her wedding, just a few months after she'd been diagnosed with multiple sclerosis.

At that time, my father—in his early twenties—was already rising as a solid construction worker. There was never any other expectation. No discussion of college or university. When high school was through, the assumption was that you'd move right into the working world. Right out of high school, Dad landed his first job on a site through my aunt's boyfriend, Scott, who worked construction.

"It was basically, 'Hey, here's a job for you,'" Carol says. "And he kind of learned it as he went."

And that was it. That connection is what defined the rest of his life. It was why I was drilling holes in the basement floor more than three decades later.

He was good at it. He knew how to follow orders. He was meticulous about getting things right, which had to have been fuelled in part from years and years of my grandfather telling him he was doing things wrong. He was quickly promoted to finishing foreman. Dad's path was set without a glance in a different direction.

Throughout my life, Dad would continually urge me to find my dreams and chase them. To hunt them down with every ounce of passion and dedication I could find within me, and to never give up. I'd never stopped to consider why.

"What did he want to be?" I ask Carol. "Did he ever tell you?"

"He liked the idea of learning how to fly. Like, to be a pilot."

She bought him a few lessons as a gift, she says. "He was really interested in that."

One night, years later, Carson seemed to have come down with a bad flu. A doctor in town told them he'd be fine, but it got worse over the next few days.

"Carol, I'm afraid to close my eyes," she remembers him saying.

They knew it was much worse than the flu. My father picked up Carson, put him in the backseat of his car, and drove with Carol to a hospital in Toronto to see a kidney specialist. Every bump on the road left Carson in agony. When they got to the hospital they took him right into the emergency room. A doctor found that his blood urea nitrogen levels were lethally high. Carson went on dialysis right away.

Dad and Carol went home while Carson was treated. The next day the doctor called to say that everything was going well, but that Carson needed to stay for another day because he was complaining about having a headache.

The phone rang again at ten-thirty that night. Carson had died after suffering a brain aneurysm.

Carol and my father ended things sometime after that. It was her decision—she was the one who broke it off.

"Why?" I ask.

"You know what, it's funny. At the time, I never really knew. I don't know, it just felt like something—I can't even tell you why," Carol says. "I don't even know, back then, why. But looking back now, I think what it might have been, for me, was that although he was so sweet and good to me and I loved him and everything, he wasn't the affectionate type. And I think I needed that. That's what I think it was. And I didn't realize that, probably, until just the last couple of years. You don't always understand yourself when you're younger."

"Was it tough to break up?" I ask. "How did it go?"

"Yeah, he was pretty upset. I mean, we both were. It's hard to break up for everybody. If you've been through that, you understand, right? I know definitely it was hard for him, for sure."

I wonder what Dad knew about heartache. I wonder if he remembered the agony, or if it had faded into a faint memory of what had once felt so real and endless, the way first love always does when it ends. Or maybe, beneath the sting, there was relief—and the thrill of new possibility after so much of his young life had already seemed locked in place.

A couple of years later Carol and Dale got together—and the boy with a crush on the girl dating his best friend finally got his chance.

They started a new life together, drifting ever away from those long-ago days. Carol and Dale would have two sons, making stories of their own as they rocked along heavy waves of marriage. Years later they'd divorce, but they'd still sit in the kitchen and talk for hours. And one day they'd take a long drive together to sit at the front of a packed church to say goodbye to an old friend.

I wonder if Dad ever thought of them. I wonder if he thought about how life breaks into fragments and leaves pieces behind as time barrels on. Or if he ever thought about what might have happened if his heart hadn't been broken and a first love had lasted forever. Did he think about how close the course of our lives can be to taking us somewhere else entirely?

After he and Carol broke up that spring, I know that Dad did take more flying lessons. In an old box of his things I found a Brampton Flying Club logbook that charted the hours he spent in the sky. Also in that box was a pilot's operating handbook for a 1977 Model 150M Cessna Commuter. On October 23, 1977, he earned his solo flight certificate in that plane.

I know that he flew to Waterloo on June 10, 1978—and to the airports in London and Brantford, Ontario, on June 24. I can see his signature written neatly and proudly at the bottom of the page in the logbook, confirming that Rick Robson had indeed soared through the clouds.

I know that a few weeks later, on July 11, 1978—convinced by a couple of friends who were trying to get him over a broken heart—he walked into a bar in downtown Toronto.

That night, Dad met Mom.

15

We drive through our neighbourhood, along the streets I used to bike as a kid—down Corkett, where our ball hockey games were halted by passing cars, and then down Burt, past the house where I'm told Carol and Dale lived for several years before moving north to Barrie.

Mom is driving, which is odd. Since Dad died I've always been the one at the wheel.

We turn left onto Major William Sharpe Drive—which I've just realized was likely named in memory of a soldier whose history has otherwise been wiped out. I'd walked, biked, and driven down this road thousands of times and not once thought to wonder who this man was, let alone that he was an actual person. As kids we'd even dropped the "Drive" altogether, referring to it only as MajorWilliam Sharpe—as though Sharpe were another word for Avenue or Street. Whenever our school bus reached MajorWilliam Sharpe, my sisters and I knew we were almost home. And MajorWilliam Sharpe was the boundary for how far we could bike. Now I wonder who this Will Sharpe was—and why he became a major, and whether he lived to see the street that was named for him.

Probably not. Streets are rarely known to the names they've been given.

Mom turns right on Flowertown Avenue, which for a couple of blocks is lined with houses built in the eighties, like ours, until a sudden shift to houses built in the late fifties and sixties. This is where the old farmer's field began. This is where Dad would have biked to the edge before charging in. We leave the stalks and drive down the same road. We roll to the intersection of Flowertown and Cumbrian Court, where Dad and I sat stalled in the Honda, me grinding the gears as cars honked and sped around us.

My grandmother's bungalow, with its pink brick and beige siding, is the second house from the corner, with a maple tree out front that I used to climb. Dad's blue truck sits at the top of the long driveway. I picture him leaning beneath the raised hood of a green Land Cruiser as we park over a pattern of old oil spots.

Auntie B has done her best to keep the grass cut and the roof from leaking, but it's been hard since Dad left us. After my grandfather died, it became his job to keep the old house standing. We were only five minutes away. He'd go over to the house to fix anything that needed to be repaired. A few years back, he had the old pool filled in because no one used it anymore. He hired someone to do that, though Pa probably would have given him a hard time for not doing it himself. It was an act of erasure, I thought—filling the hole he'd dug and along with it any trace of the blue liner, the steel siding, the whirlpools that pulled kids around in a circle when the adults moved as fast around the edge of the pool as they could. The grass was fresh above it, as though sitting on a grave. You could see the outline of what was there, but only because you knew. In the decades ahead there'd be no sign of those summer days spent by the water.

I wonder what Dad thought standing next to the filled-in hole. Did the sweat and tears of digging it seem futile, or did the years hidden beneath the grass seem like treasure?

Dad enjoyed taking care of the old house after his father died, I think. We used to be here all the time.

I've kept his truck here because there are no other cars at my grandmother's place now that she's in her nineties and can no longer drive. And these days the blue trash bin at our house is taking up half the driveway.

But tonight we're buying a toilet and a tub. And only a truck can carry that.

It's seven-thirty on a cool spring night. There's a hole bored halfway through the side of our house and a muddy trench system dug into the basement floor. The sun sets pink and orange. And Home Depot is open until ten.

Big box hardware stores are tough for me. Dad used to complain about them all the time. He much preferred Guest Hardware, the shop he favoured most of his life. I remember going there with him when I was young. There was so much stuff packed into a small space on the main floor and down in the basement. Any screw you needed. Any bolt. A lawn mower? A table saw? You named it, they had it. Whatever you needed to keep your house standing.

But then, in the 1990s, big box complexes with their massive parking lots were built on the north and south sides of town. I distinctly remember when they arrived. Giants like Home Depot and Lowe's filled spaces that could be airport hangars. The rows seemed to stretch for miles. For every item the old hardware store carried these mammoths had dozens more—and with endless brands to choose from, stacked on grates you needed a mechanical lift to reach. You'd think that, for my father, it would be like a trip to Willy Wonka's Chocolate Factory. But it wasn't.

There was something impersonal about the wide aisles, the endless inventory, the staff in their orange work-apron uniforms with name tags to create the illusion of a personal connection. But the big boxes could never be the old-time mom-and-pop hardware stores that their aesthetic tried to emulate. There was no heart or soul in the place. No connection to the people who bought the tools they'd use to bring shape and structure to their lives. There's something about a store that knows the generations that have passed through it—something that connects it to the tools it sells and the people who buy them. People they know by name; tools they've sold for years. There's an intimacy to it.

And inevitably, just as Dad had worried, the big box stores put the small local shops out of business. Guest Hardware closed down shortly after Dad had done that first renovation on our main floor and basement. The only convenient option left was the leviathan that had consumed it.

My father never found the same joy there. He'd go in, get what he came for, and leave. Sometimes when we went together he'd lament the end of that old hardware store as he scanned the rows. I always felt lost in Home Depot, despite the huge signs hanging in front of the aisles. It's one thing to know where something is in theory and entirely something else to know what you actually need when you get there. Dad could glance at a wall of nuts and bolts mere seconds before grabbing the exact size he wanted. I'd stand there for at least ten minutes until I was frustrated enough to pull out my phone and ask him.

I've been inside a Home Depot only a couple of times since he died. Each trip was draining. It's weird what sets off the memories.

I only ever went there with Dad, so it was impossible not to associate a trip there with him. I once walked the aisles for more than twenty minutes on an errand to pick up light bulbs. They weren't hard to find, but I wasn't really looking. I just needed to walk around the place and feel like he was beside me. It was an odd nostalgia, but I felt as if I could have walked those mile-long aisles for hours.

But this time it's different. This time I'm with Mom and Tim, who's met us—and we're on a mission. Since Dad died my mother has become particularly hostile to salespeople. She carries an automatic defensiveness, as though every store employee sees her as a helpless widow and is trying to con her. She seems to believe that there's always a deal to be haggled over, and that if she doesn't try she'll get ripped off. "That's the best deal you can give me?" has become her go-to phrase during nearly every transaction she makes.

There's much more variety in the Home Depot toilet section than I expected—an entire aisle is dedicated to porcelain thrones. You don't really notice the different designs and intricacies of each until you see them lined up side by side. I had no idea how expensive and complicated toilets can be. In my entire life it never occurred to me that there might be more than one standard version of a can. I mean, I've heard of the super high-tech ones with temperature settings, personalized music, and multiple strengths and angles for bidet spraying and blow drying. But here were dozens of toilets of the same manual wipe and flush variety. There are different shades, shapes, and sizes. Some have long tanks, some short. Some have oval seats, others round. Some even come in a yellowy-beige hue that makes them look vintage in a weird way.

It's overwhelming.

The three of us spend at least twenty minutes walking back and forth down the aisle, considering style, features, and price. Mom wants the perfect one. She's set on a Kohler because that's the brand Dad liked, she says. I don't know how this is a thing she remembers, but it seems sweet to me that somewhere in the past my father had made a comment about the quality and comfort of a Kohler toilet and that moment had stuck with my mother. It's the little things that make a marriage.

If Dad can't be here, we're at least going to take care to honour his memory properly.

The Kohler Highline Classic Comfort seems to be the best in class. Its overview boasts of simple design and efficient performance, which conserves water without sacrificing flushing power. The tank curves inward with a seductive elegance. But it comes in at more than $300.

We waver at the price and check out another Kohler model for $269. I'm starting to see the difference now. The lower-priced model seems plain and forgettable compared to the siren song of the Classic Comfort. Mom seems to agree, quickly moving past it.

"Look at this one, Dan," she says.

It's the Highline Dual Flush. It has a long, solid tank—without insisting upon itself. It's stylish but understated. Mom stops to consider it.

"It's more money though," she says.

It comes in at $290. I suggest that there might be value in spending a few extra bucks to get the kind of toilet you want to spend the rest of your life with.

"The last thing you want to do is sit on a brand-new can and think '*Shit*,'" I say out loud.

That was quite clever, I think, but Tim carries on as if he didn't hear while Mom gives me a cross look for cursing.

We finally settle on the Kohler Cimarron, Comfort Height® The Complete Solution® with a round bowl—"Patented Flush Engine: No flapper, No leak, No problem"—which is equipped with AquaPistin® flush technology. It comes in at the high twos, but Dad would appreciate the quality. It's the shit.

Tim and I pull one of the boxes out from beneath the display and put it on our orange cart. We move on to the next step in our journey: a tub. As we turn around to look at the bathing options on the rack behind us, a man in an orange apron appears.

Before we walked in, I had specifically asked Mom not to speak to any of the salespeople. I knew how it would go, and I was right.

"Can I help you with anything?" the man asks.

"Yes, we're looking for a tub," Mom says. She points to a white tub beside us. "I want a white one. Not like this one."

The man looks at us, confused.

"This tub *is* white," he says, defiantly. That was a mistake.

"No," Mom says. "It's not."

This is tense. It looks white to me. But if it's not *white* white, it's absolutely in the white family. Maybe an off-white? Eggshell? I don't know.

The Home Depot man doubles down.

"This is the colour of all our tubs," he says.

Mom is not pleased. I give her a look that suggests we need to step away from the situation. I can tell she doesn't like this man and his strong stance on tub colours.

"Okay, thanks very much," I tell the man. "We'll figure it out."

As he turns and walks away, Mom sends daggers through his Home Depot apron with her eyes.

It takes us much less time to find a tub she wants than it did to decide on the toilet. She's frustrated, and I'm sure it has very little to do with the tub salesman. Mom has to feel like I do. This was Dad's territory. He would have walked through these aisles with an aura of infinite experience. Dad would have known which toilet and tub to buy right away. I would have followed him with a rolling cart and helped load up whichever one he pointed to, and we'd have been at the checkout within ten minutes. Instead we've spent nearly an hour here trying to figure out what to do. It's not the time that matters. It's not the differing shades of white. It's the not knowing. It's the hesitation. It's the inescapable absence. I can see it in Mom's eyes. She wants to go home now. And so do I.

We settle on a sixty-inch acrylic tub. It's white, we agree, and it holds water. It'll do. We put it on the orange cart next to the Kohler Cimarron, have them rung up at the checkout, and push them out the door. Tim and I load them into the bed of the truck while Mom gets into the front seat. She's always hated pickup trucks. They remind her of the farm where she grew up and then spent the rest of her life pushing away from.

I climb in and turn on the engine. The truck shakes to life.

"This thing is so big," she says.

"You're such a city girl," I say.

She smiles and we listen quietly to the truck rumble as it takes us home.

Later that night we sit at the kitchen table we've had since I was young and my sisters and I would complain about the tuna pot pie

Mom made at least once a week. We had an old-fashioned, every-one-at-the-table-for-dinner rule in the house, one that the three of us always met with frustration. But now I'm glad for the memory. Tonight it's just me and Mom.

I can tell she's aching and is trying not to show it. But she's breaking. I ask her how she's doing without him—and she's honest.

"I'm not doing good at all," she says. "It's been a shitty year. It's been a shitty life."

I've heard my mother use the F-word exactly once in our lives, and it's seared in my memory. She *never* swears. I'm glad she's allowed herself to now. But it breaks my heart to hear her.

She wipes a tear off her cheek.

"I have no one to do nothing with," she says.

My mother doesn't talk much about the past.

Not the fun parts, anyway—not about her rebellious years, back when she left the farm and the Mennonite church behind and set out from Punkeydoodles Corners, a hamlet named after a nineteenth-century tavern off the old bumpy road she grew up on, near Stratford, Ontario. I know that she grew up very poor. That she hated the barn, having developed a lifelong fear of mice from the many that ran across the rafters and dashed beneath the hay. I know that she went to college in nearby Kitchener, to become a nurse, and that at age twenty-six, after a breakup of her own, she moved to Toronto to work in the Emergency Room at Women's College Hospital.

That's the point where she starts to colour between the lines of her history.

"I didn't really know the city," Mom tells me.

She'd been in Toronto for only three weeks before the night of July 11, 1978. A friend from nursing school, Ronnie, took her out to a popular bar called Brandy's on the Esplanade. It was packed most nights, even Tuesdays. The place swirled with music, cigarette smoke, and booze.

"We were sitting near the bar," she says. "I noticed him walk in."

My father was twenty-three. He had short, light-brown hair, broad shoulders, and a recently broken heart.

One of the two friends he arrived with tried to hit on my mom and Ronnie. They weren't interested.

"I told him I'd rather dance with him," she says. Mom nods across our kitchen table towards the other end of the room as though Dad is standing on the far side of a busy bar.

Dad's rejected friend returned to let him know that the brunette was interested. But even with a sure-thing sign like that, my father still had to work up the nerve.

"It took him a while to come over and talk," Mom says.

They didn't dance that night. They chatted over drinks at that table near the bar while the music and smoke went on swirling around them.

"He was shy and quiet," she says. "But I thought he was a good-looking guy. He seemed nice—I thought he was a school-teacher."

Before the end of the evening, with a sudden surge of dashing courage, Dad asked for Mom's phone number. She scribbled it on a napkin and smiled and the two parted ways. Mom rumbled north on the subway beneath the street. Dad went west, driving his imbibed pals home in his Land Cruiser, the digits that would unlock the rest of his life tucked in his pocket.

It took him four days to call—so long that Mom had already assumed he wouldn't. She suggested dinner at the Crock and Block near her apartment in Toronto. Dad told his older sister about the girl he'd met. It was the first real date of his adult life. He bought a new shirt for the occasion. The yellow polo.

"He was all nervous," Mom says.

Beneath the glow of our kitchen light she smiles, still impressed by the effort.

"We were married two years later."

Part IV
Blueprints

16

The alarm on my phone goes off at six-fifteen a.m., but I ignore it until quarter to seven. An early start after such a full day seems an unnecessary cruelty, but we're way behind schedule. Matt wants to keep the project on track, and I can spend only so much time in this imaginary life before my real one falls apart.

It's been a year now since I've worked at my actual job as a sports-writer—ever since a book leave turned into an extended mental and emotional departure. I've been back on the payroll since the New Year, but I haven't done much to earn it. Like my relationship with Jayme, back in Toronto, my career has been out of sight and mind. I haven't really confirmed whether these are "vacation days" or not. They're just days when I'm here. And they're running out.

I stumble out of bed just before Matt and Jonathan pull into the driveway in the old mint-green truck. It feels as though every muscle and bone in my body is objecting. I'm thirty-two—not young, but not old—and it's too soon for my body to revolt like this. It feels like it's giving up.

I'm still shaking out the sleep when I meet all three guys downstairs. It's dark in the basement. The uneven trenches stretch across the floor like unhealed gashes. It seems like a lot of damage and not a lot of progress.

I yawn wide and loud. Matt hands me a black coffee from Tim Hortons.

"Today we wire and finish up the plumbing," he says.

He holds a coil of white plastic wire. Matt apprenticed to be an electrician, so we'll be paying even more attention than usual to what he has to say. It's clear he wants to get moving—he jumps right into our instructions.

"Outlets have to be three metres apart, maximum," he tells us. "But we'll obviously put them a lot closer." I'm already thinking ahead, planning where a TV will go, where dressers and bedside tables will sit.

Meanwhile, installing the outlets, it turns out, is an easy process. The electrical boxes pop into place with the tap of a hammer against the side of a stud in the desired location. Little tabs on the end wrap around the edges of the wood to hold the box in place with a screw.

I tap in six boxes. Perhaps it's overkill, but I don't want any outlet regrets. I put two on each side of an imaginary bed, and then one along the far wall separating the bedroom and bathroom, where the TV will go. The last one goes beneath the prospective TV screen, where it'll be hidden by a dresser.

Matt and I unroll the white wiring to connect the boxes I've knocked into place.

"When you support wire, you have to support it every three feet, and twelve inches from the box," he says.

On the top and bottom of each box is a little tab meant to feed the wire through. We pull the first wire around behind the studs and loop it up through the bottom of the first box. There's a tiny screw that we need to loosen and clip the wire behind after several inches of it has been pulled through. Matt flips around the attachment for his screwdriver—"It's a Robertson," he says helpfully—and then twists the square head into place.

Now he pulls out his box cutter, twisting the knob to extend the blade.

"Then you take your knife and strip it back," he says. "You've gotta get it right in between like that." He presses the tip of the knife into the middle of the white casing around the wires. Then he pulls down, sliding the knife across the casing as it splits apart like a banana peel. The excess is cut away with the knife, leaving an orgy of naked copper wiring.

Matt offers a quick history lesson in home electrical as I watch him do it again.

"If a live wire touched the side of the box it would become live," he says. Anyone who touched it, in other words, would be electrocuted. "So about forty years ago or something they added this wire." He pulls back one of the three lengths of copper. "It's tied onto the box. You stick it under this screw." Now he twists the wire around the small screw near the bottom of the box. "You want to put it on clockwise, so that tightening the screw pulls the wire tighter," he says, turning it.

"Now it's grounded, so it's safe," he explains. "You tie the line to the panel, which connects to another ground wire, which goes directly to the ground."

It's one of those moments when you suddenly realize something that should have been apparent all along. "So it grounds it," I offer. This feels terribly obvious as soon as I say it.

"Yeah, so if this touches it will trip the breaker," Matt says, pushing the "live" wire against the side of the box. "So you'll never have the problem of somebody getting electrocuted."

Matt pushes the excess wiring back into the box. "You can fold those in like that, and then that's it."

With the next box, he shows me another veteran trick.

"Sometimes you'll install a box and then realize, 'Oh crap, I need to move it another foot,'" he says. "So you just leave a little loop, and fasten it here." He bunches up the wire and then clips it to the stud with a plastic staple that has two small nails attached. "One to set, one to sink," he says, giving the clip two whacks with his hammer, driving the nails into the wood.

We've been repeating that phrase a lot during the renovation: "One to set, one to sink." It's a well-known construction mantra that is used repeatedly in a YouTube video Matt's shown me by an old-school carpenter named Larry Haun, who made instructional videos that look to be set in the mid-1980s. He's a frail-looking old guy who's basically a superhero of home building. Matt and Jonathan are obsessed with him, and have been showing us clips every day. Larry Haun is a throwback to what seems like a bygone masculinity. He's skinny, but you know he can probably lift a car. He wears tank tops or works shirtless. His skin is sunbaked and worn like leather. He could probably drink you under the table but would never sully a job site with a beer. He's a tough-son-of-a-bitch kind of man—a do-it-your-self, build-your-own-damn-house kind of man. He's the kind of man who sets with one whack and sinks with the next. Every. Damn. Time.

But every Larry Haun had to start somewhere. I'm well on my way—spending the next hour weaving electrical wire through the bedroom walls.

"You're going to put another box maybe three feet over," Matt says. "And here's a little trick. When we're doing any interior walls we'll have to drill a hole and run it right through the stud. But since it's an exterior wall we'll just bring it back behind the stud. It's much faster."

"So when we get to this box, what do we do?" I ask, pointing to the next electrical box that I've clipped into place next to where the bed will go.

Matt pulls the wire along the wall and flips it over top of the next electrical box. Then he grabs his wire cutters, cuts off the wire from the coil, and with his screwdriver pops out the top and bottom tabs. "We're going to put in a second wire that jumps to the next receptacle," he tells me. "And we just repeat the same operation."

He pushes the large coil of white wire with his foot across to the next box.

"And you know what to do from here," he says.

Maybe.

"All right," I say. "I'll give it a try."

"Right on," Matt says.

On the other side of the reno, we begin to lay our pipe into the long trench across the concrete, making sure we've got the slope right. The rule, Matt reiterates, is that there needs to be a quarter-inch decline over each foot of pipe.

Tim measures the depth of the hole closest to the big black pipe at nine and a quarter inches. Then I help him measure across the length of the trench that runs from the pipe to where the tub will sit. It's about eight feet.

"So our rise is going to be eight times a quarter," Matt says.

"Two inches," Tim translates.

We need to bring the depth to seven and a quarter inches where the tub drain will sit. I measure it at just under six inches right now, so we'll need to do some digging to get it right. Tim breaks up some ground around the trench with the sledgehammer. When we dig away the rubble we uncover another large copper pipe that appears to run across the back wall.

"That's the main three-quarter-inch waterline," Matt tells us. It's a long piece that enters the house before the shut-off valve by the furnace.

It seems important.

"So—what happens if we hit that?" I ask.

"Well, if we break it, it's a huge disaster," he says. "Water pours out until you can get somebody to come from the city and shut it off in the street. They open up a little tiny hole and they have a pole that comes down, and they turn a valve."

"This is just somewhere out on the street?" I ask. I'm kind of amazed at how inefficient that process sounds. And where *is* this hole? I'd played ball hockey and tennis-racquet baseball out there for years and never knew that something so important was beneath me. It's a literal artery of water.

"Yeah. And it's an emergency kind of thing. You call the city."

"And the whole time your basement is flooding?"

"The whole time water is just pouring into your basement," Matt avers.

"So . . . we avoid that."

"Yeah," he says. "You don't want to hit that. What you *can* do, what some guys do—like kind of risky contractors, confident guys— they'll break up all around the pipe and then they'll cut it, and then as the water is pouring out they'll put these fittings where you can slip them on—SharkBite fittings—and you tighten it down. They just try to do it quickly. That's a lot of water pressure coming out of that three-quarter pipe. A *large* volume of water."

"So they cut it and let the water just come out?"

"They cut and the water is pouring out. I'm sure they'd be drenched by the end of it."

"But you're not supposed to do that."

"No, it's not recommended. That's how a cowboy does it. You've got to be pretty confident that everything is going to go smoothly."

"You've got to be Larry Haun," I say.

"Pretty much."

Shortly after Dad met Mom, the company he worked for—Costain Construction—went under and he was out of a job.

Dad spent a couple of years getting by as a contractor while making plans to start his own company. He'd previously enrolled in architectural technology and construction management at Ryerson Polytechnical Institute, now Ryerson University. But it seemed like a waste to pay for a piece of paper to show that he could do things that he *already* knew how to do.

He dropped out, which was something that would become one of his biggest regrets in life. But his focus then was on starting his own business and being his own boss—the working man's dream.

Dad's plan was to design and build custom houses, Mom tells me. After learning the trade with Costain, he knew he could start something by himself. And he hoped to one day buy some land and build a house for his family to live in.

"Dad would have loved that," she says.

Every fall we'd drive through the escarpment north of us, just past the farmers' fields, our school, and the Brampton Flying Club.

The trees in the hills would hang over the winding roads like a canopy of blood red and burnt orange, leaves falling like giant snowflakes, blowing in the wind. As we drove we'd gaze out the car windows, watching the colours swirl. Then we'd stop near an entrance to the Bruce Trail and hike in. Not for long, maybe five or ten minutes, just until we'd find an opening next to the trees. We three kids would jostle one another while Mom tried to settle us into a pose for a family photo. Dad would balance his Canon AE-1 camera on a rock to line up a shot. He'd press the timer and then run across the path to be with us. We'd count down from ten, readying our smiles before the flash.

Later, on the drive home, Dad would always comment on the country houses we'd pass, with acres and acres of land between them. One day, he said, he and Mom would buy land and retire somewhere up there, somewhere in the hills beneath the trees.

I believed that he would.

Dad started Robson Renovations in 1981, the summer after he and Mom married. He bought a burgundy work van, with large magnets bearing the company name that would eventually stick to our basement fridge. It was his first office. He even pulled the seats out of the back to make room for the $3270 worth of tools he'd bought to get started. That August he pencilled out a list of the items on graph paper for an insurance company. And when I found that list, folded neatly in an envelope in one of the boxes in the basement, I recognized some of the names from the tools that had been tucked away in old milk crates in the garage. The list gave a sense of purpose to what I'd known only as a tangle of unusable machinery. These were the things Dad carried as he built our life.

There was the Model 77-c Skilsaw ($300), the ½" Milwaukee hammer drill ($200), the Black and Decker screw gun ($120), the

Craftsman 1½-hp router ($170), the Viking sabre saw ($100), and the Skil ⅜" rev. car speed drill ($100). Some of the other tools listed sounded pretty badass, like the propane torch kit ($65), a steel bar ($40), and a 10-lb. sledgehammer ($25), which I'd used to smash up the basement floor. Many of the other, smaller items were still in his tool bag: fourteen assorted screwdrivers ($65), a 20-oz. True Temper framing hammer ($20), a 16-oz. Estwing trim hammer ($24)—and a leather carpenter's belt ($35), which I now wore every day.

Dad also listed a Canon AE-1 camera ($380)—the one he'd used to take those photos on our fall colour tours.

Driving around in his burgundy van with its orange and brown decals, Dad was a one-man show trying to get his company off the ground in the beginning of a recession. He'd work for days on little sleep, often going from early in the morning right through until midnight to make sure the job was done on time and done well. And he was meticulous. He had to be: one bad job could sink him. The pay was never worth the effort, but he was building equity in his reputation.

A person's reputation is all they have to keep them going, I remember him telling me.

Mom worked constantly, too. While he was sleeping she'd be pulling evening or overnight shifts in the emergency room at Etobicoke General Hospital. Their young life together was a constant loop of long shifts and odd hours. It was the kind of work that could rip a couple apart. And there was certainly tension, but it was never enough to break them.

"One time I got so mad that I threw a pound of frozen hamburger at him," Mom tells me, smiling at the memory of a fight. "He just caught it and laughed."

Those were lean times. But Dad stayed afloat by landing a couple of big gigs in the first two years. When he was hired to turn an old house in downtown Brampton into a swanky new Italian restaurant, he ripped out the old main level and replaced it with a dining room floor, complete with a solid oak bar that he built. The reno earned him a reputation for fine craftsmanship. More jobs arrived. But it was always scattered, unsteady work.

Soon after they were married they bought a townhouse in Meadowvale, a leafy suburb west of Toronto. It was a small place in a complex called Treetops.

"It was cool and funky," Mom says. "It was unique." (Nostalgia may have coloured her memory. On Google Maps it looks like a pretty standard 1970s townhouse complex.)

It cost them $52,000, which they certainly didn't have. When they bought the mortgage, interest rates in Canada were a low 12 percent. The next year they rocketed to more than 18 percent, and would soon tip over into 20 percent. Many people just couldn't make the payments and had to sell their homes. But young and broke, Mom and Dad benefited from their blind luck. If they hadn't locked in for several years when they did, no way could they have kept the house.

"We had no extra money," she tells me. "We would have been in serious trouble."

It was a bad time to start a business and a tough time to start a family. But a few months after Robson Renovations was launched, my sister Jaime was born.

The snowflakes were huge on that January night in 1982. They fell softly outside the window of their townhouse in a way that my mother would never forget. It's the first thing she remembers about that night: the big, slow-falling snow.

The second thing she remembers is Dad running down the stairs of the townhouse and rushing to the carport to start up their blue two-door Firebird. She was waiting at the curb when he pulled up. He got out of the car and looked at her standing there. He smiled and shook his head. "What have we done?" he said.

She smiled back. "I don't know what we're doing," she said.

Dad helped her into the passenger's seat.

During the prenatal course my parents took he'd scribbled diligent notes and studied the material as if there'd be a final exam. Then, in the weeks before the due date, he'd put the finishing touches on the nursery he'd built for Jaime. He'd made a change table out of wood and a frame for a tiny bed she could sleep in when she was old enough.

That night, though, there was little he could do—and nothing either of them could control.

Mom tried to breathe slowly while her contractions increased. Dad drove quickly, nervously through those big snowflakes, on their last ride together before everything changed forever.

In the hospital he dabbed Mom's head with a cold cloth and held her hand. He ran through the breathing exercises they'd learned. None of it was really of any use. The one thing she asked for—a larger bed, she felt claustrophobic—he had no power to provide.

There wasn't time anyway. Three hours after they left the house, around one a.m. on January 6, their first child was born.

Dad held her first.

"She has perfect lips," he said.

"He was overwhelmed," my mother tells me. "He was just beaming and crying."

Like when it rains on a sunny day.

17

It's ten a.m. We're just a few hours in, but it feels as if it's been an entire day. Our pace has improved.

I'd managed to get the rhythm of the wiring down, finishing much faster than I imagined I would. The drain pipes have been laid on a meticulously measured slope, ready to be connected and tied into the main sewage system.

Now Matt rifles through a Home Depot bag, searching for something he can't find. He forgot to pick up the couplings for the plumbing. He doesn't seem concerned.

"Your dad probably has some in the garage," he says.

"He probably does," I agree. But I have no clue. I just assume he's got at least one of everything. We all know about the stockpile of tools and hardware in the garage, but beyond what I wield around my waist, I've remained quiet about bringing any of it into the mix. I'm still careful to not leave any of his tools lying around to get picked up and used by someone else.

The truth is, I don't want Matt going through my father's stuff. I've been trying to avoid the very obvious reality that we have everything we need for the reno in the garage. The other day, I'd brought one of Dad's drills downstairs to use, but lost sight of it when I set it down and it got mixed in with the general tools. After I hunted around and found it again, I'd quietly put it back in its base and taken it upstairs. It was a weird quirk, and I couldn't admit how much it bothered me. So later, when Matt asked if they could borrow a couple of drills to help speed things along, I dutifully went upstairs to get them. Dad had printed *Robson* in permanent marker above the Milwaukee logo on the red case that held two of his drills. I grabbed that one. That had stressed me out enough.

Since then I've tried to keep tabs on who was using the drills and where they were left. When no one was around, I'd carefully place them back in their cases. I'd never experienced obsessive-compulsive disorder, but I was feeling borderline at least.

I tell Matt he can look for the couplings in the garage because there's really nothing else for me to say. He heads upstairs with Tim, and a few minutes later they return with several copper fittings they've found in an old fishing tackle box.

We had enough T's, Matt says, but we'd run out of couplings. He shakes the copper pieces in his hand like dice. "But now we're back on track."

He mentions that he saw a bunch of tools up there that got him excited. "Man, there's an awesome old-school Skilsaw," he says. "Like, a pro one. That one's pretty sweet. I got giddy when I saw it."

He also noticed the "amazing pro mitre saw" that Dad had recently bought—the one he'd pack in his truck and bring down to my place to help me build the shelves and the desk I work at.

I grin. "Yeah," I say. "It's pretty cool." I'd only ever touched it when I helped Dad carry it from my patio to his truck.

I know the request to put tools like that to use will soon follow. There's no doubt that it would save us a lot of time. They're going to want to use these tools. It's inevitable. And of course, why let them sit there, going to waste? Still, I just don't know if I'm ready yet.

But no need to worry about that at the moment. Matt's quickly moved on to his next task: firing up a blowtorch.

We have to solder together the junctions for the new waterlines, which means first building a makeshift workbench by balancing one of the old doors we've taken down atop two sawhorses.

Now Matt scatters the couplings on the surface. He takes a piece of steel wool and swirls it around inside one of these little pipe fittings, scuffing off the oxidization and exposing gleaming copper. He gives it a blow, then cleans up an inch or so at the end of the pipe. After that he takes a bit of flux—a chemical paste used to join metals—from a jar with a small brush, and spreads it around on the inside of the fitting and the edge of the pipe. I didn't know this (not that I'd ever thought about it), but the solder won't stick to copper on its own. It will just bead off in unsightly blobs. It certainly won't seep into the joint.

The blowtorch hisses as Matt turns it on, and then a flame bursts out of the nozzle. It sounds like the static on the snowy channels that didn't work on old analog televisions. He pinches the joined copper piece in a big pair of pliers and holds it over the flame, rotating it slowly as if he's toasting a marshmallow. Grey steam rises out of both ends of the pipe.

"Once it heats up it just sucks right in there," Matt tells me.

I find myself fixated on the flame kissing the copper. The solder disappears into the seam between fitting and metal. When it was cool it was dull and lifeless. But now, as the tip of the solder touches the hot copper, it melts like wax, seeping eagerly into the joint and glowing like mercury wherever the flux has been applied to the pipe. It's the melting of one thing into another, forging a union. It's like how strangers find each other—and whatever form or shape that union takes, it creates a bond that makes those two things one. Or the way a child is always connected to their parent, part of each other, for better or worse, forever. It's incredible to watch the melding of a connection that creates something that wasn't there before. Maybe love is just a way of melting.

"Sometimes you'll find that it's not sucking in," Matt observes, breaking the spell. He's still holding the flame to the copper matrimony, but it's not taking. It seems destined for divorce. "The problem is likely that there wasn't enough heat all the way around, so you need to make sure you rotate nice and slowly across the entire surface."

The soldering takes time. We work carefully, since the smallest mistake caused by a shortcut can lead to enormous problems.

"If you forget to clean one thing, we'll have water spraying everywhere," Matt warns.

The plan is to cut into the current waterlines that run across the rafters above us—then slip in the new copper junction we've soldered. It creates a way for two new lines to tee off from the waterline for the washroom.

The meticulous nature of this process strikes me as something akin to the way my father always carried himself. If he hadn't shown that to me through his tools, he'd certainly stressed its importance in life. Everything was built with careful execution, slow and steady. There were no shortcuts. If melting is love, effective love takes patience and care.

Back in the soon-to-be-bathroom, we've smashed out a giant crescent-shaped hole in the floor, revealing two large "sanitary pipes," which

I learn is a nice way to say "shit pipes." One runs parallel to the stairs and the other runs on an angle, connecting to the other pipe somewhere farther down beneath the basement floor. We need to saw into both pipes and add junctions to drain the new shower and toilet, Matt explains.

This seems a potentially disastrous idea. The massive crescent hole looks like a muddy lake—and it's rising rapidly.

Matt goes to press his Sawzall against the pipe.

"Have we turned off the water?" I say, quietly concerned. He doesn't hear me—but because it isn't under pressure, nothing unsightly comes flooding out as the saw rips through it.

The new junction is supposed to slip over top of the edges of the old pipe after we've cut out an opening. We'll have to slide it over one end of the opening and then shimmy the piece back, splitting the difference between the two ends and overlapping about half an inch on either side, which will be slathered in glue. It won't take long to dry, so we need to move quickly. We're eyeballing the length here. The initial gap isn't big enough, so Matt uses the Sawzall to trim off a bit more of the pipe until we have enough room to manoeuvre.

The water rises around the operation at a concerning rate. There's much more than the day before.

"We're going to need to bail as we go," Matt says.

I rush to the stairs to grab a few Tim Hortons cups that held our morning coffee. We each kneel around the hole, trying to scoop the water. Matt pretends to take a sip from his while Jonathan empties out a garbage can to pour the water into. We go cup by cup, which is not close to being quick enough to keep the water from swallowing the sewage pipe.

Although the four of us are working away on the junction, it's a slow, inefficient process. I feel that everyone should be much more concerned than they seem. We try to slather the glue on the edges of the pipe, but it keeps getting washed away.

It's soon apparent that the coffee cups are a bad idea. It feels even more ridiculous when I remember that there's a Shop-Vac in the garage. "Will that help?" I ask.

Matt's hands are drenched in glue and muddy water as he struggles to connect the pipes in the muck. "Yeah," he says. "That would help."

As expected, the yellow industrial vacuum—which of course bears the name *Robson* in permanent marker—works much better than the coffee cups. It sucks back the water and holds it from rising just long enough to allow us to apply the glue and screw the pipe in to fit. Still, the base of the vacuum fills quickly and I have to dump it out into the garbage pail several times before we're finally able to get the junction glued in place.

I'm covered in the muddy water of whatever's come up from the ground—or possibly what's leaked out of the sewage pipe.

We move on to carry out the same process on the other side of the crescent mud lake, sawing a large chunk out of the sewage pipe that runs on an angle beside the first one so that we can add a junction for the toilet.

We have no margin for error. This time Tim works the vacuum while I stand ready with channel locks—a long blue wrench the size of my forearm—in case we're unable to twist the junction into place and have to force it. Fortunately that particular call to battle never comes.

With the junctions connected, we head up to the garage to unpack the brand-new porcelain throne. We need to make sure that we place

it in exactly the right spot above the drain and an inch off the wall—
which means we have to factor in another half-inch from the frame
to account for the drywall still to come. We're starting to think ahead
now. Getting smarter.

"You'll go to some people's houses and you'll see the lid tilting
forward because they put it too tight to the wall," Matt tells us.

He measures the width of the toilet tank. "We're at ten and
five-eighths," he announces. "So off the stud, add a half-inch for
drywall—and that brings us to eleven and an eighth."

I nod, but I don't really understand math with fractions off the top
of my head.

"Let's add, say, an inch and three-eighths," Matt says, holding his
tape measure across the back of the toilet. "So let's make it a nice
round number of, ah, twelve and a half. That's where the centre of
our toilet drain is going to be."

I nod again, still not knowing what he means. "All right, okay—
cool," I say coolly.

Matt is correctly unconvinced that I understand the measurements he's talking about. I clearly have not reviewed my notes on the
original lesson he gave me on how to properly read a tape measure.
He extends it and explains that anyone who can properly read a tape
measure is able to build a house.

"Some of the familiar marks are going to be your twelve inches,
obviously—a foot—and then you have your twenty-four," he says,
pointing to each number, highlighted in black. "And you have
your sixteen in red, so you know sixteen on centre," he goes on,
repeating the one lesson I learned while framing. "Other materi-
als that are going to line up with your sixteens are your insulation
and drywall."

I nod once more, following the lesson so far. But it's about to get more intricate. Matt holds the tape with his thumbs at the fifteen and sixteen, then moves his left thumb along on the longer marks between the numbers.

"Everything is measured in halves of halves of halves of an inch. Just keep dividing in half. Quarters, eighths, sixteenths. You'd have to be the king of finishing carpenters to measure in thirty-seconds. So, when we're measuring, you use the largest number of the largest fraction you can. Three eighths, but not four. Five sixteenths, but not six. Because six sixteenths is three eighths, and four eighths is a half."

It seems like a riddle.

He shows me what each of the shorter lines between the numbers indicates, pointing to each one moving across: "One eighth, two eighths—two eighths is a quarter," he says, moving his thumb along. "Three eighths, four eighths—five eighths."

It seems way too specific for me to ever use, but Matt insists it's important. Any carpenter worth the name can look at something and tell you within an eighth of an inch how thick it is. And they don't just talk in fractions of inches, they *see* in fractions of inches.

"Some guys will say measure that stud to the sixteenth," Matt says. "So you've got to be real accurate. Once you've mastered the sixteenth…"

"You're ready to build a house?"

"You're ready to build a house. People think I'm ridiculous when I say 'Learn to read a tape measure, you can build a house.' They'll be like, '*Anyone* can read a tape measure.' Well, no."

Not me. In construction, I'm learning, knowledge is competence. But that's only half of it. Your hands know things your brain only suspects. No amount of theory will help you sink a nail in one swing or rip a straight line into a sheet of plywood with a Skilsaw. You can do almost any job if you understand the principles and your eye and your hand know their way around. My trouble is, I don't have either. Not the theory, not the instinct. And the rules—the skills of the trade—it all feels like a different language to me. It's a language I've had plenty of time to learn. A language I should know.

I feel both stupid and guilty for not knowing about something as simple as the markings on a tape measure. Dad gave me my first one when I was two years old. How did it take me thirty years to find out how it works?

There's no time to dwell, though. We have pumping to do.

We've laid out the wide black tubes inside the trench in the floor. One leads to the toilet. The other to the shower.

"Now we need to think about flow," Matt says, returning to his drainage philosophy. "Good flow is essential."

Pipes often get backed up when they've been installed with poor planning, taking weird turns on odd angles. I've never considered where the pipe beneath a toilet or shower drain leads, and how obvious the points that clog things up actually are. It's fascinating to see the skeleton of a house—all the hidden bits you take for granted. Like a human body, you often don't know something is wrong until it's too late.

I look down into the drain where the new toilet would sit, and flash back to an unfortunate incident involving the washroom on our main floor that I'd caused.

I was in the basement playing video games when I saw several drops fall—and then noticed the giant wet spot pooling across the ceiling tiles. A clog, combined with a running toilet, had resulted in an overflow that flooded the downstairs bathroom and then leaked through the hardwood and into the basement. I did what any proper teenager would: I bolted upstairs to find someone else to take care of the problem. That person was Dad, of course. He was in his room, about to fall asleep, when I came bounding in with all the gory details. He quickly stopped the flooding and replaced the ruined ceiling tiles. It took days to dry out the carpet.

I'd been the last person to use the downstairs bathroom before the great flood, but I never told anyone. Its hardwood floor remained rough and darkly stained, the scars of my irresponsible flush management still visible today. It was my great shame, and I planned to take it to my grave.

The memory haunts me as I peer down the toilet hole with Matt. He's pondering ways to ensure the optimal angle for effective release.

"I imagine if you wanted to you could put in two forty-fives here," he says. "That *might* improve the flow."

"It's all right," I say. "I think we're good."

It's been a long day and I'm done talking about flow. We settle for the ninety-degree bend and hope for the best.

That evening I go to a Mexican restaurant downtown with a close friend, Marco. He's been around our family since we were kids, and spent many hours sitting at our kitchen table chatting with me and my father.

He asks me how the renovation is going. "Like, what are you really learning?" he says.

"I think I'm learning how fun this all is," I say. "And how much I wish I'd spent the time doing it beside my dad when he was here."

In a way, I say, it also feels like he is. It's more than just physically using his tools. It feels like he's swinging the hammer too, guiding me. I know it's stupid. It's silly. Overly nostalgic and self-indulgent, and whatever else people who repress their emotions always say.

But that doesn't change the fact of the feeling. I feel him smiling and laughing, and I feel him huffing when I screw something up. I can feel him telling me to keep going.

When the waiter brings out beers and guacamole, I realize that my eyes are red and wet. I look down, but I can't stop now. I can feel the tears on my cheeks as I look back up at Marco. The other people in the little restaurant pretend not to notice.

It's the first time I've cried in a while. The first time since we started to rip the basement apart. I was sad and I was mad then, because I knew what I was really trying to do—and I knew I'd never really accomplish it. It was impossible. I wanted to find him, but my father could only be an image in my mind now—a ghost beside me that no one else could see and that I could never fully feel. A ghost that would fade with time no matter how hard I willed my mind to make him stay. It was an incomplete connection.

I just want to see him again. To have him squeeze my hand again. And learning how to swing a hammer could never fully give me that.

"I don't know what I'm trying to discover here," I say. "I don't know what I'm trying to accomplish."

That I can hammer and screw? That I can cut some wires? Smash up concrete?

It's more than that.

I can see how a house comes together now. I can see its bones and muscle, its veins and its heart. I can see how a home really is alive. How it holds up—and how when you cut into it, the water rises.

How it bleeds and crumbles. How it falls apart.

18

I arrived a year and a half after my sister, on a warm Sunday evening in the middle of July.

They'd barely gotten the hang of one child before a second arrived. Once again, Mom did all the work while Dad tried to stay out of the way. In the first minutes of my life, the nurse passed me to him. He held me against his chest with one arm and held my tiny hand.

Rain in the sun again.

"The perfect family," Mom tells me he said.

It was far from perfect, though.

With a baby and a toddler to take care of, Mom took a leave from her job in the ER. They had to find a way to make life work with Dad's scattered renovation contracts alone. But after a year of struggle—trying to juggle work and kids, trying to make enough money to pay the bills—Dad knew his dream of owning his own company wasn't going to pan out. He had to find something more consistent and manageable or his family would starve.

A friend offered him a lead with Bramalea Limited, a company that, after its founding in 1957 as Brampton Leasing, had become one of the largest real estate developers in Canada. In the early 1970s it sought to create a new planned town—known as a satellite city—that would serve as a kind of suburban utopia. The company bought a large swath of land on the outskirts of Brampton from a local farmer who called his land Bramalea—carving the name out of the two small towns it lay between, Brampton and Malton, and adding the pleasant-sounding Old English word for meadow, "lea," at the end. The company rebranded itself and went to work building the houses, apartment buildings, civic centres, and shopping malls that would become the suburbs of Toronto. Then, through the late 1970s and 1980s, Bramalea Limited continued to expand its reach, developing real estate across the country and throughout the United States. It was growing rapidly, with a vision for the future.

Dad took a job as a construction site manager with them in 1984.

He sold the burgundy van, replacing it with a light-blue Ford F-150 issued by Bramalea Limited, and stored away the custom-made Robson Renovations magnet signs in case he might get to use them again one day. The pay was a little more than what he could make on his own, and the hours were consistent.

With Dad home in the evenings, Mom was able to return to the ER part time, working night shifts. She'd take care of us during the day while Dad was off at a construction site. Then she'd drop us off at our grandparents' place before she drove into Toronto for her shift. At the end of the day, when Dad was done, he'd pick us up and take us home to bed. Mom would get back sometime in the middle of the night.

It doesn't sound like an ideal way to start life as a family, but Mom doesn't seem to have any regrets about it. They were still young and they were moving in the right direction.

By the mid-eighties they'd saved enough to upgrade from their townhouse to an old bungalow near downtown Brampton. Dad built a workshop in the basement and a deck in the backyard. He commissioned his two-year-old son as an assistant, buying him that small silver tape measure engraved in his consistent scratch: *Danny Robson, 1985.* Back in a hazy, distant place in my mind, I can still see him cutting the boards and hammering them into place while I try to help him measure.

Those years on Norval Crescent formed my earliest memories.

I nearly choked to death on an orange slice, and Mom had to give me the Heimlich. Dad held Jai and me as we said goodbye to Mom before she left for a night shift, and we both wriggled free and fell hard to the ground. I learned to bike without training wheels on the street in front of the house, with Dad holding me steady and pushing me from behind. I can remember the rush when he let go and I went soaring down Norval for the first time without him. And the pebble-marked scrape down my leg when I lost control and crashed.

There were the stories during evening baths and as they tucked us into beds Dad had built in his workshop. Tales of the Berenstain Bears. *A Fish Out of Water, Mud Puddle,* and *The Paper Bag Princess.* There were prayers for everyone and anything we knew of in our young lives. *"Now I lay me down to sleep, I pray the Lord my soul to keep. God bless: Mommy, Daddy, Jaime, Danny, Grandma, Grandpa, Auntie B, Uncle Larry..."* There was Raffi at Christmastime and "Old toy trains, little toy tracks"—and the patter of reindeer on the roof. There was the soft strum of Dad playing his guitar as he sang about snow falling on Douglas Mountain while we fell asleep. There was a panicked rush to the doctor after Jaime fed me half a bottle of

Flintstone vitamins. The chill as we learned how to skate under the arched wooden roof at Brampton Memorial Arena, and the smell when Jaime threw up in her helmet.

There was the day when Mom left us in the Toyota Corolla in the driveway while she grabbed something from the house and we managed to push the gear to neutral and rolled backwards across the street, over the curb, and onto the neighbour's lawn.

With no sense of time there was no concept of an ending—just the long stretch of childhood that seems a lifetime in itself.

Mom almost didn't make it into the hospital when my little sister was born in early January 1988. At seven a.m. they'd sat in the parking lot of Etobicoke General, Mom refusing to budge: she knew the overnight nurses were getting off their shift and she didn't want to be that person who strolls in to give birth right when they were about to leave. She finally relented and they went inside a little after seven-thirty. Dad had just made it back from filling out the paperwork when Jenna showed up.

My aunt brought Jaime, who'd just turned six, and me, four and a half, to the hospital to meet our baby sister. She pointed at her in her crib through the glass. Jenna was a tiny ball with chubby cheeks, wrapped in pink. I was unimpressed.

"I'd rather have a puppy," I said.

And then we were five.

We moved from the bungalow to our house on Bates Court shortly after Jenna was born.

Our parents had hunted for months for the right place to raise three kids, but nothing fit until they saw the house on a cul-de-sac on the western edge of Brampton. Twenty-Six Bates was a two-storey brick four-bedroom with a slightly pink hue. It had a brown roof, a two-car garage, a bay window into the living room between two evergreen trees. It had space and room to grow—a garage for tools, an unfinished basement to renovate. It had a decent-sized backyard where Dad could build a deck big enough to host barbecues by a pool, if they could save enough to afford it. Our parents could see our life unfolding there. At $200,000 it was beyond their budget—more than double the price of their bungalow—but it was perfect. They'd managed this far; they could get through the rest.

I remember the day we moved in. I stood on the lawn and watched the movers unload their massive truck. Our names were taped to the bedroom doors our parents had chosen for us—I felt proud to have a space to call my own for the first time. Still, the house was bare and bland. The carpets were beige, the kitchen tiles had a faint yellow pattern, the backyard was just a long stretch of grass with some grey patio stones. And the basement was dark and empty—like a cold, concrete dungeon. I was afraid to be down there alone.

The house was a stranger to us then.

We didn't know which part of the floor creaked when you tried to sneak out of your room. We didn't know which vents allowed birds to nest. Or the best way to get on the roof whenever a tennis ball got stuck in the eavestrough. We didn't know that the dining room off the kitchen was the best place to call a crush without anyone hearing. That the kids' shower had the best water pressure. Or that the best spot to sit on Christmas Eve was just to the right of the crackling fire, and the best place to find hidden gifts was at the top of Mom and Dad's closet. We didn't know that the breeze coming in from the farmer's field just beyond the rows of houses to the west would land perfectly in our backyard on warm summer nights. Or that the sewer grates on the court resembled the bases on a diamond, that a throw against the top of the bay window would result in the perfect shallow fly ball for a diving catch, or that the streetlight at the end of the driveway offered just enough glow to score one more Stanley Cup winner before bed.

The house formed around us. It became us. And the creaks in the floor, the heat in the fire, the concrete chill of the unfinished basement, the backyard breeze on a summer night—they belonged to us. They were ours, just like Michael Jackson's *Thriller* on the CD player at Halloween and Douglas Mountain and Dad's soft voice on dark winter nights. We carved our stories into the walls. A stranger couldn't read them, but we could. We knew they were there. In the pen marks climbing farther up each year on the edge of my closet, in the garage where Dad wrote his name near the door in large white letters, in the pocked eavestrough, in the cracked and water-stained hardwood of the downstairs bathroom. In the young trees that we planted in the backyard and that grew with us, rising beyond the roof.

But back then, on the day we arrived, I didn't know any of this. I sat on the bed in a room marked *Danny* and wondered if we'd like it here.

At the time, Dad had excelled as a site manager at Bramalea Limited and was quickly promoted. The company went on a spending spree in the late 1980s, picking up swaths of vacant land it planned to develop—spending more than $1.5 billion to purchase property just as the market started to peak. It was a frantic, booming time. Dad would be out of the house before six some mornings, managing the construction sites of several residential apartment buildings and subdivisions at once.

Mom took care of our hectic mornings a couple of hours later, Jaime and I darting through the neighbour's backyard to make it to the end of the court as the bus arrived. We'd still be pulling the burgundy sweaters of our school uniform over our heads as we ran. Jenna, meanwhile, would always be there on time, prompt and waiting. Sometimes we'd miss it altogether, Jaime and I, and Mom would rush us into the back of her ancient blue Toyota Corolla hoping we'd luck out at the train crossing on Chinguacousy Road.

"Go! Go!" Mom would yell—I swear, in a housecoat with rollers in her hair—as the two of us charged out of the tiny four-door sedan like an elite military team on a life-or-death mission. Our bus driver, a charming faux-grump named Mr. Prankard, would see us in the side mirror darting up the side of the road, past whatever cars lined up ahead of us, and pull open the bus door for us to swing in just as the tail of the train passed and the bells and lights stopped ringing and flashing as the safety arm rose. (We were just up the tracks from where Dad, Bill Plunkett, and the gang blew up signals and dodged trains.) Mr. Prankard would smirk and say something sarcastic about the Robsons always being late. And Jenna would grin victoriously, a couple teeth missing, from one of the seats near the front where the young kids sat. It seemed to happen almost daily.

By now Mom had a part-time job with Saint Elizabeth Visiting Nurses, a home health care company. It had meant giving up the adrenalin rush that came with treating victims of gunshots and motorcycle accidents for cranky patients who needed to pee out of a tube. Whatever had been lost in excitement, though, was made up for in the mornings and evenings she could now spend at home.

Mom would travel around with a bag of needles and catheters in the trunk of her car, coffee splashing out of her cup as she navigated the streets of Toronto's western suburbs using a well-worn road atlas. It was always a long day, filled with complaints from overstressed families dealing with seriously ill loved ones. In some cases these patients had come home to die. It was Mom's job to make sure they had the dignity of peeing through a properly inserted tube or that they remained hydrated with an insulin drip.

Every night after school we'd hear the garage open and the squeak of the laundry room door—and then Dad's voice calling, "Family, I'm home . . ." He'd smell like sawdust and grass after it rains.

And then it was dinner, a story, a prayer, then bed. I'd dream through the night until that distant but familiar beep. Until the creak of my father's feet on the floor and the rush of falling water. Until he'd peek through our doors, just to be certain.

"What have we done?" he asked her that January night under those thick, soft snowflakes.

"I don't know what we're doing."

But each new day they'd do it all again.

19

Matt examines the thin copper waterlines that run across the ceiling rafters above the bathroom. Then he holds up one of the fittings we've soldered together and lines it up with the pipes. We'll cut through the pipes and slide the new fittings into the gap, tapping in off the mainline to bring water to the bathroom. He points at another thin pipe that runs directly beside the hot and cold waterlines.

"We just have to be careful of this gas line here," he says.

I stand up on the edge of my toes to get a look. "That we don't hit it?"

"Yeah," Matt says. "So we don't blow the house up."

There's a long pause.

"How would we hit it?"

"There'd have to be a gas leak—and then we'd put the torch on it," he says. "And *boom*." Matt mimics an explosion with his hands, and lets the thought sit there for a moment. "We'll have to turn off the water and drain all the lines," he tells me. "And then we're off to the races."

The main shut-off for the water is on the other side of the new bathroom, beside the water heater. There's a meter near the wall, connected to the heater. I've never noticed it before.

"On the city side of the water meter, you've got your shut-off," Matt says. It's another small copper pipe that comes up out of the basement floor, running into the meter gauge gizmo. There's a little knob to twist, on and off.

Before this moment I had no idea where it was. If we'd had a leak or a flood, I wouldn't know how to make the water stop. I don't mention that fact. It's embarrassing. So I pretend that I knew all along.

Matt points to a wire that runs across the ceiling to the electrical panel and then down, entering the floor next to the main waterline. It's a ground for the house, he says. It ensures that any excess current will want to move to that point and find ground, for safety.

We shut off the water and then check the valve on the hot water tank, which is also pressurized. We have to open up the taps to let the water drain out. If the taps are closed there's a vacuum in the system, like a giant hypodermic needle. When you open the taps the air flows in and gravity pulls the water down. Something else I didn't know.

We use the Sawzall to cut open the hot-water line in the rafters above the bathroom.

I push over a bucket to let the warm water drip after the cut.

If we hadn't opened the taps there'd still be water left over in the pipe—and it would start to trickle down and cool the pipe so much that the solder wouldn't melt.

As the warm water bleeds out, we move over and take the saw to the cold-water pipe.

"You have to start the cut on the opposite side of where you're standing, and pull towards you," Matt says. "If you start on the side you're standing on you'll get a bunch of water right in the face."

"You cut towards yourself?" I say. Doesn't seem safe. Dad always said to cut away.

"Yeah," Matt says. "But it's better than getting splashed in the face."

We connect the drain piping to the tub and the T-junction that breaks off towards the sink. We have to fiddle with it to make it happen, taking about half an inch off to make it fit before soldering it in place.

Later, Matt gives us a crimping tutorial. He slides a small ring—the crimp—over the end of the pipe so that it covers the two lines engraved on the skinny end of the pipe junction. Then he uses a tool called the "crimper" that looks like a giant pair of pliers, but with differently sized crescents where the ends meet. They close around the Pex tube and crimp. He pulls the handles tight, and with some difficulty, before it closes fully with a snapping sound.

He holds up the white tube now attached to the copper fixture. "It's a lot easier than soldering it," Matt says. "And you've got your water tank line."

In the bathroom, we stretch a coil of Pex tubing from the new junction over to the hole where the toilet will sit. Matt holds the line where it will run down the wall that isn't yet there.

"You have to be careful with Pex because you only have so much room to be able to make that crimp. If you trap yourself—if you put it through and then decide you want to crimp something inside the joist base—it gets tricky," he says. "There are crimping tools that go in a joist base, but I don't have that. So we'll just be smart."

He calls for the biggest auger bit we have—about the width of my index and middle fingers—and connects it to my father's drill to bore a hole through the plate around the toilet. A long piece of Pex is pushed through the hole, sticking out the top. We add an elbow and snap it onto another piece, which allows the waterline to run horizontally through the joists and then down the wall.

Jonathan is the tallest among us, so we have him do the work up high. The rest of us stand around the toilet hole and watch him.

"He's the crimping man," Matt says.

Jonathan tightens the crimper around the new connection point. "The Bloods and the Crimps," he says in a tough guy voice.

"The Bloods and the Crimps," Matt repeats.

Tim shakes his head, disappointed in us. "I knew someone was going to make that joke," he says.

Jonathan clips the crimper, pinching the connection in place with impressive speed.

"*Nice* crimp," I say.

"Good crimp, *good* crimp," he agrees. "Very tight crimp."

"Water tight," I say.

"*Water* tight," Jonathan offers.

"Water *tight*," says Matt.

We are men at work and this is our worksite banter. It's silly in a truly unfunny way, but deep in the basement it is proper comedy. The days spent working side by side have forged a connection that is unique to us. We make jokes about Larry Haun, the king of contractors. We find terrible puns hilarious. We repeat each other's words with exaggerated inflections, just because—like the guys in that old "Whassup" Budweiser commercial. It's odd, juvenile behaviour. But it's the language we speak after spending hours, exhausted and dirty, cutting through sewage pipes and drilling into the damp dirt beneath us. We are building something, together—and the shared work creates a unique kind of union.

Water tight.

Water *tight*.

We go through the process a few more times, setting up waterlines to reach the vanity and shower. Both hot and cold lines are connected where the tub will sit, the cold-water line with a connection that extends over to the link we just set up with the toilet. Another connection brings the waterlines down to where the sink will sit on the other wall. A web of Pex tubing brings it all together through the joists and studs. We just need to tie into the hot and cold mainlines we cut through earlier, using the two T connections we've soldered together.

Matt takes the blowtorch to the cold-water mainline pipe to make sure there's no moisture inside.

He's dangerously close to the gas line, just above it.

I take a few steps back and bump into Tim.

"It won't matter," Tim says. "If he hits that, the whole place goes up. If you're on the second floor you're still going to feel it."

I wait on the stairs around the corner until Matt switches off the blowtorch.

Soon we're connecting the waterlines to the tub that Tim and I have carried in from the garage and set in place. We set up a laser level to shoot a line up the middle of the tub, lining up where the faucet and handles will go.

When everything is tied in and connected, we turn the water back on to test it out. Water sprays out of one side of one of the connections in the joists above the tub. We forgot to crimp it. Jonathan reaches up—and pulls the tubing apart. Now water is gushing everywhere.

"Leave it in!" Matt shouts.

Jonathan manages to reconnect it. I hand him the crimper and he snaps the connection in place. Crisis averted, but we're soaked.

"That always happens," Matt sighs. "You miss one crimp."

Crimping ain't easy, but even we can't bring ourselves to say it.

The waterlines are connected. The plumbing and electrical work is almost complete.

"And that's it," Matt says. "Throw up some drywall and Bob's your uncle."

By six that evening we're still hard at work finishing up small bits that need to get done. We build a wooden frame around the electrical panel, which is still a mess of wires and dormant wifi routers. We fill in the space between the studs with pink insulation, so the new bedroom walls—held together by half-sunken nails sticking out at crooked angles—look as if they're packed with cotton candy. We cover the insulation with plastic sheeting and staple it into place. I discover that the sheeting is called "poly."

Tim pours bags of gravel over the plumbing we've connected in the holes we blasted out of the floor while Jonathan smoothes it over with a shovel, so we can cover it with concrete.

I walk out to the side of the house where Dad left his old green wheelbarrow and the long ladder we used to hang Christmas lights and retrieve tennis balls from the eavestrough. The wheelbarrow wobbles on its single wheel as I try to steer it over the grass, through the gate, and around to the front door. Once I've manoeuvred it downstairs, banging it into a couple of walls along the way, we fill it with concrete mix and water. Matt mulches it with a shovel until it becomes a thick grey mud. Finally we heave globs of the wet concrete over the gravel and use a trowel to smooth it out.

The day doesn't end until half past eight with final touches to the concrete, which we leave to dry overnight.

On my father's desk there is a cream-coloured pamphlet bearing a blueprint sketch overlaid by a green triangle, the name *Paramount Design, Build & Management* printed beneath it. I've stared at it for months. We must have workshopped dozens of names before the family landed on that one.

I remember we had swimming lessons scheduled the day he lost his job at Bramalea Limited. Mom and Dad sat us down at the kitchen table to tell us. It felt oddly formal. Dad explained that the company had gone bankrupt, and that it meant he no longer worked for them. He didn't sound concerned when he said it, but he must have been. After all, only serious news, like our grandfather's death, required a family meeting at the kitchen table.

"Everything is going to be okay," he said, anyway.

So we did the only thing we could: we believed him.

With time you learn that when a parent goes out of their way to tell you everything is going to be okay, there's a good chance it won't. But as a kid you nod your head and maybe give them a hug. Then you pack your bathing suit and towel and they drive you to the YMCA to watch while you learn how to tread water.

Only once did I ever see fear in my father's eyes. He was lying on a sheet of ice on a cold winter night, gasping for air. Christmas lights sparkled in the trees and music was playing as people drifted around the oval rink at Gage Park across from Brampton's City Hall. Dad had been skating backwards with me when he hit a divot in the ice and landed hard on his back. I remember falling to my knees on the ice beside him as he tried to breathe. I didn't know what to do. No one stopped to help us. They just glided by, moving with the music. I asked if he was okay, but he couldn't speak. His wide eyes locked on mine. I'll never forget them. I'd never seen them look that way before. I thought he was dying—and worse, I knew he did too.

"Dad?"

He grabbed my hand.

"Dad?"

He squeezed. It felt like minutes. I cried. Finally he gasped as though he'd found the surface of the sea. Then he lay on the ice, breathing deep and slow, our eyes still locked and his hand in mine.

"I'm okay," he said at last. "It's okay, buddy."

We slowly got up together—and then pushed off on another lap as if nothing had happened. Fathers aren't supposed to show fear, and he took his back as quickly as the breath had left his lungs. I'm not sure why that's the rule, but I know that a child never forgets the look of terror when they see it on a parent's face. They're the barometer of security, and it's impossible to forget the moment that our true vulnerability is exposed.

It was a flash, but it lingered in my mind. Dad never spoke about it, and I never brought it up. He never let me see his fear again. I still don't know if that was a strength or a weakness.

In the months following the collapse of Bramalea Limited, Dad set out to start his own company for a second time. What did it take to jump into that uncertainty without showing fear? He must have been stressed or anxious. He must have thought about what could happen if it all fell apart.

But if he did, we never saw it.

We still went to the private Christian school on the edge of Caledon, just beneath the flying club, which we'd attended our entire lives. It was run by Kennedy Road Tabernacle, the Pentecostal church my parents were married in and where we went every Sunday. Neither of them had really practised faith—aside from attending church as kids—before going to the occasional service and deciding the purple-carpeted rotunda was where they wanted to get married. Neither had been particularly religious before, but the church offered community, structure, and purpose. It became central to our social lives—and a framework through which I understood the world.

Kennedy Road Tabernacle Christian School was built in the late 1970s as part of an effort to promote conservative Christian education. Jai and I went there as soon as we reached kindergarten. We wore burgundy and grey uniforms and recited the Lord's Prayer, read out over the intercom every morning, before singing the national anthem. It was a small school, with only a few hundred students. The walls were lined with fuzzy grey carpet, and if you brushed against it you'd often get pricked by pins left over from work that had been displayed. For the first several years the gymnasium floor was covered in a green carpet that caused terrible rug burn anytime you fell playing hockey with a Wiffle ball or during "Indian tag," a capture-the-flag game that I now understand was quite racist.

Dad helped build the playground and the small wooden bridge that crossed a ditch just beyond the paved blacktop out back. In warm months, through elementary school, the boys in each grade played a blend of soccer, football, and rugby that had essentially one rule: a point was scored by getting whatever kind of ball we had between the baseball caps set up to make a goal line. The pitting of grade against grade created a tribal competitiveness that spilled across a battlefield left strewn with bloodied noses, gory scratches, bruised bodies, and ripped uniforms. These brutal conflicts, waged during our half-hour recesses, were banned several times—only to re-emerge as more civilized games of soccer or touch football inevitably regressed to their natural schoolyard state.

In the age of barbarians, the wars lasted seasons. Winters brought a different kind of combat. With the wind ripping across the open acres, biting into any inch of exposed flesh, we'd build forts, digging into the drifts that rose where the schoolyard pushed up against the farmer's field beyond us. Snowballs were amassed, stored for sieges or in defence against other classes that came looking to smash our strongholds. Behind the middle-school portables, a range of plowed snow mounds would pit every boy for himself in King of the Castle epics. Alliances broke as the peak neared. A best friend could send you crashing down the snow mountain onto the icy pavement.

Recess was survival. The best kind of education.

It was from that playground that I watched the framework of the school's new wing form into the building that would house my adolescence. Managing its construction was my father's first gig for his own new company.

In his office at home are hundreds of photos from that year when he built the school. The blueprints, corners withered and brown, are still in the closet. Boxes of invoices, project plans, and contracts tell the story of his decade-long journey developing that little construction company—until it was bought by an expanding engineering firm that eventually grew into a global company called EXP. It was there that Dad turned the leap of faith in himself into ownership shares and a regional management role running construction projects. He was one of the only senior employees without an engineering degree—let alone not having a degree at all.

That EXP office is around the corner from the warehouse where I pick up the new flooring that my mom and sisters have decided on for the basement. I don't drive by to see the tree his colleagues planted there to remember him. I'm worried that its frail roots didn't survive the winter, that the tree is already dead. I'd rather imagine it thriving than to know for sure.

I fill the bed of Dad's truck with stacks of grey laminate and close the gate. It's starting to rain, so I have to rush home.

Given the extra hours we spent on the plumbing yesterday, we agreed on a late start this morning. We've earned the rest, though I don't imagine that real handymen go in for this kind of lethargy.

Today we put up walls.

I'm tasked with cutting out the space for the electrical box as we put up sheets of drywall. We want to have a bit of a gap between the pieces, Matt says. We measure out the distance to the electrical box, already attached to the frame, from the floor. There'll be a small gap between the floor and the drywall when it's put up, meaning I need to subtract a quarter-inch when measuring from the bottom of the sheet.

The electrical box sits fourteen and a half inches from the edge of the drywall, so I have to measure that across the sheet and mark the centre of the box. Then, from the floor up, I measure fifteen inches— and the resulting point of intersection is where the electrical box will sit. The depth of the box is three inches. So I draw the box's outline onto the drywall, adding a quarter of an inch around it as a margin for error. While measuring this out, I notice a marking on the back of the drywall sheet that reads "Aligns with sixteen-inch stud spacing"—which reminds me of the sixteen inches marked in red on my measuring tape. Carpentry's secrets revealed.

As I consider the prospect of being able to build my own house one day, I fiddle with what looks like a serrated hunting knife with a wooden handle. I found it in Dad's tool bag.

"It's a drywall knife," Matt informs me.

First things first. I need to use it to carve out the holes for the electrical outlets.

"Just take your time," Matt says.

He knows I'm likely to botch this. I grip the knife with Dad's work gloves and saw into the drywall. It's not pretty. Not being able to draw a straight line means I'm also unlikely to saw one. The expected rectangle comes out more like a narrow octagon with uneven sides. It's reminiscent of the felt snowman I'd made in grade four—one that was unintentionally derivative of Picasso, and that Jai hangs on our family Christmas tree every year next to her own perfectly round and proportional snowman.

"That'll do," Matt says, surveying my art.

Matt has hammered the pot light into place along the joists above us, taking special pride in the strategic layout he's come up with in the bathroom. He fastens the last fixture in place, tilting its head to demonstrate how it can be adjusted in any direction.

"So you can highlight the throne," he says, aiming it towards the toilet.

Another bit for our reno-humour comedy tour.

We operate by the glow of the one lit bulb in Dad's work light and a sunbeam that streaks down from the window. The hole we carved into the ground to lay the piping is now sealed by a scar of dark concrete.

All conveniences are considered before we entomb our frame with drywall. I suggest putting a nailer in place to add extra support for hanging a television in the bedroom—and adding an extra electrical outlet above it so that its wires can be hidden. I'm quite proud of the suggestion.

The pot lights are linked up and finished. We flick the switches and they all work. We're making progress now. Jonathan and Tim affix the drywall sheets to the frame at one end of the bedroom as Matt and I start at the other, the four of us listening to an old Bob Dylan playlist as we go. We work quietly, efficiently—each in our own minds, but moving in symmetry.

I cut the drywall to encase a bulkhead in the bedroom. It's even worse than my butchered electrical box opening. The edge of the long narrow strip extending down from the ceiling is a wavy, sloping line. It's dreadful. Dad would never settle for this. I remember him once commenting on my lack of fine motor skills. Back when I was a teenager, I'd tried to help him with something—I can't recall what—and he'd noted that although I had no problem stopping a puck or shooting a basket, I couldn't seem to master the intricate movements required to use a saw or hammer. I don't think he meant to hurt me; it was a compliment: I was good at things he couldn't do at the cost of the things he could. But it felt more like an indictment. I just don't have the talent that a handyman requires.

I groan.

"Shit."

What a mess.

I finish off the job with an even worse effort on the sheet that runs along the bottom of the bulkhead. The drywall looks as if it's been ripped out instead of cut. Straggly pieces dangle from the uneven corner, which jags in and out along a line of overcompensation.

Within a couple of hours, the bedroom walls are done. The wall between it and the bathroom is complete and we've put in new door frames side by side, leading into each.

Eight days after we cleared it out, the old basement is starting to look like something new.

Now we have to measure out markings for the bedroom pot lights before we can put the pieces up for the ceiling. We've sketched out a plan indicating the centre of each spotlight based on the distance from the edge by width and length. Each square is forty-eight inches wide by ninety-six inches long. And we have to mark out the corner where the ceiling drops into my Frankenstein bulkhead.

We also need to put up the bathroom drywall, which is different from the stuff we've used in the bedroom. As we place the heavy green sheets around the shower, Matt gives me a lesson on the different kinds we need to use. We have normal drywall, bathroom drywall, and then shower drywall, he says. The bathroom drywall is moisture resistant. The shower drywall is for heavy water use—it's basically waterproof.

While Matt and I put up the drywall in the shower, Tim and Jonathan are charged with measuring the drywall for the bathroom ceiling, accounting for the bulkhead and the location of the pot lights. Jonathan scribbles the measurements on a scrap piece of drywall that looks like a stone tablet.

We cut and then raise the bathroom ceiling panels into place. Next, using the drywall knife, we cut around the circles they've drawn for the pot lights.

But the edge of the ceiling doesn't align with the wall. Something is out of square. It's a mistake we've just noticed. It went undetected several steps back.

We'll have to pull it down and fix the problem.

"Then we'll throw it back up," Matt says as if it's no big deal.

Jonathan smirks and raises an eyebrow.

But fortunately, the ceiling tightens down when we keep screwing, closing the gap enough that we can cover the imperfection with some compound.

"We'll get some nice twenty-minute setting stuff and fill it all in," Matt says. "And that's it."

It's the kind of quick-fix solution I know my father would have avoided by making sure it was done right the first time. I picture him shaking his head, pulling down the crooked frame, and starting again—plumb and level.

Even with the gaps filled in, I'll always see the imperfection in these walls.

20

I stand in the faded goal crease and look around. I can see right across the basement from this spot. The guys are busy. Tim and Jonathan use a Wonder Bar to pop off the remaining old baseboards, one by one, before we lay down the flooring in the living area of the basement.

The old door is still a workbench. Stacks of drywall lie in one corner. Two grey garbage bins are full of wood and drywall scraps. Wide stripes in three shades of grey have been painted across the wall, ready for Mom's final decision.

It reminds me of clouds before a storm.

The silver tinfoil-like underpadding is rolled up next to the stacks of laminate panel that will soon cover the crease once more. The moisture barrier looks like something from a 1960s spaceship. It doesn't soak anything up—it's just a layer that keeps it from moving through to the flooring we're going to put down. It also acts as a barrier so that the pieces won't lie unevenly if there's an imperfection in the floor.

We put a small piece of laminate against the wall to leave a gap for the floor to shift—and then lay out the pieces of flooring from there, row by row, like a giant puzzle. Each thin, rectangular piece has a ridge that clips into the side of the one next to it. It creates an audible click. The first couple of rows try to push upward and don't settle flat.

Each row of laminate will have one piece that's cut shorter when it meets the wall. We've cut a smaller section of flooring to fill the gap. A mitre saw would make an enormous mess, so we use a special punch that creates a clean cut and no dust. All we have to do is set the piece at the right length to cut and then pull the lever forward.

Tim and Jonathan measure the angle of an alcove that I used to call my trophy shrine—cutting the ends of the laminate on an angle so that they'll fit into the curved corners.

I'm not sure how they've figured out what the proper angle is for each piece.

"We just measured the left side to the wall and then the right side to the wall, and drew a diagonal," Jonathan says. "And then cut it."

I have no idea what he means. "Ah, cool," I say. "It's *perfect.*"

And it is.

Later that afternoon, Matt holds a trowel in one hand and a grout knife in the other. He uses his knife to pick up a glob of mortar that's been mixed in an orange Home Depot bucket. Next to the bucket sits a stack of large tiles with a faint grey marble pattern. There's already a thick layer of mortar spread across the bathroom floor, above the heating panels.

"What you do is called 'back buttering' them," he says.

"Back butter?" I repeat.

"So yeah, so butter the tiles. You just put a thin layer—and then it adheres a lot better. You just stick them down."

He spreads a thin layer of mortar across the back of one of the tiles. Then he kneels down and slowly lines up the tile's edges, laying it down in the corner, snug against the tub.

"They are going to look *all right*," he says.

A few tiles are laid out already, to show the spacing. The marble design on two of them lines up and I get excited about it. "I like that. Let's keep those two together."

This is my contribution.

"Yeah," Matt says.

I'm certain he's done with me.

"Let's do it."

I have significantly hampered this process. Matt started with a schedule, which we're now days behind. I've slowed down every step, asking him to explain it again and again. Much of the work I've done has had to be closely monitored or fully redone. I'm a menace to efficiency.

The accent wall above the vanity is half finished with the black subway tiles we've chosen. Plastic spacers are clipped between each one, holding them in place while they dry. The tiles surrounding the vanity might get splashed a little, but they carry no weight. They're decorative.

But we have to be much more careful with floor tiles than the tiles on the wall, I'm told. We need to make sure we get the floor tiles right the first time.

Matt butters another one.

"Even if you didn't do this you'd probably be fine," he says. "But why take the chance? If one tile cracks because maybe the floor is uneven and you step in that one place, you're done. I've seen homes where the tiles are cracked. That's terrible, right?"

It does seem terrible.

He puts down his scraper and flips the tile over, placing it gently next to the other two, easing it into place and running his hands over it to make sure it's flush.

"You want to try to get your corners to line up," he says. "See, like this is off a little bit"—he points to the corner where it meets the last tile.

Now he reaches for a flat-sided tool and slips it under the tile, wedging it upward. Holding it up, he dabs on some extra mortar from a glob beside him and then smoothes it. Then he puts the tile back in place, again eyeballing it to see that it's as even as he can make it.

"Have to make sure it's nice and flush," Matt says, running his hands gently across the tile again. Then he takes his pencil and runs it through the gap between the two squares, cleaning out the excess grout.

Jonathan walks in as we prepare another slab.

"I can't believe this room," I say, looking around at the white tile rising up around the tub and the fully enclosed walls. "It's like a *room* now."

"Yeah," Jonathan says. He sounds a touch sarcastic.

"Weird, eh," Matt says. He's on his knees, clearing more mortar out of the grooves with his pencil.

It *is* weird. My entire life, this space has been unfinished. Now it has shape and purpose. We've created something, step by step, covering up the cold concrete that lies beneath it all. The tiles shine in the light. The room smells brand new, just like the ones in the construction sites Dad used to take me to.

This is a beginning, not an end.

Jonathan and I are quiet, watching Matt place another tile. He looks over at us.

"You guys want to start cleaning up?"

Part V
Measure Twice

21

There are many people I want to speak to about my father, people who might help me build on his memory and keep him alive in my mind. But there was one person I needed to speak to more than any other. I didn't have a brother, but my father had another son.

Josh Spilchen and his mother, Christina, entered our lives shortly after Jai and I moved away to university and Jenna was finishing high school. Christina had worked reception at the office for visiting nurses that my mother managed. She'd been going through a tough time. My parents became very close to her and Josh, her eight-year-old son, and eventually the two of them moved in. They lived at our house while Josh was in elementary and middle school.

He was a skinny twerp of a kid, with short blond hair and big blue eyes. He was shy at first, but deep down he was mischievous. The day I first met him we played basketball on the old Fisher-Price net in the basement. I was twenty then. He practised his dunks off the steps while I tried to teach him how to shoot, keeping his elbow in and putting some spin on the ball.

I didn't grow close to Josh in the way I could have. I was consumed by university life, on my own for the first time. He was always there when I came home, and I loved that. But I never allowed him to become like a brother to me. And I didn't really see him as part of the family.

A few months before his death, Dad called and asked if I'd go with him to take Josh out to dinner for his birthday. He was in his early twenties now and working in construction, trying to find his path.

Dad picked me up on the way. On the ride to the east end pizza place, he told me he hoped to start seeing Josh more often. It had been hard to connect with him since he and Christina had moved back to Toronto when Josh was in high school. They'd visited often for a while, but with time they became less frequent.

I suggested that we go to a Toronto Raptors game sometime. We never did.

Josh came to the hospital when he learned what had happened. We were sitting next to Dad, watching him die, when I saw Josh standing outside in the hallway. He seemed unsure whether he should be there. I went into the hallway and told him he could come in. Dad would have wanted him there.

Josh wept as deeply as I had.

A while after Dad's death, I took Josh out for lunch. It had been too long and it felt like a failing, because he'd been so important to my parents.

My father was different with Josh than he was with me. I'd talk with Dad on the phone nearly every day while I was away—walking home from class, on the way to hockey practice—one of us calling the other whenever we had some time. I remember him telling me about how good Josh was with tools. He thought he might have a future in construction. I didn't think much of it at the time, to be honest. I thought it was nice that Dad had a little kid around to teach things I'd never shown an interest in.

When I pull up to meet Josh, he looks a decade older than the skinny blond kid I pictured in my mind, with wisps of facial hair and thick shoulders. I hadn't noticed that the night Dad died. In memory, he was still a kid. We settle on lunch at an East Side Mario's in Scarborough—a nostalgic nod to a suburban favourite.

I order a beer, which I feel guilty about—and he orders a Jack and Coke, which seems wrong. But he's a full adult now and has already endured more than I ever will. After my father died, Josh's older cousin and closest friend, Paul, was murdered by a stranger who started a fight outside an east end bar and stabbed him. Josh was supposed to be at the bar with Paul that night, but had decided to stay home.

He's still spinning from both deaths, he tells me.

"Your dad was like a father figure to me. That's what I always explain to people who don't really understand the situation," Josh says. "He did everything for me. He always picked me up from school. Whenever anything was wrong, he always knew. When I got hurt at school he was the first one to come and get me."

In grade five, Josh was climbing on a friend's back at recess when he fell backwards and cracked his head. He bled everywhere, but the cut was actually pretty small. Dad left work to come get him at school. While Josh cried, Dad took a photo of the back of his head to show him that the cut was really nothing.

"He was tough like that sometimes," Josh notes. "Tough love."

When you knew you were doing something wrong, Josh adds, he had this look like he knew it too. I know it well.

"Rick knew exactly what he had to say," Josh says. "Not too much. He'd say what he had to say to get the point across."

In the evenings, Dad and Josh would always sit at the kitchen table and do his schoolwork together. Dad was the person who made him erase his work and start again if it was wrong, or even if it was just too messy. He'd buy Josh giant erasers and make sure he used them.

I didn't realize what it had meant to Josh to have someone to do his homework with, to teach him to use tools, to pick him up from school when he'd smacked his head.

"We were like a family, eating dinner and breakfast," Josh says. "Then we'd go out, go to church."

The unlimited garlic bread arrives.

I don't have a single memory of my father checking my home-work, let alone sitting down to work on it with me.

Josh smiles, thinking of those frustrating hours spent beside my father over math problems. "He always used to say, 'You've got to get this perfect.' I wish I had that now."

Christina and Josh moved back to Toronto when he reached grade nine. After that he'd return to Brampton every other weekend. His father, Trevor, and his stepmom lived there. And he'd often stay over at my parents' house. But as he got older, he says, he made his own decisions and didn't need to visit them as much. He stayed in Toronto, went to parties, hung out with his friends.

He pauses as his eyes well up.

"I miss your dad," he says.

I bite the edge of my lip. "He was really proud of you," I say. "He always told me how good you were with tools. And I wasn't, right?"

He smiles.

"Did he teach you?" I ask. "Did he show you how to do stuff with tools? Would you ever do projects with him?"

"Tons, yeah," Josh says. "He would also give me Lego and small stuff like that, and would kind of see how well I would do with it— not using instructions, just using my own imagination—and how it would go. I think he just kind of picked up on that."

"He'd do it with you?"

"Yeah, he'd do it with me. Yeah, lots. But he was also just proud when I'd finish, and I'd show him . . . It was just small little things, but—I don't know. I didn't really know what I wanted to do back then. And now I do a lot more. It's a lot more clear."

He pauses again.

"And I don't know," he says. "I wish I had him here."

My eyes are blurry.

"I wish I had him too."

The waiter drops off a second loaf.

"I talked to him almost every day," I say. "You could call and just say, 'Hey, I'm not doing great right now.' He'd talk you through something calmly and smartly. Like, wise."

"Yeah," Josh says. "He wanted to listen."

"When was the last time you saw him?" I ask.

"I don't know, to be honest with you. One of the last times was with you. We went to that pizza place. That was a nice memory . . ."

We sat downstairs at Margherita Pizza, because it was quieter than sitting upstairs. Neither of us remember exactly what we talked about.

"I don't know," Josh says. "I wish I did."

But I do remember the way Dad smiled at him. It was the way he smiled at me and my sisters. It was the way he smiled at Jerry, our long-time family friend, on his wedding day.

We eat some bottomless salad. Josh's memories start spinning.

"I remember when my bike got stolen. I told your dad. In like two minutes he was dressed, ready to go. We hopped in his truck and drove out towards the Hasty Market, up the street. We found my bike right away. With a group of like fifteen teenagers."

"Seriously?" I say. "What happened?"

"We drove straight into them. I literally thought he was going to run them over."

"No."

"I swear on my life. He slammed on the brakes, skidded the truck towards them, and hopped out of the vehicle. I stayed inside. Then he walked up to them—in the middle of fifteen kids, like teenagers, like young adults—and asked them where they got the bike. The kid was so scared, I could tell by how he was presenting himself. He was shaking, looking all nervous. He was like, 'Oh we just found it in the parking lot.' Your dad was like, 'Yeah, okay, sure, whatever.' He said, 'Give me the bike.' The kid gave him the bike. Your dad rolled it over to the back of his truck, and with one arm picks the entire bike up, puts it into the back, stares at them like this"—Josh furrows his brows, mimicking Dad; it's a touchingly accurate impression—"and then jumps into the vehicle. And then we drove back. He didn't say anything to me and I didn't say anything to him on the ride home, which was just down the road. But I was like, 'Yes!' That was the most amazing memory ever. We never talked about it again. I don't even think I said thanks, I was so nervous."

I shake my head. I'd witnessed Dad's angry side before. He was usually patient and mild-mannered, but when he was mad you did not mess with him. He once stormed out of the house to yell at a friend of ours who was doing doughnuts in the cul-de-sac in his Firebird. All of us went silent and white. Another set-to happened at one of my hockey games. When I was the goalie on the bench, Dad would volunteer to run the score clock. One night he was mad at the referee about allowing the other team to play rough, which had ended in a fight. So later in the game, when the ref came over, Dad told him to fill out the scoresheet himself. "You do it," he said. "You caused this mess." He was booted out of the scoring box and another parent had to take his place. To twelve-year-old me, it was a real scandal.

You never wanted to see Dad's angry side, the flaring nostrils. Josh laughs, picturing it. "He gave those guys the look he would always give me," he says.

Josh's parents had split up when he was young. They were both kids themselves when they had him. Christina was only nineteen at the time; she was just twenty-seven when they moved into my parents' house. She adored her son. His father, Trevor, did too. But they were still trying to sort life out themselves.

"My dad was going through some of the roughest times when my mom met your parents. And your dad never judged my dad, the things he did and the issues he had," Josh says. "Your dad helped my dad get a job. Your dad gave my dad his personal tools. And my dad still has them to this day."

"Seriously?" I say. "He gave him his tools and said . . ."

"Pull yourself together," Josh says. "It was nice."

His father is doing well now. His life is on a steady track and he's a constant in Josh's life.

"He has a full-time job. He works hard. He's been clean for twelve years. No drugs or cigarettes," Josh tells me. "He drinks a little bit every now and then—has a beer every once in a while—but he's fortysomething now and he has another kid. He's responsible. He's got his shit together."

Josh loves his little brother. He says he plans to give him the blue BMX bike that Dad rescued for him. He's kept it all these years. It reminds him of my father.

"My dad, he is that person now," Josh says. "But back then, he wasn't there as much as I would have liked him to be. Your dad was."

I wasn't able to see, as a young man, how much we need to lean on the male supports in our lives. It's what the other guys who hung around our house have been telling me since my dad died—friends who had more complicated relationships with their fathers, or didn't have them in their lives at all. They'd come to our house and sit on the deck or around the kitchen table and chat with Dad, listening to stern advice given with a smile because it was something they'd craved in their own lives. I didn't understand that then. I didn't get it until I saw them crying by his hospital bed or in the weeks after he was gone. They told me the things they loved about him because it was too late for them to tell him themselves.

One friend, Steve Farley, lost his father in an industrial accident when he was six years old. When he started his own renovation company he sat down with Dad several times to get his advice. "Especially missing that male aspect in my life, anytime there was someone you had a lot of respect for, you took it," he told me.

Sometimes Steve did contracting jobs at the church. One day he was adjusting a duct and had to open up the wall in the basement beneath the old sanctuary. Dad walked in just as he'd bashed through the drywall and found a carjack that someone, years ago, had spray-foamed into the wall to hold up the floor above. "The look on your dad's face was just comical. Absolutely hilarious," Steve told me. "He says, 'Man, when will this church learn that volunteers just will not cut it sometimes?'"

Dad would often check on the work being done. "He paid a lot of attention to detail," Steve said. "You knew. He'd give you a look of approval, or he'd make suggestions for how to *adjust* things."

Another time, they were sitting in a Kelseys restaurant near the church while Steve went over the details of a business plan he'd laid out for his renovation company. Dad sat there relaxed, not saying much at all. "The detail I was going into he didn't need to hear. He'd seen it and done it," Steve said. "He kept reiterating to me, 'You need to get guys. You're worried about the product. Your job is to *manage guys.*'"

It was the first time, Steve told me, that he understood that his job in the field wasn't the job itself—it was to oversee it, and to make sure it was done the way it needed to be done. "I never realized that your dad had run his own *renovation* company until later," Steve said. "I'm sitting there going, 'Come on, Rick, you don't understand what I'm talking about.' But you come to realize years later that he *did* know what he was talking about—and I just had to trust that the information he was giving me was exactly what I needed to hear."

Sometimes it takes years to learn the lesson. It takes time to understand what you were really being told and why it mattered more than you could have known. It took Dad's death for me to realize that, all along, my father's job was really about managing men. Keeping them honest, but inspiring them too.

At that East Side Mario's table, I tell Josh that I think he appreciated what I'd taken for granted. That he was able to understand how Dad was different. But that I didn't *really* know what I had in my father.

He nods.

I'm jealous of the time they spent together, I say. I envy the natural talent he had working with his hands—the talent Dad had gushed to me about. I regret that I hadn't tried harder to be like him when he was alive, and that I feel an enormous void because of it.

I tell Josh that I'm trying to make up for it now. I'm trying to be the kind of person who can take care of himself and fix things for his family. And it's making me feel closer to Dad again. It's making it feel like he's not fading away.

"It's weird how you carry them with you," I say. "When people you love die, they're still part of you."

It might be a cliché, but it's true. I can see that Josh knows what I mean. Of course he does. He knows it even more than I do.

"You look back and just know you were better off for knowing them," I say, "even though they're gone. Because you *had* them. And they're part of you. They're part of everything you do. Part of the way you think. You can actually hear them saying things. Mostly for me when I'm trying to use tools, he's just like, 'Son, how are *you* my son?' He would say it in a loving way, but—you know—because I was just *brutal*."

We both use the laugh to wipe away tears.

"I didn't learn a lot of the things you spent time learning from him," I continue. "I was doing my thing and he was doing his kind of thing. I admired that he could do it, but . . . Later on, in the last couple of years, he'd come down to Toronto and fix stuff in my apartment that I couldn't do but should have been able to, and I remember telling him, 'It's pretty amazing that you can do all this stuff.' And I'm really glad I had the chance to say that to him, because I hadn't before. I think he understood that I respected him, because it was something I couldn't do at all—and now I'm lost, trying to learn how. Totally lost. Anyway . . ."

Our pasta is getting cold. We order another round of salad and bread, intending to pack up what's left so that Josh can take it home.

I know Dad would have wanted us to get together, and I feel terrible that it's taken this long. I also know that it'll be a while before Josh and I see each other again. And that will be on me, because I can't be the man he was.

Josh looks up from the table.

"He was an amazing person. But that doesn't give it justice, you know what I mean?" he says. "He was honestly the best guy ever."

22

Matt is clearly frustrated by the pace of the project so far. And to be fair, we are significantly delayed. We stand in the bathroom, hands on hips, taking a tally of what still needs to be completed.

"You're driven to get this done," I note.

"I have to be. If I want to get this business going, I have to be organized," Matt says. "If I'm not organized . . ."

One of the many delays is the fact that the wall across the back of the bathroom, where the tub sits, wasn't built perfectly plumb. That seemingly small mistake leads to huge headaches. Most of the tiling in the shower is done, but the joints between each white rectangle tell the story. Tiles leave no room to hide mistakes.

Matt is diplomatic about it all, trying to hide his irritation. Working with a crew seems efficient, but it also means they can mess up on you. It's about *managing* people. When you do it yourself, you have control—and no one else to blame.

Matt points to the corner of the shower, where several rows of tiles end with a gap before meeting the other wall. "It's kind of annoying now," he says. "Because each cut is out by a sixteenth. So up here it's different from down here." He points to the unfinished top half of the shower wall where the head and faucet are. "But if we'd done the wall perfectly level, we'd just go out and cut them all the same." He smiles and sighs, and then rotates his forearm in a small circle—the universal sign for *speed it up*. "And we have to take the extra time. That's why we have to make sure everything is square, plumb, and level."

"So now we have to do a bit more detail on the corner," I say, shaking my head like a frustrated craftsman.

"Yeah," Matt says, and sighs again. "Yeah . . ."

I'd never heard the phrase "square, plumb, and level" before starting this project. Apparently it's one of the most common and important concepts in construction. It's pretty simple in theory, but it's also essential to making sure that each element fits in place and functions in support of the next step. It's about planning and precision. It requires that the surface of the foundation you're building on is perfectly horizontal—or level. The tiniest slope will create problems as you build.

When building up, like framing a wall, it's imperative that every vertical element stand perfectly upright. From top to bottom, ceiling to floor, each wall has to be straight up and down—that is, plumb. The idea comes from a tool called a plumb line, which is just a string with a weight on the end that uses gravity to show you what a perfectly vertical line is. And every angle has to be ninety degrees—or square—because the smallest incongruity can lead to massive problems later. There is nowhere to hide a mistake when you're a framer. If your wall is square but sitting on a floor that's not level, then the wall that runs perpendicular won't be plumb. And if you're not paying attention when you're laying out the footings, chances are the framer will see it when he's putting the plywood on the roof. You can try to hide your mistakes somewhere, and there are definitely tricks. You can spread your mistakes around so evenly that maybe only another carpenter will be able to spot them. But who would you rather be, the guy who masters the tricks or the guy who builds things square, plumb, and level?

When you get it all right, everything is "true." But right now, everything is wrong.

"What about on this side?" I ask, turning to the black tiling above the vanity that Jonathan is busy working away on. "Is it level?"

Jonathan is trying to fit a small square of tile into a gap in the corner, twisting it around as if it's a puzzle piece. There are several small gaps of varying sizes running up the corner.

"Well, that one," Matt says. "I mean . . ."

"We've already had to cut pieces," Jonathan says, mumbling as he fiddles with the tile that clearly doesn't fit the space. "I don't know if it's level or not."

"Right," I say.

It's not level.

"This one's a little more tricky," Matt says.

"Matt, your number eight broke," Jonathan tells him. He runs his finger across a gap closer to the top of the tiles. He's referring to one of the pieces of tile that had to be custom cut to reach the corner.

"There was one on the floor that *might* fit," Matt says. "Maybe an extra piece that's not . . ." He bends down and picks up a grey slab. "Maybe this one here."

Jonathan doesn't seem encouraged by this development. He tries to fit the piece of tile in his hand into another gap a few rows up.

Matt holds the new piece, examining it. "No, this is too big," he says, and drops it.

"So, it's a bit of a puzzle, putting a wall together, eh?" I say.

"Oh yeah," Matt says. His voice is flat. "Oh yeah."

Jonathan tries to force the piece into the gap again, this time pressing it in with his middle finger. It doesn't fit.

On its own, each step in this process is easy enough, but combined with small imperfections, the big picture falls apart. Bringing everything together in a way that functions, that will stand through time—making it *true*—that part is much harder than it seems.

Later that morning I'm tasked with cutting the new baseboard trim. I take a big step and suggest using Dad's saw in the garage to help speed up the process. It feels like taking his prized sports car for a joyride. Dad bought the saw within the last couple of years before he died. He'd talked about it for weeks, hemming and hawing over the cost until he finally convinced himself that it was justified. Then he went to Home Depot and bought it, a Milwaukee mitre saw with a wheeled portable stand.

Dad loved it. He packed it up and brought it to my condo in Toronto several times, setting it up on my front patio and spraying the courtyard in sawdust. This was how we built the ten-foot bookshelves downstairs and my desk on the second floor that looked down over the loft. We picked up the lumber together. He measured out what we needed based on a design drawn up by one of our friends who's an architect.

I remember Dad joking that architects and builders often live in different head spaces. The architect dreams something up, but it's the builder who has to somehow make that crazy vision happen. It felt like Dad had let me in on an industry joke—something that only someone who wore a hard hat every day would get. It was the kind of banter Dad always shared with his workers at the job sites we'd visit when I was younger. There they spoke in a construction-site language I didn't understand and made jokes I didn't get.

It was also like the banter Dad shared with the men working at the loading dock when we went to pick up the large piece of Douglas fir I'd ordered from British Columbia. The idea was to mount it on an early twentieth-century punch press I'd bought at a vintage store and to use it as a kitchen table. I'd paid too much for a piece of otherwise useless industrial equipment; and I'd ordered a special slab of wood to make it into a piece of furniture. It was a *very* Toronto thing to do. Not the kind of thing Dad would have done. But he took me to pick up the wood when it arrived.

The loading dock was somewhere west of Toronto, in the kind of industrial area off the 401 highway that I never went to but that Dad seemed to know by heart. We drove up to this gigantic garage door, raised about six feet off the ground. The man at the dock asked us what we needed—and Dad started talking and joking with this guy in that strange language. It was English, but somehow foreign. Dad had lit up, smiling with a comfortable confidence, chatting away with a stranger about loading docks and lumber.

In the maybe ten minutes that it took for our order to be retrieved and delivered, Dad and this middle-aged guy in grey coveralls were laughing as if they'd been best friends for years.

They loaded the Douglas fir tabletop into the truck. Dad gave the man a friendly wave before he climbed back into the driver's seat. Then we rumbled out into the street, my industrial-chic tabletop furniture hanging out the bed of the blue F-150.

I pull the big mitre saw out from the corner of the garage, steering it into an open area and plug in.

Matt pauses with a wide smile. The saw is a beautiful machine. It makes me proud. But also afraid. It's powerful and dangerous, a stunning, ferocious beast. It could build a house—or take a finger, without a pause.

Matt and I fiddle with it, finding the different safety locks and gauges that allow you to tilt the blade on different angles and along different guides to ensure you'd make a precise cut.

"What was one of our marks there?" Matt says.

I pull my notebook out of my tool belt and flip for some recent scribbles.

"Seventy-four," I say. "Back wall."

Matt rests a long piece of baseboard on the saw. Then he smiles and walks away.

I pull the end of the measuring tape, stretch it out to seventy-four inches, and mark it with a line. I place my left hand carefully down on the wood several inches from the blade, holding it steady. Then I grab the handle of the saw and brace the trim with my other hand.

I can feel my heart beating. I press the trigger and the saw whirls as I push it down slowly—much slower than I should. A car pulls into the driveway just before the blade hits the wood. I release the trigger as though I've been caught doing something I shouldn't. Jai gets out of the car with a tray of coffees. (It's job site etiquette: Never arrive without coffees.)

"Careful," she calls, walking by.

I shake my head and get back to it. The saw whirls to life again. I pull it down—slowly, still—but fully through the wood, pushing the blade back across the width to complete the cut. I feel the tension release in my left hand. I let go of the trigger and slowly raise the blade.

I stop to survey my work. A perfect line.

Matt walks around the corner balancing three more pieces of trim. "You can cut these three at the same length," he tells me.

I used a pen to mark the line on the first piece of trim. I'm feeling self-conscious about it now as Matt looks at my work and I realize there's a bit of ink still visible.

Damn it.

"I'll get a pencil," I say. "I used a pen, but maybe it'll rub off—or we can paint over it?"

"It's okay. But is this the seventy-four mark?" he says, pointing to the still very visible line.

"Yeah, this is seventy-four right there," I say. "Or, a little more than seventy-four. Do we need it to be right on?" This feels as dumb as it sounds.

"Yeah, you're going to need to cut an eighth off that," Matt says. "What I like to do is, in my mind I say, 'I need to make that mark disappear.'"

We measure and mark the length on the next piece of trim. I straighten the blade on the line and give it another push. The line turns to dust.

"Beauty," Matt says.

"You're pretty precise with that, eh?" I say. Again, it feels ridiculous as it comes out.

That's the benefit of a mitre saw, Matt tells me. The Skilsaw we used downstairs is better for cutting pieces of wood for the framing because it's more of a rough cut. We can move around more easily on site with the smaller saw, he says. The table saw is more cumbersome. We're confined to wherever we set it up. But it's also much more exact. We can cut angles with it—like with outside corners, he says, where you have to make sure they are cut perfectly and everything lines up, or it'll leave a gap. "With the table saw you can be back on down to a twenty-fourth," Matt says.

"If I knew what that was it would be impressive," I say.

Matt laughs. "A twenty-fourth is what machinists use."

It's not much of an explanation.

He walks away again, and I keep going. I try to run the tape lengthwise along the next piece of wood by myself, but it slips off several times. This works better with a crew: one measures, one cuts. Alone, it takes me at least ten minutes to cut a few pieces.

Matt returns with more wood to cut, then leaves with the pieces I've finished.

I get much steadier with the process. I find a rhythm. After about a dozen tries, I become quick and firm with each push of the blade.

But the measuring tape still gives me trouble. And the thin trim keeps flopping when I lay it out across the table saw. The tape snaps back and rips towards me several times. As soon as I get it in place and am about to measure, it unclips and falls. This happens at least five times in a row—and all I can do is struggle with it and keep on going.

Matt comes back up from the basement and I swallow my pride.

"Hey man, can you just hold that end there?" I ask. "It keeps falling off."

He hangs on and watches me fiddle with the measurement. "Mark it with the other hand maybe," he says.

"Yeah," I mumble. "I was going to . . ." I look up and realize he's walked away from the other end of the measuring tape. He's somehow clipped it in place.

I line up my new cut and attempt to keep the speed and confidence going. I place the blade right on the piece of wooden trim without pressing the trigger to start it. When I do, the wood jumps up beneath the blade. I scrunch my face, and Matt sees me. We've already talked about this. He goes to say something, but I rev the blade and start sawing again, drowning out his voice.

The wood drops to the floor. I shake my head and scratch my nose. It feels like it's my father who's been telling me how to do the job.

"Hold it steady . . ."

"Try again . . ."

Again. Again. Again. Every time I try and fail, I can hear his voice. Not angry or impatient, but knowing. No matter how many times I try, I won't get it right.

I can't hold it steady. I don't know how. For the first time since we started, I want to quit.

"Steady, buddy. Try again . . ."

Matt turns his attention back to his own task.

"All right, so I'll pass these through the window?" I say casually, as if I hadn't just cut him off with the blade.

"Sure," Matt says. "I'll run down there."

He heads through the laundry room as I pick up the pieces of baseboard.

"Ugh," I sigh.

When I join Matt in the basement, he hands me the nail gun, attached to the air compressor. He tells me to use the gun every sixteen inches or so to shoot two small nails into the baseboard, holding it in place. If you don't hit a stud, just put it in on an angle, Matt says, so the nail will have a better grip in the drywall.

I nail the baseboard pieces to the wall, roughly sixteen inches apart, as instructed. I'm not really sure if I hit the studs or not. But the pieces are holding.

The corner poses a new challenge: we have to cut the pieces on an angle to make them join properly. The mitre saw turns on precise degrees, so Matt shows me how to shift the blade to a forty-five-degree angle. Then he holds the baseboard in place with his left hand while pushing the saw handle down with his right. His fingers are incredibly close to the blade as it cuts through the wood.

As the cut piece of baseboard falls to the floor, Matt sees the concern on my face. "I'm not afraid, really," he says. "So, there's our forty-five."

Easy enough, it seems. But we're not done.

The forty-five-degree cut has revealed the contour of the baseboard's profile. Matt picks up one of Dad's saws that looks like just an enormous handle with a thin grey blade sticking out of it. A jig saw. The blade moves up and down rapidly as he pulls the trigger. He runs it across the contour, trimming away a triangular offcut. This is supposed to allow the piece to fit tighter on the inside corners. I have no idea how the random cuts he's made can possibly do that.

He joins the new edge with the end of the other piece of baseboard, making a corner.

"You just fill that," he says, running his finger across the exposed end. "And it's perfect."

"Perfect," I say.

But now it's my turn.

We have to move the saw from forty-five degrees on one side to the other side. We clamp a brace on the table to hold the wood in place. I have to cut away from me—so I push down and away with my right hand, bracing the wood with my left. The saw whirls to life. I hesitate just enough.

"Oh, you have a little bite here," Matt says, pointing to the small nubby in the edge of the wood. "Hit it again."

I try again, but miss the wood completely. One more time—I have to nudge the wood over. This time sawdust flies. The nubby is gone.

"Right on," Matt says.

But now I have to cut the edge, which seems much more complicated as I hold the saw in my hand.

"You just have to follow this line all the way," Matt says, running his finger across the decorative ridge at the top of the baseboard. "It might be easier to go in at an angle."

I move around and line up with my left hand, which feels like an odd way to start with a saw I've never used before.

"Just take it nice and slow," Matt encourages. "Make sure you're going straight and right along this line."

The saw sputters as I start it, pushing forward—but halts about a centimetre in.

"Keep going," Matt says.

I push further and it sputters and stops and then jolts forward, ripping up a puff of sawdust.

"Nice and slow," Matt repeats. "There you go. The easiest way is to just hit it from this side now."

I move to the other side, switching the saw to my right hand and readying myself to cut through the ridge. But when I try to cut the shorter angle slowly, the blade begins to sputter and jump again. I flip to the other side, on my left, to try and get the final ridge. Matt says something about how there are mitre saws you can buy for $15, but that the one I'm using is way more expensive and professional. I nod—and then bump and bumble with the saw through one last cut.

"That's it," Matt says. "Perfect."

I'm dubious.

"Is that notched enough?"

"Yeah, yeah," he says.

"This part too?" I ask, rubbing the longer butchering job I did.

Matt grabs the other piece I cut and holds them together at a ninety-degree angle, making a corner with the baseboards. "That's going to be a nice finished joint," he says.

"Perfect."

He leaves me to take on the rest of the baseboard pieces alone. I line up the first forty-five-degree cut, trying to decide whether I'm actually on the line or beside it, and not really confident that I know either way. I move the saw up and down a few times, seeing where it lands—and continue to hesitate. I look up and down the piece of baseboard, as though it will provide an answer. I put my hands on my hips and look out across the court. It's a sunny afternoon. There are birds chirping. I sigh.

"Shit," I say. "Ugh."

Then I pull the saw back to the centre, take a deep breath, and press down. The end of the baseboard falls to the floor.

When I pick it up, I realize that I've cut the wood on the wrong angle and to the wrong length. It's a truly incredible failure.

Start again. It takes a couple more attempts to get it. When I finally have it figured out—the right length, the right angle—I try cutting out the edge with the jig saw, just like Matt showed me. I fiddle with the jig saw and the wood for a minute, but I'm afraid to ruin the work I've done already, so I pick a piece of scrap to practise one more time. The wood bounces around again as I saw into the edge. I toss it on the floor in disgust.

Twenty minutes later, I've successfully sawed and notched out a *single* piece of baseboard. I deliver my masterpiece downstairs.

"Let's see the expert cut," Matt says.

I lay the piece against the corner I've been trying to complete. It nudges out just beyond the edge of the wall.

"Too long?" I ask.

"Perfect," Matt says. "I never should have doubted you."

"Perfect," I repeat, unsure. "*Is* it perfect?"

"Let's line it up with the other piece," Matt suggests. He takes the adjacent baseboard for the corner and sets it in place. He pauses. The piece I cut extends just beyond it. "It's a *little* long," Matt concedes. "By an eighth. You could shave a bit off."

He's trying to be encouraging.

"Just disappear that line and it will get you right on this corner," he says. "It's like *pretty close* to perfect."

"Thanks," I huff.

23

I head back to the loft Jayme and I share in Toronto for the weekend, and it's quickly apparent just how much I've neglected. There is so much work to do. The painting Jayme asked me to hang has been leaning against our concrete wall for months.

She mentions that maybe it's something I can finally get around to doing.

Metaphors are rarely so neatly framed. While I've been trying to build something from my old life, I've completely forgotten the one we were building here. Meanwhile, Jayme's been busy at work while planning our wedding.

I'd had a designer make a custom ring, right before Dad died. I'd planned to tell him about my intention to ask Jayme to marry me over a round of golf on his birthday, which we would have been celebrating only a week afterwards.

I ended up proposing to her on my parents' anniversary, November 1, a month after Jenna and Tim's wedding. It should have been an exciting step forward—a catalyst. But beyond the proposal, I've let everything else fall to her. We've set a date: October 1 in the coming year. She's taken on every task it requires while I've been in my parents' basement playing toolman. I figure it's time to show her the value in what I've learned.

Having bored through a brick wall and smashed through the foundation of a house, hanging a frame on a concrete wall will be simple. I packed Dad's hammer drill in the truck to get the job done, intent on using it just the way he did when he installed the bookshelves that rise up next to where the painting is supposed to hang.

It does not go as planned. No one is around, but I feel nervous. I stop and start several times. The drill fires up and bounces off the concrete even as I try to press into it with both hands.

"Ah!" I shout in frustration.

Henry, our miniature Goldendoodle, gets frightened and hides in the corner.

I try again.

Nothing.

Steady.

Piercing whine. Concrete dust. Another millimetre.

Push with all your weight.

I shout an expletive and push in again. Nothing—I barely move a millimetre.

I look at the drill, checking to make sure it's the right one, the one with the hammer. I've used whatever bit I could find that fits.

"Come on . . ." I say.

Hold it steady, buddy, straight—and push.

Nowhere. And the drill stops. I swear again, softly, close to defeat this time.

"The battery. Ugh."

Done.

The dog shakes.

"Henry, buddy, it's okay."

I pack up the drill and lean the painting back against the wall.

The next day I decide I'm ready to caulk our shower, which has been leaking down into our hallway for several days.

I go out and buy a special blade to remove the old caulking and a new tube and a gun to squeeze it out with.

I overdo it. There's no consistency to my squeeze—no delicacy, no art. It looks like the excess glue on the popsicle-stick bridge I constructed in a competition in high school, which I decided could be held together by adding more glue than anyone else. I lost.

My caulking is one long uneven blob, right around the base of the shower. It might be the most amateur job ever done. But nothing—not a single drop of water—will be able to seep through. I've stuck to my long-held belief that when in doubt, more is always better.

"What are you going to write your next book about," Jayme mocks, "caulking the bathroom?"

"Yes," I defend.

She's mad. It's more than just the past couple of weeks in Brampton. It's the last year of our life, which I've spent trying to take care of a house that isn't ours. Trying to be my father, which is a role no one asked me to take on. And no matter how I try, I can't replace him.

The biography I'd completed after Dad died had been successful and earned decent enough royalties. It had taken everything I had to get it done. I dedicated it to him.

"For my father, Rick Robson, a builder and a fixer. With me, always."

He would have been proud. I should have been thrilled.

But I can't feel joy in it. I don't care about much beyond my anger that he's gone.

I'm upset because Jayme doesn't seem to understand what I've lost. She wants to push us forward and for me to pull myself together. She either refuses or is incapable of understanding why I can't. At least that's how I view it.

In reality, she was there the night he died and she stood by me for months, helping me finish the books that needed to get done, while still balancing her own career with one of the best investigative journalism teams in the country.

I remember when we first met, the year we were interns at the *Toronto Star* and we sat next to each other. I couldn't focus on my work because I was enamored with everything she did. She rolled her eyes at me every time she caught me peeking over the cubicle. When she was sent to Cairo to cover the Arab Spring, I helped her get ready to leave, frantically running through all the things one is supposed to pack for an uprising. Her flight was just hours after she'd been given the assignment. It was a huge opportunity for her— the kind you don't turn down—but we were both still interns, both still scared. As we waited for a cab to take her to the airport, she turned to me and said, "I want you to know that I love you." It was the first time that either of us had said that.

I didn't hear from her for nearly a day after she landed. It was rather busy in Tahrir Square. But I kept refreshing my e-mail, waiting to see her words. I kept swallowing, swallowing. Finally, a few rows away in the newsroom, I overheard an editor repeating copy about the rising demonstrations as she took dictation over the phone on a headset. I walked over and interrupted.

"Is that Jayme?" I asked the editor.

She looked up from the phone, confused by the intrusion on deadline. Very few people knew that Jayme and I were seeing each other at the time.

"Yes," the editor said, shortly.

"Tell her I say hi."

She looked back at the copy on her screen, newsroom body language for *go away now*.

"Dan Robson says hello," she repeated into her headset.

There was a brief pause while the editor continued to typing.

"Jayme says *hi* back," she said.

I smiled and walked away.

I love you too.

We built our life together over the next half decade, supporting each other through shared dreams and embarking on global adventures.

This was the second half of me—the part that was supposed to have it all figured out. But I'd fallen apart on her.

The drinking is still a point of contention. She thinks it's a problem—and I think she's overreacting, searching for a way to tear me down while I'm weak. The truth is, I can't really see what I've become; what it looks like on the outside. I can't see what it is to be in a relationship like that. I can't see the absence. The lack of attention. The disappearance of my heart.

The argument that quickly escalates into a shouting match is one it seems we've both been waiting for. My heart is pounding. I'm spiralling. And I resent Jayme for not comprehending why.

I can't process what we're saying. It's just anger. My anger. I don't know how to get rid of it.

I stare through her.

"You're scaring me," she says. "Where have you gone?"

"I don't know," I say. "But I don't think I can come back."

I don't live in the present anymore. I walk around in a constant dream, trying to grasp old memories that slip away like sand. That night, I take another long detour through the past.

When I was finally done playing competitive hockey, I went and sat in a gazebo in a park by a lake and cried. By that time I was at Queen's University, where I'd been the second-string goalie for a few years, never playing a full game. It was embarrassing. An upper-year goalie was the starter—and it was clear I'd never get a chance to actually contribute to the team.

We were on the ice six days a week with practices and games. It consumed a ton of my time. But over those few years away from home, I'd become a different person. I got involved in other things, beyond hockey—like, actual *school*, and extracurriculars like running my Concurrent Education program's Frosh Week, which involved painting my body silver, wearing a toga, and learning choreographed steps to "The Dancing Queen." I was the only hockey player in the production.

I'd shed the fanciful dreams of my youth, which always ended in me somehow playing in the NHL even though the highest level I'd ever actually played was Tier II Junior A. We'd won a provincial title with the Brampton Capitals—it felt as big as the Stanley Cup—and then some key players went on to the NCAA and OHL. When I was accepted into Queen's (a real shock to everyone at my school) and recruited to play for its hockey team, I decided to head there instead of hoping for a scholarship to arrive from the States after playing another year of Junior.

In terms of hockey, it was a terrible mistake. Queen's was very bad at the sport. And without a spot to play regularly as a rookie, the coaches asked me to get some time in with a Junior C team a half hour away in a small town called Gananoque.

It was a nightmare. In my first game there, one of the players picked up a spider off the bathroom floor and ate it. It was his pre-game routine. I hated taking those trips out to play for the Gan Flyers. I hated carpooling with other players who'd either been set aside by the varsity team or weren't good enough to make it. It shredded my pride.

Just before reading week that February, Dad called. He told me to sit down—and then told me that our golden retriever, Brandi, had died. I was gutted. We'd had her since I was in grade three. She was a gorgeous blonde who never barked or bit or did anything wrong except sleep on the couch.

We were just finishing up our season in Gan, so I wasn't going to be able to go home for reading week. Instead, Dad took a week off work and drove three hours to stay with me in Kingston.

I showed him around campus—all the beautiful old limestone buildings, the library that held first editions, hundreds of years old. I took him to the Epicure, an amazing little breakfast spot named after an ancient Greek philosophy I'd learned about in the first year Classics course I was failing. I took him to the park by the lake, where sometimes I'd go to sit between classes and call him. I showed him my new world, a world he'd never had the opportunity to be part of.

Then we drove out to Gan together for a hockey game. It was a quiet ride through a snowy night. And it was during that ride when I first realized that I didn't really like this sport very much at all.

It stressed me out. Being a hockey player carried too much of my perceived value. I'd tried to build my life on a dream that was never going to work out. And frankly, being a goalie is really, really hard.

It just hadn't been the same since I'd left home. It wasn't the same without the hot shower after a nap in my childhood room, or the plate of tortellini I'd wolf down as the garage door opened and Dad came in, changed quickly, and then rushed out to the rink with me.

It wasn't the same without those stars streaming past the window through the night. Or without Dad's whistle rising above all the noise in the stands.

It wasn't the same without him.

I started that game, and it was terrible. I let in four goals in the first period. I was anxious and angry. Every shot seemed to find its way in. Dad was in the stands and I was devastated. I'd wanted to show him that all the time and money he'd spent on my hockey dreams hadn't been a giant waste. I knew my heart wasn't in it, but I didn't want him to know. In the second period, the goals kept coming. I could feel my heart panic. I could hear the other team chirp. I could see my own players slam their sticks. Another goal—and another. It was a nightmare.

I could hear Dad's whistle above it all. I could see him at the top of the stands, at centre ice as always, clapping his hands together and signalling to me as loud as he could.

I looked at him—and then I left the ice. Before the ref could drop the puck after that last goal, I skated towards our bench and motioned to the coach to take me out.

The coach waved at me to go back in, but I kept skating. I felt a lump in my throat. I couldn't look at my father. I sat on the bench with my head down and the game went on without me.

Dad didn't say much when I loaded my gear into the back of his truck afterwards. He gave me a hug, and on the ride home he patted my leg. We drove in silence while I looked at the stars.

He knew it was over too.

I stuck with the Queen's varsity team for another season, knowing I was really just a guy for the players to shoot on in practice. I don't know why I stayed, except that it was all I'd ever done. Then, during training camp in my third year, a talented first-year goalie showed up. Our starter would graduate in a year and they'd need someone to take his place. It wouldn't be me. I was called into the coaches' room after one of the training camp skates and told I no longer had a spot on the team.

It stung like hell. There was no getting around that. I was angry. But deeper than that, I felt a relief I'd never experienced before. I felt free. I went to the gazebo by the water and sat alone.

The next day, I called Dad. My heart was pounding. I was upset because I'd failed and also because, despite all the time he and I had spent chasing this game, I knew I didn't want it anymore. It took me ten minutes to dial his number.

"Hi, buddy," he answered.

I went right to it, because there was no way around this shame. I've been cut from the varsity team, I told him. I went on to say that I was pissed and that the coaches sucked and all the other things you're supposed to gripe about. And then I said what I'd really wanted to say.

"Dad, I just want to say thank you."

He didn't say anything for several moments. When he came back, he sounded rushed.

"I'm sorry," he said. "I have to go."

And he hung up the phone.

I didn't know what happened. I sat down on my bed and stared at the floor. Five minutes later, my phone buzzed.

"Dad?"

His voice broke.

"It was always about you, son," he said. He took a deep breath, and then his voice cracked again.

"It was always about you and me."

24

After the weekend off, Jonathan and Matt arrive in the basement looking like characters from a Dickens novel, their faces covered in soot. They've spent the morning bringing down a century-old ceiling in Matt's bungalow. The night before he'd stood in the shower and thought about how exposing the attic beneath the steep roof would open up the narrow hallway that felt tight and dark.

Matt got out of the shower and told his wife his plans. Without flinching, Rachael said, Do it. So the next morning, before he and Jonathan came in to continue our reno, they demolished his ceiling.

Now Matt sits in the tub, smoothing putty—"grouting"—over small white rectangles as we attempt to finish off a tiling job that's already taken us two days.

"So how did you take it down?" I ask.

"We pretty much got in the attic and started kicking out the ceiling," Matt says.

"What if you fell?"

"Well," he says. "That wouldn't be great."

They just stood on the joists and stomped until the old ceiling fell. It was dicey. They taped the adventure with a Go Pro, and proudly promise to show me the footage later.

"Jonathan is like two hundred something," Matt says. "So I tried to stay away from his section."

Jonathan huffs a laugh as he returns to his puzzle, piecing together the accent wall above the sink. I suspect the ceiling demolition was a welcome distraction from my constant questions and interruptions while we piece together the bathroom.

It takes as much time to put up the little tiles on the walls around the tub and vanity as it does to lay the larger tiles on the floor. It's more intricate, Matt says, requiring more cuts. Sometimes the smallest things take as much time as the big things.

He uses a grinder to cut the tiles around the tub's faucet. It has a diamond blade, but it's on a hand-held wheel, so he just scrolls and breaks the tile as he goes. He's already used the grinder to cut out a hole for the toilet in the big floor tiles.

"You have to be brave," he says. "Because a wheel is spinning in your hand that could cut you. And when you first pull the trigger it torques, so you have to be ready with a good grip, and then you just . . ." He mimics the action of cutting through the tile. "And the tile particles are flying everywhere and you have to squint—or wear your safety glasses."

Matt smiles and smoothes down another glob of putty.

I've learned that mortar is the paste plastered under the tiles and that grout is the putty that separates them. There's a cement board behind the first foot or so of tile, above the tub. Mould can't develop on it, Matt explains. The rest is waterproof drywall. It's all finished with a special drywall compound.

Jonathan wipes down the dark tiles above the sink with a wet sponge, removing the excess grout, which is black instead of the white stuff used around the tub. Measuring and cutting the small pieces that fill the gaps between the tiles and our flawed corners has been a two-day headache for him. But for all the fatigue and dirt, for all the uneven angles and impossible-to-fill gaps, the tiles have brought life to the bathroom. As we lay them, the room keeps getting brighter and brighter.

"This is going to look great," I say.

No one responds.

I take the grout blade from Matt and start working it side to side, up and down—right into the cracks between the tiles. I scoop more grout onto the blade, working my way down the side of the tub.

It's just filling the cracks, really, Matt says. It's mostly aesthetic.

It's repetitive. We work in silence. Just a few handymen, grouting. Putting in an honest day's work. Getting the job done.

After a few minutes, Matt opens up the worksite small talk.

"Jonathan's ready to build a house because he watched a whole hour-and-a-half video of Larry Haun," he says.

"Oh, yeah? Nice," I remark. "What did you learn?"

"Stairs," Jonathan says.

"Stairs?"

"Well, that was the trickiest part of the video," he says.

"Is that where you're learning all your stuff from?" I ask. "Larry Haun videos?"

Jonathan shrugs and places another tile.

"Larry Haun, what a man," I say. "A visionary."

I realize that the unnecessary chitchat has taken my focus, and become immediately self-conscious about the row of shower tiles I've set in place. I've reached the corner.

"What am I doing wrong here?" I ask pre-emptively.

Matt assures me I'm on the right track. Then he takes the blade from me and slaps a glop of grout across the edge. "What you have to do is grab a nice chunk at the corner and try to push it up to there," he says. "That should be the trickiest part."

He hands me back the blade.

"Grab some more material," he says, pointing to the bucket of grout. I add a glob to the blade and spread more across the wall.

"Yeah, you have it. Yeah, there you go," Matt says. "Give it another drag so there isn't any more excess. Use the edge."

"Inside or outside?" I ask.

"Yeah, at forty-five degrees," he says. "That's perfect."

I step back and admire the smooth layer of grout halfway up the shower.

"Look at that. Grouting for Dummies," I say. "Larry Haun would be impressed."

It's a segue to more proper worksite banter.

"So what else did you learn from Larry?" I ask.

"Me?" Jonathan says. "Some of the more beginning stages of building a house—how to square a corner—"

Matt points at the still untiled top third of the shower. "Maybe start working your way up this wall," he says to me.

"Okay," I say, and go back to Jonathan.

"You learned how to square a corner?"

"Using the Pythagorean theorem," he tells me.

"Seriously?"

"It's simple," Jonathan says. "You just have to measure out two measurements. If you measure eight feet and six feet, then you get ten feet on a diagonal."

As I push those numbers around in my head, I realize I'm incapable of grouting and doing math at the same time.

"Press it around," Matt reminds me, watching over my work.

"Sixty-four plus thirty-six is a hundred, right?" Jonathan says. "So all you have to do is measure eight feet one length, straight to the wall. Measure six feet on the other, mark it. And then measure from the marks on each wall, the diagonal measurement. If the diagonal measurement equals ten, that means you have a right angle—which means that the corner is square."

I try working that out for a moment.

"You don't have to do the math," Jonathan says. "You just have to know that one corner is six, the other corner is eight."

"I can skip the math then? Pythagoras did it for me?"

"Because six squared plus eight squared equals a hundred, and the square root of a hundred is ten," Jonathan explains, again.

I don't know what this has to do with building a house, but I nod as though I do—and spread another glob across the wall.

"So I can build a house now," I say.

"That's it," Jonathan laughs.

Matt smiles. "All you need is a tape measure," he says.

"And set and sink," Jonathan says. "Two licks."

He's repeating the words of Haun, our great teacher, who has showed us how to be better, more efficient old-school builders. But Larry didn't explain the math or that it was the Pythagorean theorem. Jonathan says he just knew that it was.

"It's just math."

"He didn't even give Pythagoras credit, eh," Matt says.

I'm still glopping on the grout and then sweeping it back with the edge at a forty-five-degree angle. Jonathan continues his lesson.

"If your corner is less than six-by-eight long, then you're going to have to actually do the math," he says. "If not, you just get a square."

I'm overly impressed by Jonathan's ability to apply this theory to real life.

"Pythagorean," I say. "What grade did you learn that in?"

"Junior high?" Jonathan says.

"Junior high?" I repeat. "*Really?*"

My father was always very good with numbers. He had a knack for doing quick math in his head. His notebooks are filled with small equations scribbled on the spot whenever he came across a problem on a worksite that required some visual thought. He didn't pass that talent on. I was so bad at math that my high school principal banned me from practice during the start of basketball season until I pulled up my grade eleven math marks. That was embarrassing enough for me to put in a modest effort to get back on the team. I just didn't see the point in math. I was rather daft about the whole thing, obviously. But numbers bored me—and I'd decided I didn't need to know about them anyway because I wasn't going to grow up to be like my father.

My identity was built on the idea of being what he wasn't. I didn't fully grasp that then, but I didn't feel I needed to excel at what he did because that's the role he filled. I was going to fill a different role; I was going to become what he couldn't. And so I didn't value learning even the basics of what he knew. I don't think it was out of a lack of respect for him. I felt he understood—and that, all along, it was what he wanted for me.

So I would never need to know the Pythagorean theorem to build a house. Instead I'd be a professional athlete, or a writer, or a world traveller. And, after all, Dad would do the math *for* me. I'd be too busy living my dreams to have to get up before the sun and sweat out life on a construction site.

It seems arrogant now—and it was—but I was young and blind. And dumb, yes. Very, very dumb.

You never realize how lucky you are to have survived your own ignorance until you're somehow standing on the other side. I studied "the arts" in university—literature and history—with a plan to become a teacher. I was quite terrible at it, too. But I was at *university*, which was one step further in life than my father had taken. At least that's what I allowed myself to think—and it's also what *he* told me. I was in a world he'd never had the opportunity to join.

He was proud of that. I was too.

But now I can't even recall in what grade they teach the Pythagorean theorem—and I'm bewildered by basic math.

I wonder if my university degrees hold any more value than the experience my father gained on the job when he was still just a teenager, or if it was all just an illusion we bought into. All this time, the unspoken contract was that I was supposed to surpass him in some way. But here I am, no better suited in life than he was, and trying—and failing—to figure out how he managed to hold everything up.

Matt has moved from the shower where I'm grouting and has started wiping down the black subway tiles next to Jonathan. He tells me he went to trade school during his electrician's apprenticeship, but that it really just reinforced what he'd already learned on job sites.

"The fun part is making connections," he says. "You see things on site and then you see it in class, and you're like, 'Oh right, of course, that's why I did that.' That kind of thing."

It was the reverse, too: seeing stuff in class and then making it work in practice, he says. But it was also the people he met along the way.

"There were tons of characters, man," he says. Like the guy from Iraq, a former soldier, who showed him photos of the rifles he carried and the friends who'd been killed. And a guy from North Bay—super smart, but with a serious attention deficit disorder—who would sit at the back of the class and cause trouble, distracting everyone, playing games and stuff. He was just there because he needed to finish trade school. He already had a job as a lineman working on hydro lines.

"He was already making a thousand a week as a third-term apprentice," Matt says.

"What does third term mean?" I ask.

"He has another two years before he can make his full wage rate. If you can get in, it's good money. You have to travel a bit." They'd work all over the place for a year, putting in their time. "It can be rough that way," Matt tells me. "But when he's done he finally gets to go where he wants. Those guys, when there's an ice storm, man they make a lot of money. Overtime is like double. They'll work sixteen-hour days—doing whatever they have to do to get everyone back online."

I picture these linemen clipped to the side of hydro poles in blistering snowstorms or in violent rain in the middle of nowhere, trying to get power restored to families in houses nearby who'll never know their names and never appreciate the work they do.

We keep grouting the tiles, nearing the finish. Matt stops to admire the work. "It's pretty crazy to think that two weeks ago we were just tearing down walls and putting up walls," he says.

He's right. The bathroom looks large and bright. I'm astounded. This space was nothing for so long—grey and dank and forgotten. There's a shiny tub and marble-print tiles where Dad's tool bench sat.

Matt seems proud of the work he's done—and maybe, in a way, of what he's taught me.

The drywall is done and patched. The bedroom still needs to be painted. The doors on the electrical box still need to go up. The wires are a mess. The pot lights are finished, except for one that dangles in the bedroom from the fixture. The job is almost complete.

"It's amazing how things can change," I say.

25

Gord Holmes was a person I'd often heard about but had never met. He'd become a close friend of Dad while I was away at school. They met one day at church, when Gord walked in hazy and blurred by constant drug use. He'd served in the navy for three years, but at twenty-one he started using cocaine heavily, spiralling into addiction once he learned how to make crack. I remember Dad taking Gord's phone calls, and I'd heard about him driving to Toronto in the middle of the night to get him help.

I found Gord on Facebook and asked if he'd tell me about my father.

"Hi Dan," he wrote. "I'd be honoured to share with you my memories of your father. Quite honestly, I don't think I'd be alive today if it wasn't for his friendship and guidance through some difficult periods of my life."

I didn't know how Dad would have managed to connect with someone who lived on the margins as Gord had. But when I reach him by phone, it's obvious. Gord is a toolman too. They spoke the same language. Today he does carpentry work. He's building a custom closet company, and does some plumbing on the side.

"Basic plumbing is pretty straightforward," he laughs. "You could basically teach a monkey how to do it. I've got some skills that I'm happy with—and I guess proud of. But I'm not going to build a house from the ground up, either."

I tell him about my own renovation project and what I'm trying to learn. My hope is to use these tools as well as Dad did, I say.

Gord says he had the chance to witness Dad's proficiency first-hand when he helped him build a set for the church's Christmas performance. Dad led the way, as he usually did when volunteers gathered to build or fix things at the church and school.

"Your dad wanted things done his way," Gord says. "He was very assertive about expressing that."

We both laugh. My father had little patience for doing things the wrong way, which meant a different way from *his* way. Watching Dad work, Gord hoped to learn how to use tools in a way that could help support him on his journey out of addiction.

In his darkest place, Gord was dependent on crack. It hits you in a different way than cocaine, he tells me. It's an immediate, aggressive high. The euphoria is all-consuming. It became psychologically addictive. "It's not a cheap habit," he says—it was costing him $200 a day. Gord tried to work odd jobs, "but it was hard to have a job where you had to show up on a regular basis. I had lost the ability to be that responsible."

Some of the addicts he hung out with were tradesmen who worked as roofers when they could. He'd live with them, and during the months they could work they'd find roofs to repair or eavestroughs to clean. But if he couldn't make money at that during the day, he'd have to go out and "boost." He peddled drugs when he could in exchange for being able to use them for free. And when he needed to earn a bit more, he'd break into garages and steal tools and bicycles. But the best hauls were always the tools, for which there was a market that was both consistent and easy to access. "I was committing crime pretty much every day," he says.

Sometimes Gord would walk tools right out of big box stores like Home Depot and Rona—at the time, he tells me, they were pretty easy to steal from. Often he'd sell the goods directly to contractors. Or he'd go to pawn shops—known as "the fence"—that would ask few questions and buy at a third of the retail price. It was a risky operation, though. Gord was busted several times—once by a Home Depot loss-prevention officer who'd been looking for scams like his. Another time he was caught during a break-and-enter in a Dodge Ram he'd stolen. (He'd often steal cars to use for a few days and then dump after his theft spree.) "The police pulled up right behind me basically when I was in the middle of doing the job," he says.

He ended up in jail several times. He'd spend a couple of weeks in holding cells, keeping his head down and avoiding fights, until he could see a judge and be released with time served.

It was a constant cycle. Just like rehab. He'd been to treatment for addiction six times, his last stint lasting a year before he was out, couch surfing with old friends who helped thrust him back into drug use. He didn't have a place of his own. "That's classified as being homeless," Gord says. "But I never spent a night on the streets."

Outside of jail and rehab, there were times when he'd managed to pull himself out of drug use for long stretches of time. Once, he was clean for six months. But when he tagged along with a girlfriend to church the morning he met Dad, Gord was thirty-four and on the edge of another spiral.

Dad introduced himself. They talked for a while and exchanged numbers. After that, they spoke often. Gord started coming to the church on Wednesday nights, and sometimes Dad would drive down to Kipling Station in Toronto to pick him up and bring him to Brampton.

There were times when a few weeks might go by if Gord was using. Sometimes he'd dial my father's number but hang up before he answered. "Your dad would know," he says. That's when Dad would drive into the city to find him. When he did, they'd sit in a coffee shop until the world felt manageable again. "Every once in a while he would give me a blast of crap, because I needed it. If your mom was there she would always whisper in his ear and the tone would change."

He pauses.

"I'd forgotten about this," Gord says. "I'm getting a little emotional about it. I called him at eleven-thirty one Friday night and said 'I can't do this anymore.' And him and your mom drove down to pick me up in Toronto, and drove me to a detox out in the east end." He laughs. "I think he did that twice. I can't remember. I know it's because I was too messed up to, to be honest with you."

They spoke often about life on the other side of addiction, Gord continues. He had hope. He wanted to learn more about the trades he knew and to emulate the work Dad did. He wanted to design and build stuff. He applied to the architecture program at Sheridan College.

"I'd never had that support before," Gord says. "Or that *person*— that sort of rock or foundation of a relationship with somebody where I could be honest with them and know that they would still love me unconditionally. I didn't grow up in that environment."

But the cycle was vicious, and he kept spinning back to the places he was trying to escape. "My addiction wouldn't allow for it," he says. He couldn't be the person he wanted to be. "I like to look at my work at the end of the day and take pride in what I've done."

In August 2007, he called my father again. Dad picked him up in the blue F-150 and headed to a London rehab centre three hours west, Gord sleeping most of the way. In the months that followed he'd call Dad on a pay phone, using a calling card he gave him. My parents drove down to see him at Christmas. Gord spent a year there.

When he left, he says, he finally felt he had control of the disease he'd grappled with for so long. He and Dad continued to hang out while Gord pieced his life together. He completed an addiction and community service program and started working with others who suffered from drug use. And he worked as a carpenter, using the kinds of tools he used to steal.

"That's why your dad was so important to me," Gord says. "Honestly, Dan—and I don't say what I'm about to say very lightly— but I wouldn't be alive without your dad and the love that he showed me. He didn't treat me any differently than he treated anybody else, even though I kept slipping up. He was always there for me."

In 2010, Gord got married. My parents were there. He became a step-parent to a lovely daughter. They moved north, to Barrie. He has six dogs, three cats, a bunny, and three birds. He kept studying in school and working with addicts in their recoveries. And he kept a garage full of tools.

Then one day, Jai called him and told him Dad had died. Gord was standing in his kitchen when he got the call.

"I was shocked," he says. It'd been several months since they'd last spoken. He regretted that. Gord went into his e-mail and found the last message he'd sent Dad. It was a note thanking him for never giving up on him.

"I wouldn't be alive," he says. "When I needed your dad the most, he was there. He was just always there."

We both go quiet, suddenly feeling the same absence.

"I don't know how you view it, Dan," Gord begins. "I view it as God saying, 'Job well done—and I'm taking you home.'"

"Yeah," I say—meaning, I don't view it that way at all.

We're quiet again.

"He absolutely saved my life," Gord says. "You should be proud of him."

Part VI
Square, Plumb, and Level

26

In the late afternoon I drive in from Toronto to meet with my mom and Jenna for a final walk-through of the new basement.

On my way, I take a detour to the Brampton train station.

I think of it as Dad's station because he spent several years managing its massive renovation, including the construction of a pedestrian tunnel that runs beneath the tracks and connects to the street on the other side. I park the pickup on the road beside the entrance. Although the project was a huge undertaking, the tunnel itself is a forgettable concrete pathway. Now hundreds of people stream along it every day, rushing through the routine of their lives. But I walk through it slowly, as if it's an architectural masterpiece. Something that will be remembered.

The tunnel is just one of the great wonders I've quietly visited over the months since my father's passing. There were the townhomes around the corner, the residential apartments across from the mall, the Sunoco gas stations scattered across Toronto and its suburbs. I've returned to every place I remember visiting with him while they were still being built. I'm not sure what I hoped to find. Each location is just a small part of everyday life for everyone else. It carries its own kind of beauty that way. There's no sign at the tunnel's entrance, no public record of the man who was in charge of building the walkway you follow to catch a train each morning. The families living in those apartments and townhouses have no notion of the day my father pulled his truck into an empty lot and showed his son the blueprints of what would rise there. The kids dreaming in the backseat while their parents stop for gas after a weeknight road game would never consider the people who put it in place.

Dad's structures were canvases for other people's lives.

I walk the length of the dark, grey tunnel and up the stairs into the light at the end. The station is quiet. I remember Dad dropping me off here when I was a young reporter at the *Toronto Star*, still living at home. It was just a few years ago. We'd roll up in his truck in the morning rush. Sometimes some of his crew would be there, working on the tunnel. Sometimes he'd remind me that this was one of his sites.

He could sense the stress I felt about the chaotic world of daily news. He didn't pretend to understand. "You've got this, buddy," he'd say. "I love you."

And when I came back at night, sometimes on the last ride before midnight, he'd be there waiting.

That year, my sisters and I gave our parents a family photo shoot as a Christmas gift. We took the pictures at the train station. Dad and I stood side by side on the platform, next to the tracks' edge. He was still finishing the job then. He pointed out some of the work he was doing, but we didn't take much notice. It was just a boring tunnel.

Soon it will be tagged by graffiti. A drunk man will relieve himself on one of the walls. The fresh concrete will grow dark and damp.

Rodents would find refuge there. One day, rushing commuters will do their best to avoid it. In fifty years, maybe a hundred—maybe two—it will decay beyond repair and be replaced.

But right now, I wish my father knew that someone felt that this tunnel was the greatest underground commuter pathway ever completed. I wish he knew how proud he'd made his son. And all the piss, graffiti, and rats to come would never change that.

Mom and Jenna are at the house when I pull into the driveway. I give them a tour of the basement.

Jai came by the night before and took a critical eye to the project. She marked imperfections that needed to be fixed with little yellow sticky notes. Agreeing with her, Mom and Jenna now point each one out to me.

There's a crooked piece of tile near the ceiling. Mom tells me she wants that changed.

The tiles on the wall with the shower are uneven, Jenna says. They jut out a fraction in places.

"That needs to be changed too," Mom says.

We've already taken down all the tiling we put up around the faucet and shower head—the part I had done—because it wasn't even. Now just a faint outline of the old grout remains.

I'm frustrated. They have no idea how long it took to put these tiles up. I can hear Jai's voice, too—the three of them are driving me crazy.

"And I'm going to tell Matt this grout should be grey, not white," Mom says, pointing to the lines between the tiles on the floor.

"No," I say. I'm exasperated.

"It shouldn't be yellow," Jenna puts in.

It's not yellow. "Oh geez, guys . . ."

Jenna doubles down. "No, but it shouldn't be dirty."

Dirty?

In her assessment, Jai also pointed out how messy the grout work was around the base of the toilet.

It looks fine to me.

No, the grout is too wide around the toilet, Mom insists.

She says it feels as if we rushed at the end to get the job done. She refers only to "Matt"—not acknowledging that I'm part of this too. I feel the same frustration I've felt towards Jayme. They just don't understand.

I sigh—a deep and angry sigh. "The colour is nice," I say, pointing to the walls.

Mom can see that I'm getting upset. "The colour is great," she says. "It's better than what Jai said . . ."

I'm thinking of all the little details that went wrong along the way, knowing that the imperfections are probably a result of things I failed to do properly. I'm defensive.

"Okay, you know what, the honest truth," I say. "*That's* fine." I point to the thin strip of dark tiles that have been cut to fill in the edges of the subway pattern above the sink. "You can't fix that—I, like, that's—how do you even do it?" I say. "Think about it."

"I don't know," Mom says. "But why did they do that?"

I did that.

It's a replay of the scene at Home Depot, grilling the man who was selling us the toilet. Without Dad around, she feels that people are going to try to cut corners—or to finish them improperly. She's a tough, smart woman. She will not be pushed around.

"Well, it's not even right," I say. I mean the framing—that it's crooked and that it's likely my fault.

Jenna interrupts: "But someone in *construction* can fix that."

"Guys! Think logically here," I say. "This is a row that goes straight across . . ." I'm pointing to the row before the crooked tile that finishes the job.

"So something isn't level," Jenna says. "If it was, it would be flush—but it's not."

"See, it's low there and then it's higher there," Mom says. "Why is that?"

I know the answer. It's because the bulkhead above the tile isn't straight. Something's wrong with the framing. *Square, plumb, and level.* One imperfection led to another, more obvious one. But the fix? That would require taking down the already painted bulkhead, breaking through the drywall, ripping apart the frame—and somehow building it again, this time level—that is, if the problem is even fixable at that point. Who knows where we went wrong?

"Well, let's just ask Matt," I offer.

"I will," Mom says.

I brush the sweat off my forehead and run my hand through my hair three times. "Okay," I say. "Okay—so, anyway, let me . . ."

But Mom has already left the bathroom. "And this wall . . . ." she says, her voice trailing off, leaving Jenna and me behind.

"I just need to sit down," I say. I take a seat on the toilet, in the alcove I was so proud of planning—the one that's allowed us so much extra space.

"This is a *pretty big* bathroom," I say loudly.

"It's a *great* bathroom," Jenna says. She's leaning against the likely crooked wall with her arms crossed.

"And Dan," Mom says from the rec room, "let me show you a couple other things."

We walk into the open area by the stairs.

"This was only half done here, but it looks like he's fixed that," Mom says, pointing to the paint around the window at the ceiling where we'd passed the lumber through from the backyard. "But here— see here?" she says. "He's got to paint here." There's a patched-up section at the top of the wall that needs to be painted over. She points out a few other spots on the wall that require another coat.

In the bedroom, we debate whether there should be a trim around the electrical-panel door. We don't have one because we wanted it to blend into the wall. But Mom and Jenna think it looks sloppy. "It's never going to fully blend in," Jenna says. "It just doesn't look finished."

Matt and Rachael arrive a few minutes later. Right away, Mom asks him about the crooked finish of the tile beneath the bulkhead.

"Yeah, the framing got messed up and this end should have been slightly lower," he says. "So we could demo that drywall and take it down . . ."

"It just looks obvious there," Mom says.

"No, no, it bugs me," Matt agrees. "It's been bugging me."

He looks weary. I feel for him. My family is being polite enough, but they've never been good at hiding what they really feel. He's a friend, but they're thinking of him as a contractor first. And I don't believe they would have been happy regardless of the end product. This isn't about the work, it's about the absence of the only man truly capable of it in our minds.

"I don't know what you can do about it," Mom says to Matt— meaning, You need to do something about it.

"The only thing I can think of is putting it lower so that it gives the illusion that it's lower," he tells us. "Right?"

No one says anything—we have no idea what he means. He tries again, explaining that we can build up the edge with some putty so that it'll be white—basically, filling in the gap with white instead of the dark tile.

"Yeah, pulling this off would be tricky," he says. "Pulling the tile off would destroy it. And then we'd have to cut a new one—and then we'd pretty much have to build that up with some putty."

I still don't have a clue what he's planning to do. I'm just tired—and angry that this conversation is happening.

"Anyway, think about that a little bit," Mom says. "That sort of, it just looks . . ."

"Well, I'm pulling this apart, so I'll just do that one too," Matt says, pointing to the wall of tile he's already stripped from above the tub. "I'll do whatever it takes."

He's a sport.

"I like the toilet," I say. "I think it looks good, man."

"Yeah," Mom says. "And then I just have one more . . ." She points to the caulking around the toilet. "Is there a reason why this is so . . . like in here . . . it's not even?"

"Yeah, when I was dropping it we started chatting," Matt says—meaning he was chatting with me. "And I came back to it, and it set up on me. So I gotta get a sharp blade and cut around it, and then I'll do it again."

"That's okay," Mom says. "Just so you see it."

"What about the grout?" I ask.

Matt offers his response before Mom can critique. "The grout I'm going to redo, just because it's so dirty. I tried cleaning it and—"

"Can you do it with grey?" Mom interrupts.

"That might be a good idea, because it gets dirty so easily."

Rachael seems to agree with Mom and Jenna's assessment, which adds some clout to their claims. She gives a vote of approval for light grey grout to avoid the dirty look.

Matt takes a seat on the toilet, and notes how warm the floor feels. "It's so sweet," he says.

Satisfied, the committee takes their leave upstairs.

We sweep the basement of dust and debris. The remaining paint cans, brushes, buckets, and rollers are packed together neatly in the middle of the room to give it an "almost finished" look. And we are, despite the criticisms and the final touches. The pot lights shine down on the floor and in spaces on the wall as though we're in an empty gallery.

Little work remains, in the grand scheme of things.

When we're done, I take off Dad's leather belt and place it back on top of his tool bag in the laundry room. His work gloves stick out of its pockets next to the exposed, plaster-caked blade of his drywall knife. The tools are still a scattered mess of instruments that feel useless in my hands.

He's never felt so far away.

27

Lightning brightens grey clouds and rain slides down the windshield as I steer off the highway into Brampton. It's still raining when I park the truck in the driveway, open the garage, and walk past the mitre saw, tucked neatly away. The laundry room door creaks as I push through, past the tool bag and jackets falling off the hooks. There is a wall of heat in the hall. The air conditioning has stopped working. I'll need to figure out how to fix it.

It's the middle of the morning and Mom is already sad. Her eyes well as she talks about her weekend.

It's May 30. The day we've dreaded.

The four of us have agreed to get together later today for the first anniversary of Dad's death. But none of us knows what to expect. I walk down to the basement and survey our work.

The tiles have been fixed. The tiny black ones around the vanity look straight and the white floor glistens with a marble pattern, highlighted with lines of grey grout between each piece. The toilet, tucked in my alcove, looks cozy and inviting. It flushes without the confidence of a perfect slope. Hot water rushes from the shower without a leak. The bedroom covers the space that used to hold our past. The closet door requires a bit of a shove to close completely, but the walls looks straight—and any internal imperfections are hidden behind the freshly painted drywall. The new door frames divide the space between the bathroom, bedroom, and the large open living area. Every angle of the baseboard meets its mark. A trim has been added to the stairs. The grey laminate that covers the floor is the perfect shade, matching the rain-cloud hue of the walls highlighted by the soft glow of pot lights.

The basement renovation is officially done. It looks as new as it did the day Dad finished it the first time. We've even put some of the old furniture back in place: the blue leather recliner, the old brown couch, the green hutch with our childhood graffiti on it.

I stand on the stairs, looking around. We've created the illusion of square, plumb, and level. I'm almost proud of it. And considering where this all started, I wonder if Dad would be happy with how it ends.

Our lawn mower rumbles past the window in our backyard, pushed by our neighbour's son. I switch off the lights and head upstairs.

We're done here, but there's still so much to do. The deck, for one thing, is splintered and rotting to pieces. It'll have to wait, though.

I walk into my parents' bedroom—my mother's bedroom—and pull a small box from the top shelf of the closet where the Christmas presents used to hide. Dad kept all his valuables in this box: his birth certificate, his passport, and a few hundred in fifty-dollar bills. I'd stowed his wallet inside it after the funeral, to keep it safe. Now I open it up and pull out the tokens he'd tucked there for buckets of balls at the driving range. Most have expired, but one is still good.

So it's one last bucket on Dad.

I grab a pair of his white socks, neatly folded on his shelf. Then, back in the garage, I pick up his clubs and black golf shoes, still keeping their form with his wooden shoe stretchers, and toss them in the back of the truck. The rain has passed, but the air is wet and humid.

At the range next to the farmer's field, I pull on his socks and lace up his shoes. I carry the bucket of balls past the other golfers to the farthest spot on the grass I can find.

For his sixtieth birthday, we'd set a date for a round at Lionhead Golf Club. I'd told Dad the game was on me. I was excited to show him the ring I'd had made for Jayme. He cleared his schedule to be there.

I start with the wedges, just as he always did. The first ball shanks to the left. I work my way up the irons, slowly finding my form. The ground is soft and wet, and slices of grass jump with each swing. I save the last of the bucket for the driver. The balls hook left and right as I swing harder and harder, until finally one flies straight and true and I lose sight of it in the sky.

I pick up Jai at the train station a couple of hours later. She's late. Mom and Jenna are already annoyed at her. She was giving blood and then went to counselling, she says. Fine, I guess.

"I don't want to go to the cemetery," she says. "I don't want to make this day about that stuff."

"We have to," I say.

I'm rarely abrupt with my sisters. They are a soft spot, and I don't like to be angry with them. But we're doing this. It's time.

We meet back at the house. I park the truck and we all climb into Mom's Passat. I drive. I borrow Jenna's big purple sunglasses because I've forgotten my own and now it's bright and sunny. We don't talk much as we drive down Mavis Road to Meadowvale Cemetery, where our grandfather's ashes are held in a wall. As we pull in, I realize that I haven't been back since he was put there.

We drive around the cemetery, looking at plots as though we're looking for potential places to live. It's a maze of headstones. There are suburban rows, side by side, and a large area for new builds— treeless stretches that are empty except for a single lonely stone in the middle of one. It feels cold and calculated.

Jai remarks that she doesn't want to be buried at all, that she doesn't even want a stone—she'd rather be recycled as ashes and planted with a tree—and the rest of us scoff.

"You won't really have a choice," Mom says.

"Well, hopefully you'll be gone long before me," Jai says.

And we laugh, sort of.

After about twenty minutes, we all agree that this isn't the place where we want to bury Dad's ashes. Too many other dead people. He wouldn't like it here.

We go to dinner at Fanzorelli's, an Italian restaurant in downtown Brampton. It was one of Mom and Dad's favourite spots for date nights. On the way we drive by Memorial Arena, where Dad used to whistle from the stands—and where we'd held a small gathering for close friends and family after he died. I drop the girls off in front of the restaurant, then pull into the liquor store to pick up a six-pack of beer.

Jai orders gnocchi. Jenna, a baked pasta special, same as me. Mom, a pizza. We order two baskets of free bread. We drink a bottle of wine. We talk mostly about the food. Afterwards we drive to the Dairy Queen, where we used to go when we were kids.

On the way Mom offends Jenna somehow. It was pretty tame, but she starts to cry. Everyone is quiet. Mom says she's sorry and feels bad, and that she's screwing everything up.

I wait a second and then insist that Jenna tell me what kind of ice cream she wants.

"Cookie Dough and Crispy Crunch," she says.

Jai and I go inside, and when we get back with the ice cream, Jenna and Mom are laughing.

We drive by the bungalow where Mom and Dad moved after I was born, and Jai tells the story about how Dad built the deck, and how she fell off the monkey bars waving at Grandma and Pa, and that that's how she learned she couldn't hold on with one hand.

"It was just a hairline fracture," she says.

I remember Dad's workshop in the basement of that old house. I remember sitting on a blue couch with small white polka dots, eating green peas while watching the Sharon, Lois, and Bram show on TV. I remember when Dad build the deck, too, and how I'd gotten stuck in mud that I thought was quicksand and worried I'd be sucked down.

When we get back to the house, we sit around the kitchen table and read the letters people wrote in green pen on graph paper at the memorial. The Robson Renovations magnets are stuck on the fridge behind us. The girls read every letter, one by one. I open one beer, and soon another. I don't read any of the letters. I can't.

Jenna finds a card from my old high school coach, Richard Fontanna. She gets through his name, and can't read any more out loud. She bites her lip. Mom covers her face with her hands, pressing in, pushing back her tears.

We try to change the subject. Jai tells us about her plans to go travelling for three months—and that opens the door. It's a stupid idea, we tell her. She gets defensive and soon we're all arguing about a dozen different things, but nothing at all. We reach the point of near shouting, every person for themselves. Any angst we carry has been laid bare, extrapolated and expanded near the edge of words you can't take back.

I lean sideways in my chair and look over to the right, remembering the wall. While the girls keep arguing, I get up and walk into the laundry room. I hunt through the tools for the smooth leather handle. The girls stop when I come back in with the hammer in my hand.

I remember where we left the box. They remember it too.

I take a swing. A picture hanging above crashes on the floor. A tiny crack stretches across the wall.

I step back and then take three whacks in a row—each one harder than the last. A wider line tears through the paint. I take two more swings beneath the hole I've started. It feels wonderful. I think of standing beside him as a kid, bashing through the wall that once stood there, the wall we took down together.

The last blow is the loudest. It shakes the wall and echoes. I bend over and try to make the hole wider by pulling it out with my hands. It doesn't budge. I take four hard, angry whacks, backhanded.

"Let me try," Mom says.

I hand her Dad's hammer. She slams it into the wall eight times, furiously, and the drywall breaks away.

The shoebox sits on the floor inside. It's a beige Solemate box with a blue lid held on by a piece of brown masking tape. There are two holes bashed into it from our heavy swings.

I reach down, pull the box out of the wall, and set it on the table. I take the lid off slowly, as though it's a treasure chest. There's a piece of white paper on top. I remember it as soon as I unfold it. My voice cracks as I read the printed words aloud.

"Saturday, June 7," I read. "1997."

"Ninety-seven," Mom says. "Nineteen years ago."

I keep going.

> To whoever finds this letter. This box was placed here today to tell you a little something about the people who lived here at 26 Bates Court—or to remind us of our past when we find this box in the future. Living in this home were Rick and Sharon Robson. And their three children: Jaime 15, Danny 13, Jenna 9—as well as Brandi, the dog, and Oliver, the kitten.
>
> At this time, Rick is in his first year of owning his own business, Paramount Design, Build and Management. Sharon is a nurse, with Saint Elizabeth Visiting Nurses. Jaime, Danny, and Jenna are all attending Brampton Christian School.

I look up at them, grinning at the next bit.

> Jaime is an actress. Jenna is a horseback rider. And Danny's a goalie with the Brampton Maroons Triple-A hockey team—and dreams of becoming an NHL goalie.

Today is the day that the Detroit Red Wings have won the Stanley Cup. Jean Chrétien is our prime minister. And Pastor Bruce Martin has just left our church, Kennedy Road Tabernacle.

We have left a few of our articles from our past in the box. We hope this has let you know a little more about our family—or has helped us remember our past a little better.

Thank you.

Sincerely, The Robson Family

The ink of the postscript is a little smudged by tears.

P.S.: The items in this box may not mean anything to you if you are not a Robson. But if you are, then they will mean a lot.

The items we'd felt were essential to tell our story to the future are piled beneath the letter.

The Patrick Roy hockey card. One of Dad's business cards from Paramount. An inspirational poem called "A Winner's Creed" printed on a shiny silver wallet-sized card. A photo of our tabby cat, with him partly out of the frame. A photo of our golden retriever. A newspaper clipping about me helping my team win a tournament. An awkward family photo taken for the church directory.

Beneath it all is a folded piece of light tracing paper. I know it right away. I hold my head in my hands and start to cry.

Jai takes the tracing paper from the shoebox and unfolds the sketch of a father and son walking side by side. They face away, moving towards the white void beyond the page. The father's arm rests on the boy's shoulder.

The date, June 7, is written at the bottom left corner. It was the day before Dad's forty-second birthday. The day we walled in the capsule. It was a gift I'd given him so that we could make sure that whoever found it in the future would know.

There is text printed above each character.

"Friends forever, buddy?" my father asks.

"Friends forever, Dad," I say.

Pieces of broken drywall are scattered across the kitchen table. There is dust everywhere. It's a mess. I look at Mom and my sisters, and imagine Dad sitting in a chair beside them.

"We just busted a hole through the kitchen wall," I say. "We'll have to fix it."

Our faces are red and wet—but we're all laughing now. I can see him smiling, too.

28

To mark my father's birthday a year after his death, I plan a trip to the clouds to see our life from an angle he loved. The lesson at the Brampton Flying Club was a gift from a friend—one whom I'd told about my father's dream of being a pilot and who had much more faith in my courage than I did. The flight was delayed three times because there was too much wind in the sky. I'm relieved by their caution, but also concerned. Surely planes ought to be able to withstand a breeze?

When I'm finally cleared to fly late on a windless, blue-sky afternoon, I'm introduced to an instructor who looks as though he's just graduated from high school. Jenna, the bravest among us, has agreed to join me on the flight. After signing away our lives on dozens of pages fastened to a clipboard, we follow the young pilot across the grey tarmac where years before our father had taken flight.

The Cessna 172 Skyhawk he leads us to looks old enough for Dad to have actually flown. It's white with orange and brown stripes, almost identical to those old Robson Renovations decals. The wings stretch out from above an alarmingly tiny cockpit. The name *Super Hawk* is written across the engine cowl. Our instructor gives the exterior a quick once-over, then he opens the hatch and we fold ourselves in behind him. It feels as if we're about to fly the refrigerator box we pretended was a plane when we were kids.

I squeeze into the pilot's seat, shoulder to shoulder with our instructor. Jenna sits on a padded ledge that folds down behind us. The control panel is a maze of dials labelled with words like *vacuum, air speed, vertical speed, manoeuvre speed*—another language I can't speak, but one that seems critically important in this moment. We're given enormous mint-green headphones with microphones.

Our instructor fiddles with the dials and flicks a half dozen switches. Then he turns towards the open window and loudly announces "Clear prop" to no apparent person. He flips another switch and the propeller coughs a few feet in front of us. It sounds like a lawn mower sputtering to life. And then it sputters to a stop. Our instructor fiddles with a few more switches, looking more confused than I'd like. We move quickly when he gets it going again. The plane rolls forward towards a runway at the far end of the tarmac.

He's not very talkative—and I'm very nervous. The silence is tense, and I need to break it.

"How high are we going?" I ask.

"About three thousand feet," he says.

I'm aware that the many commercial flights I've taken were ten times as high, but those reach heights way beyond my comprehension. Three thousand feet is close enough to see the ground—and close enough to fear it. It's not particularly hot, but I can feel the sweat on my back and hands.

We come to a stop and the plane bobs up and down as another white refrigerator box drifts to a landing in front of us and I try to figure out what three thousand feet translates to in terms I can understand. (Later, I learn that it's nearly twice as high as the CN Tower, our local marker of *really high*.) Then, before I can brace myself, we're sprinting down the runway towards the end of the asphalt and the edge of a farmer's field. The plane whines and moans as we pick up speed—and then, in a moment, we rise. The lift pushes me back in the seat.

But the jolt is only temporary. And the nervousness I've been trying to hide deep in my stomach dissipates. The engine still moans like an overheating lawn mower, but the path feels smooth and steady. We're going higher. I look back at the rows of red-roofed hangars behind and below us. They become figurines in a model landscape. The white planes look like the Styrofoam flyers we used to whip around as children. The green fields below us reach out in plots lined with tractor trails and crops, occasionally interrupted by a stretch of unsettled brush. We can see the country homes and barns laid out across the rising land of the escarpment on the horizon. A long grey line stretches up the middle, with cars moving like ants in both directions.

The instructor's voice fills my headphones.

"It's your turn to fly," he says.

The nerves rush back.

He tells me to hold the controls in front of me. I grip them carefully, like parts of a bomb I need to dismantle. He lets go of the controls in front of him. The plane is in my hands. My arms are tense. I clench my jaw and squint my eyes beneath my aviators. I try to keep my hands as still as possible, afraid to move. We drift forward for about twenty seconds of nervous silence as I try to avoid killing us all.

The instructor tells me to look ahead at the horizon as a marker and to dip the nose just beneath it, indicating a small space with his thumb and index finger.

"Push in to go down, pull out to go up," he says.

I nudge the controls and feel the first dip of an incline, like the curve at the top of a roller coaster. We wobble left and right, and I tighten my grip as my stomach pushes into my lungs. We glide forward and down for about ten seconds before levelling out again. I catch up to my breath and slow my heart.

And we are floating.

Our little world is different from above. Life feels smaller and slower from the sky. The proportion changes—the places that hold such an enormous space in our memories appear fractional. And there's a clear view in all directions. Blue sky behind and pink light ahead. The sun falls into a cloud as we follow the rise of the escarpment towards Orangeville.

I can see why Dad loved this. Just beyond the fear, above the ground and beneath the clouds, there is calm.

A deep breath.

Look around.

Dad, you can see it all.

In the fall, I'll be married. We'll dance by the glow of tiny white lights in an old barn while the rain pours in the cold night. I'll wear your wedding ring.

A young family will move into the apartment in the renovated basement and a friend will live upstairs, filling our old house with laughter and love again. Mom will never be alone.

We'll find a plot in the graveyard in a valley in the Caledon Hills, where the trees turn bright red and orange each autumn. It's a spot we drove by together many times. The four of us will pick it out. We'll think you'd like it here. But we won't buy a gravestone. We won't break ground. The plot will sit and wait.

I'll circle the world, just as you wanted me to. I'll visit faraway places and find new adventures. I'll forget for a moment and press your name in my phone, hoping to share the stories. And my heart will break again, each time I remember that you're gone. But I'll search for you in the stars at night—looking up like we used to with the red telescope in the hallway outside your room—and I'll tell you about it all.

I won't know if you hear me, but I'll dream that you always do.

And time will fly forward, revealing new views ahead of the ever-moving horizon. I'll fiddle with your tools and try to measure up.

There will be a hole above my bed where a ceiling fan should hang. I'll take apart the bed so that I can use the ladder to reach it. I'll switch off the power and put up a work light. I'll lay out the screws and the bracket and the motor and blades beside the instructions—which will suggest that there are seven easy steps. I won't get past the first one. I'll use a drill bit on a wood screw and spin it in the bracket. I'll mangle its star slot into a square, and it will stick there and linger above me as I try to sleep in a stuffy room at night—reminding me of what I am and what I am not.

Years will pass like months. The house will continue to age and creak. The deck will splinter and rot. I'll come to learn that there is no holding this place up without you. And it will be time to let it go.

Soon Mom will retire and plan to move to a small condo closer to us in the city. A red SOLD sign will sit at the edge of the lawn beneath the streetlight. I'll fill a moving truck with everything we're not ready to leave behind. I'll bring your tools. The new mitre saw and folding stand, buckets and bags of hammers, screwdrivers, wrenches, and saws. All your old blueprints. The work table you built out of a thick sheet of wood with four-by-four legs. I swear I'll never stop trying to master them all.

"I'm sad your mom is moving," a neighbour will say. "But it's for the best. There was too much to do. This house was falling apart without your dad around."

I'll nod and say "Yeah"—because it'll simply be a matter of fact. She'll be right. There was no one to keep the house from falling. There should have been.

Before we go, I'll take one last walk. I'll remember the walls we took down and run my hands across the walls we put up. I'll feel the carpet on my toes and the creak of the stairs on the third step down.

We'll sign our names where no one is likely to find them for years and years. And even if no one ever does, we will remember—and it will always mean a lot.

I'll be the last to leave. I'll go through the laundry room, past the spot you last laid down your tools, and out the white door. I'll trace your name where you wrote it in chalk on the wall.

The garage door will stutter and jam as I close it, as though it just isn't ready for this to end. But I'll force it down, one last time. I'll walk to the end of the driveway, turn and look back.

SOLD.

I'll never fill the void you left behind.

"Dad," I'll say. "I'm sorry."

That will be the mark of our new life, without you. The space between the moment you gripped my hand and I kissed your forehead and every day hereafter will continue to expand. I'll feel you slipping away in my dreams. I won't be able to imagine your face or hear your voice the way I once did. The cruellest part of the future will be the way you fade.

But as hard as it tries, time won't destroy what you built. The foundation will hold.

It will begin with a phone call, as these things often do.

I'll be off on another flight and miss several calls in the air. When I land, my screen will light up with messages.

"Call me when you can."

I'll feel the same rush of fear I felt that morning when you were about to leave the world.

I'll text her back.

"Everything okay?"

"Yes. Just call me when you can."

The plane will taxi for twenty minutes and the passengers will depart as slowly as possible. My heart will pound. We'll shuffle out onto the tarmac in the humid air of Samos, the island where Pythagoras was born. I'll dial from the baggage carousel. It will ring nearly a dozen times before she picks up.

"Hey," she'll say, finally.

"Hi. How are you?"

"Good. Just taking the dog out and then heading to the gym."

"Why did you need me to call right away?" I'll say. "You scared me."

"It's nothing," she'll say. "It's just . . ."

"What?"

She'll make me wait.

"I'm pregnant."

And I'll find myself in a hospital, all over again. I'll sit for hours, useless and waiting.

The first time I meet my son, he'll grip my hand tight with his tiny fingers. And he will know I am there. He'll have the same wrinkles in his forehead as you. And I'll see you in the dark pools of his eyes. I'll hold him against my chest and feel his warmth as he falls asleep. I'll promise to build him a home as you did for me. And I'll wonder where his first dreams will take him. Mine will stay there, with him—breathing and breathing. Breathing, forever.

We pass over Orangeville and the instructor leads me through a turn. The plane banks, tilting to the side as we curve across the pink sky. I'm calm now. The fear is gone. We level out as we face home and the sun falls beside us.

Before landing, we loop over the old red-brick school. I can see the playground and the blacktop and the basketball net. I can see the brown roof of the wing I watched my father build. I can see every piece of the moments that raised the world we shared.

Time folds over as we float beneath the clouds. The plane tilts towards the runway. We descend, gliding home to live it all again.

Acknowledgments

This book wouldn't exist without the encouragement and patience of Nick Garrison, associate publisher at Penguin Canada—so first and foremost, my thanks to him. Your belief in this project kept me going when it felt overwhelming. Your guidance helped me express things I felt but struggled to say. You kept things square, plumb, and level. Truly, Nick, thank you.

My sincere appreciation also to Nicole Winstanley, publisher of Penguin Canada, for her support and enthusiasm for this project. This opportunity is the fulfilment of a dream, and I'm forever grateful to have worked with the wonderful team at Penguin Random House to make it come true.

To Karen Alliston, thank you for your thorough and thoughtful edits. You brought precision to my uneven edges.

As always, thank you to my agent and friend Rick Broadhead. Your support throughout this endeavour was indispensable.

I'd like to thank the Ontario Arts Council, an agency of the Government of Ontario, for its generous support, which helped provide the resources necessary to complete this project.

To Matt Lockhart, Jonathan Jacobs, and Tim Dewsbury—I couldn't ask for a better crew to be the weakest link on. Thanks for your hard work and for putting up with me. Matt, thank you for the love you showed in patiently sharing your talent with me.

Thank you to everyone who took time to share stories about my father. To all of his friends not mentioned in the text, but who gave shape and meaning to his life. Your heartfelt contributions were essential.

Thank you to Carol Taylor, Dale Taylor, Cindy Coleman, and Bill Plunket for sharing your memories. To Jerry Agyemang, Jordan Campbell, Michael Grabham, Alex Warlow, Marco Luciani, and Steve Farley—and all my other friends who let me know what my father had meant in their lives. To Gord Holmes and Josh Spilchen, I know he'd be so proud of you both.

To the friends who stood beside me through the toughest days and encouraged me throughout this process, I can't possibly thank you properly, but here's to the years and memories to come.

Thank you, John and Jill, for your love and support. And thank you, Nabil, for the evening chats on Big T and inspiring settings to sit and type.

To Auntie B, Larry, and Grandma Robson for colouring in the story of Dad's life and being such an important part of mine. To Grandma Baechler for being the best storyteller I know.

Mom, thank you for the life you built with Dad and for the endless love you shared. Thank you for your faith in purpose—and in me. You're a pillar of strength and grace. I love you. Jenna and Jai, thank you for trusting me to tell this story, which is just my part of the bigger picture. I know we each had unique experiences with our father. I hope that this reflects the man you loved, but that we always tell stories that fill in the gaps in our perspectives—and keep his life and legacy growing. LUM.

Jayme, I know that for us this is the story of the hardest part. Thank you for believing that I could find my way back. Thank you for loving me through it—and for being the strength and inspiration to keep me going. I love you endlessly.

And finally, to Oliver Richard Robson, my spaceman. Welcome to our humble corner of the cosmos. We'll sail these stars together.

© David Wile

DAN ROBSON is head of features and senior writer at *The Athletic*, Canada. He has won a National Magazine Award and a National Newspaper Award for his writing. He is the author of the national bestseller *Quinn: The Life of a Hockey Legend*, which was longlisted for the RBC Taylor Prize for literary nonfiction. His book *Bower: A Legendary Life* won the Ontario Historical Society's Creighton Award for best biography. He is also the co-author of *The Crazy Game* (with Clint Malarchuk), *Change Up* (with Buck Martinez), and *Killer* (with Doug Gilmour), all of which were bestsellers.